THE SEVENTY SUMMITS

Life in the Mountains

By **VERN TEJAS** and **LEW FREEDMAN**

Seventy Summits
Life in the Mountains

Copyright © 2017 by Vern Tejas and Lew Freedman

Published by **Blue River Press**
Indianapolis, Indiana
www.brpressbooks.com

Distributed by **Cardinal Publishers Group**
317-352-8200 phone
317-352-8202 fax
www.cardinalpub.com

ISBN: 978-1-68157-047-1

Cover Design: David Miles
Book Design: Dave Reed
Cover Photo: Shutterstock / Daniel Prudek
Editor: Dani McCormick

Printed in the United States of America

21 20 19 18 17   1 2 3 4 5

Contents

I dedicate this book to all who have inspired me along the way, especially Col. Norman Vaughan and Lowell Thomas, Jr.

—Vern Tejas

ABOUT THE AUTHORS

Vernon Tejas is a world-famous mountain climber and guide who has climbed the Seven Summits, the tallest peaks on each of the seven continents, at least ten times each. Tejas broke the records for the most times ascending Denali, the highest peak in North America, and for making the swiftest ascents of the Seven Summits. He has been associated with Alpine Ascents International of Seattle, Washington for many years.

A member of the Alaska Sports Hall of Fame, Tejas gained renown in 1988 by becoming the first person to successfully climb 20,310-foot Denali alone in winter. He and co-author Lew Freedman collaborated on a book called *Dangerous Steps* about that achievement.

Lew Freedman is the author of dozens of books on sports and Alaska and spent seventeen years in Alaska working for the *Anchorage Daily News*. Freedman first wrote about Tejas's adventures in 1988, and they have been friends since. Deb Freedman, Lew's wife, transcribed all of the interview materials for this volume.

A PERSONAL NOTE

I wrote a sports column about Vern Tejas before I ever met him.

At the time, I was working for the *Anchorage Daily News* in Alaska, and Vern was high on the slopes of Denali, the mountain previously known as Mount McKinley, which is the tallest mountain in North America at 20,310 feet.

Vern was in the midst of attempting to become the first person to solo climb Denali in winter and live to tell about it. He had been flown to base camp, the Kahiltna Glacier, by famed bush pilot Lowell Thomas Jr. It was February of 1988, and the climb stretched into March.

Tejas was following in the footsteps of Naomi Uemura, a world-renowned Japanese adventurer. Uemura had attempted this challenging journey in February of 1984. He disappeared on the mountain, and his body remains there.

Thomas flew sorties periodically to keep an airborne eye on Tejas, but one day as he traveled above the mountain, whiteout conditions obscured his view and he did not spot the climber. This went on for a few days, and word leaked out that for all intents, Tejas was missing. The outside world did not know if he had perished as the result of a storm, a mishap, tumbling into a crevasse, or become trapped because of injury.

My column stressed the drama of the unknown and that those of us at sea level should offer prayers for Tejas's survival and triumphant emergence. As fortune had it, unlike Uemura, Tejas did break into the fresh air—he had been hunkered down in a snow cave for protection and preservation.

When Tejas returned to his Anchorage home, he stopped by the newspaper office, seeking photographs taken when he had landed back in town. We met. Vern thanked me for the story, and I completely spontaneously blurted, "You should write a book about it." He quickly replied, "No, you should." Up until that point, I had never entertained the idea of writing non-fiction books. Nearly thirty years later, I have written about 100 of them. Vern has made more than 100 additional major ascents of peaks around the world. It was probably a decade ago, sitting in an ice cream shop in Anchorage, that I said he should do a book about his whole life and all of these adventures. He told me that he would let me know when he was ready.

He's ready.

I dabbled in the mountains, climbing the Chugach Mountains that overlook Anchorage. I also climbed about a dozen 14,000-foot peaks in Colorado, and ultimately on Mount Kilimanjaro, the 19,341-foot Roof of Africa in Tanzania, but most of my adventures have revolved around creative writing.

Vern has always reached higher. He has chosen a riskier path. His passion for the peaks has defined his adult life. He probably has more frequent flyer miles than Charles Lindbergh and Amelia Earhart combined. He has probably traveled as much as Marco Polo, Christopher Columbus, and Neil Armstrong. Certainly, his passport is more frayed than the average international business traveler.

Of course, that is what Tejas is. As a professional mountain guide, his work year is laid out for him in a sequence of seasons and climbing openings around the world in the various countries where the best-known geological mountainous features are situated. Yet, unlike the clients who dream of once-in-a-lifetime ascents of special mountains, these places seem almost backyard-familiar to Tejas.

There is great commonality in each trip, but the cast of characters is different; the experience is different; the challenges, due to weather changes or some other intervention, are different. What that means is each trip to Denali, Everest, Vinson, Elbrus, Kilimanjaro, Kosciusko, Carstensz or Aconcagua is its own adventure.

When Vern completed his harrowing winter solo of Denali and I wrote the story, we lived only a few miles apart on the south side of Anchorage. Much has happened in both of our lives since then. Neither of us are in Alaska much these days, although we do both have relatives locked in on The Last Frontier. But for all of these life and location changes, we do stay in touch, and we do overlap.

During the summer of 2016, we were both in Anchorage at the same time attending the same two-day event. Once, a few years ago, we were both in New York City at the same time and lunched in mid-town Manhattan. I was amused to note Tejas arrived at the restaurant by bicycle, not taxi cab, and he had to chain it to a pole outside. Amazingly, it was still there when we finished.

In the interim, we communicated by email. Typically, such contact would be initiated by me with a "Dear Vern, Wherever You Are" salutation. Time would pass with Vern atop a mountain in a remote corner of the world (one of few such places not wireless connected), and when he returned to Wi-Fi civilization, he would write back. I distinctly recall hearing from Vern from Tokyo and Chile. Not from Antarctica or Everest. However, many years ago (in the late 1980s, perhaps), Tejas brought me a gift from the rock band just below the summit of Everest: a chunk small enough to retain in a letter envelope, where it has remained ever since.

I once imagined I would climb Denali with Vern as my guide. I set out on a vigorous training program one winter with plans to first join a guided ascent of the largest Mexican volcanoes. Pico de Orizaba (18,491 feet), Popocatepetl (17,802), and Iztaccihuatl (17,159), are the third, fifth, and eighth highest mountains in North America. I filled out my application, enclosed a check, and left the envelope containing the paperwork on the bureau. That night, playing in a city league basketball game, I tore a calf muscle. I went home and tore up the forms and check and never again came closer to the necessary form or shape to sign up for a Denali climb with Vern, or anyone else.

Instead, I kept writing about it, telling others stories about the mountains.

—Lew Freedman

May 2017

INTRODUCTION

The first time Vern Tejas saw Denali, he was in his late teens, almost twenty years old. He was fascinated by the concept of Alaska and had worked his way north, curious as to what the Great Land offered. He'd only seen the mountain in pictures, and knew one basic fact about it: this 20,310-foot peak was the tallest in North America.

Vern was in the flatlands, perhaps twenty-five horizontal miles from Denali's summit. He remembers having to crane his neck and tilt his head back to look upwards and peer at the summit. The summit, as often occurs with this mountain that creates its own weather, was invisible.

Each year, some 500,000 tourists visit Denali National Park. They come to admire one of the last great scenic and unspoiled places on earth, see wild animals, and gaze upon the legendary mountain. It is not certain how many of them actually even obtain a glimpse of a purely visible Denali. It may be raining with thick cloud cover where they pause. It may be snowing on the mountain. Dense clouds may obscure the entire hunk of rock or portions of it.

Those who are fortunate sometimes are blessed enough to be in the right place at the right time when those clouds dissipate and the blue sky opens up and reveals the magnificence of the humongous peak before their eyes. Tejas was open-mouthed with awe, bright-eyed with respect, and excited for an unwritten future.

It took five years before Tejas had his first chance to climb Denali. He has never stopped, climbing one of the world's most famous and impressive mountains as if it is a neighborhood playground. As of 2016, he had reached the summit of Denali fifty-seven times, a record.

For several years, Denali was a specialty. But the fame Tejas gained after completing his 1988 winter solo of the peak changed the course of his life. No longer was he just a Denali guide. He was able to parlay his experience into work around the globe, climbing the biggest mountains and catching the front end of a new wave of popularity in mountain climbing.

Dick Bass, operator of the Snowbird Ski Resort in Utah who died in 2015 at eighty-five, was looking for a new life challenge in the 1980s when he dreamed up the concept of the Seven Summits. Bass, who was neither a professional climbing guide nor an accomplished climber on the order of the world's best, invented an adventure challenge that he began with his friend Frank Wells, president of Walt Disney Company. Until then, no one in the mountaineering world had given much thought to ascending the highest mountains on each of the world's seven continents. It was not as if the world's most prominent mountaineers couldn't do it, it was simply that the accomplishment was on no one else's radar.

At the time, likely few mountaineers could even readily name the Seven Summits. Some of the mountains were not terribly well known, and some were not coveted destinations. After the appropriate geographical research and establishing their quest, Bass and Wells chased their goal.

Their list consisted of Mount Everest for Asia, Denali (then called Mount McKinley) for North America, Aconcagua for South America, Elbrus for Europe, Kosciuszko for Australia, Kilimanjaro for Africa, and Vinson for Antarctica. They went by the numbers, matching the heights to the continents. It was a straightforward selection plan. No one tried to argue that these were the seven most rugged mountains in the world. Besides Everest, all of the other six are shorter than even the second or the sixty-seventh tallest mountain in Asia.

It all began for Bass and Wells as a hobby, a later-in-life fun physical challenge. Everest, acknowledged as the most difficult, was saved for last. Alas for Wells, he climbed the first six, but could not summit Everest. So rather than a co-success, it fell to Bass to become the first climber in the world to reach the top of the tallest mountains on each continent in 1985.

Unexpectedly, Bass's achievement had repercussions far beyond his own personal gratification. He gained wide notoriety, authored a best-selling book called *Seven Summits*, sparked an entire sub-industry of mountain guiding, and even influenced geography debates on true definition of a continent. The debate continues today.

It turned out that another mountaineer was also pursuing nominally the same goal. Canadian Pat Morrow completed the Seven Summits in 1986, but they were not the same Seven Summits as Bass ascended. Instead of Kosciuszko in Australia, which by all definitions is a walk-up needing no mountaineering equipment whatsoever and very little stamina, he climbed a mountain called Carstensz Pyramid in New Guinea.

Kosciuszko stands 7,310 feet high. Carstensz stands 16,064 feet high. No one contests the belief that climbing Carstensz is the worthier mountaineering achievement, but they do question if Carstensz belongs on the list. Some say New Guinea is part of Oceania. However, the general listing of continents in most sources fails to recognize Oceania (or Austral-Asia) as a continent in lieu of Australia.

Morrow's accomplishment was significant, but it was overshadowed by Bass's. It did not help Morrow that Bass completed his journey a year earlier. Also, because Bass was more of a citizen-adventurer than a professional climber, his climbs resonated strongly with the average Joe and Joan. They swiftly came to believe that, as long as they were following a mountain guide, they too could do what Bass did. This threw open an entire area of opportunity for guide services. People clamored for the opportunity to go into the mountains, climb the high points of the world (usually saving Everest for last because it was the most difficult and most expensive), and the need arose for qualified guides.

Suddenly, the Seven Summits appeared on the life lists of many. Running with the bulls with Pamplona was one thing. Running a 26.2-mile marathon in some exotic location was another. But this, chasing the summits of seven mountains, that was something to put on your résumé. As long as you had the money and time and trained like an Olympian for stamina, a guide would help you fulfill your grandest dream.

This sudden intense interest, arising from almost nowhere, enabled Vern Tejas to transform himself from a Denali mountain guide into a citizen of the world mountain guide. Whereas before 1985, it was extremely difficult for a man of Tejas's talents to make a living year-round at high altitude, he was now in demand.

The Seven Summits quest opened a world of opportunity and a lifetime of adventure for Tejas.

Tejas removed his mask for a quick top-of-the-world selfie
on one of his first Everest summits

EVEREST ACHIEVED

Mount Everest is the tallest mountain in the world at 29,029 feet. To stand on its summit is the grandest single prize for a mountaineer.

Everest is also the best-known mountain in the world, regardless of nationality. Being the highest spot on Earth provides special cachet, and although they all may not aspire to climb it, more people in more places know about Everest's stature than that of any other mountain.

The pull of Everest has always been great. When George Mallory and Sandy Irvine set off to conquer Everest in 1924, Mallory was asked why he was climbing the mountain. He answered with the pithy comment that has endured in mountaineering lore, "Because it's there."

One reason the British were so interested in Everest, of course, was the country's history in the region. The mountain was charted in 1852 by the Survey of India and named after Sir George Everest, who was the Surveyor General of India at the time. That's the origin of the mountain's name, although there are other names applied in native tongues throughout the area. Tibetan people call Everest *Chomolungma*, which means "Goddess Mother of the Earth." Nepalis call it *Sargamatha*, which is translated as "Head of the Sky."

The British kept after the summit for many years until a British Commonwealth team at last put the first two humans on top. New Zealander Edmund Hillary and his companion, Sherpa Tenzing Norgay, finally stood on the summit on May 29, 1953.

The summit of Mount Everest loomed above my head. Almost there. I stepped. I was moving so slowly as I approached the top of the world. My lungs were bursting; my legs felt weighted down. I took another step. The fatigue made me woozy.

Another step, a short one. Another step, a long one. I took a long breath; it was a gasp. I was moving so slow. I had completed the Hillary Step, the last big obstacle before reaching the 29,029-foot summit of Everest. As I traversed the summit ridge, I bent and scooped up a rock. And then another. A few more. They were tiny pieces of Everest to keep for souvenirs, for memories, as precious as any gems. It seemed fitting at the time. Not only did I not know if I would ever be back on this small section of real estate nearing the highest point on the planet, but for two months, the biggest rock of all, this huge mountain, had been chipping off pieces of me. It destroyed my body as I sought to climb it.

The sun was out. I was fortunate that the weather was clear. It was zero degrees, not cold at all for Mount Everest. I could see for a great distance: miles and miles. I looked out and saw China, India, Tibet, and Bhutan. I thought I could see the whole world from there. I believed the view was forever. But I had to keep moving. I tore my eyes from the horizon and looked back at my own feet, willing them upward and forward. Step. Breathe. The rocks became snow. I had reached the end of the summit ridge.

There I was, age thirty-nine, a professional mountain guide from Alaska, only twenty feet shy of the fulfillment of a dream. I was closing in on the summit, the top of the world. I was about to become the third Alaskan ever to climb Everest, and the first Alaskan to climb the world's Seven Summits: the highest peaks on all seven continents. This was the seventh summit, the hardest of them all. It was a few minutes before noon on May 12, 1992.

I took a short step and a long pressure-breath. I inhaled the thin air. And then, at last, I was there, standing at the top of the world.

For me, it was an extra special moment. I had tried and failed to reach the summit of Mount Everest in 1989 and 1991. There had been setbacks and concerns, unforeseen challenges and dangers. Making it to the top this time was even more meaningful because it also represented the conclusion of another personal quest. Only in recent years had the idea of climbing the Seven Summits become a sought-after goal in the world of mountaineering. That, too, was something I very much wished to accomplish.

With those same final steps came a dual achievement. I had climbed Mount Everest, and I had climbed the Seven Summits. At the time, climbing the Seven Summits had been accomplished by a dozen people. It was a rarity. Little did I know that the Seven Summits would define the future of my guiding and climbing careers.

Year after year after that, climbing season after climbing season, my time, energy, and efforts would be devoted to the Seven Summits, traveling the world, relying on the strength of my legs to lead other people to the top of these high mountains in remote places.

At the time, as I gulped for air, trying to drink in the bottled oxygen I was counting on to get me down safely, I had no inkling I would surely be back in this place, this high on the highest mountain. My first-time completion of the Seven Summits was a milestone, yet twenty-five years later, looking back, it represented a fresh beginning.

Now that I have climbed the Seven Summits at least ten times each, that journey of 1992 seems so long ago. Yet it was a critical one. As it was said long ago by the Chinese philosopher Laozi, who dates to around 600 BC, a journey of a thousand miles begins with a single step. You cannot climb the Seven Summits over and over again until you complete them a first time.

At the time of my third attempt to climb Mount Everest, I had climbed Denali more than twenty times. I was a regular spring-time guide on the tallest peak in North America and the chief defining characteristic of Alaska. In 1988, I became the first person to complete a solo winter ascent of Denali. It earned me a considerable amount of renown. I was a fairly identifiable figure at the time, anyway. I stood five-foot-nine and weighed about 170 pounds. I also had a very thick, bushy black beard and shaved my head completely except for a small pony tail trailing off the back of my skull. Put it this way, if you saw me walking down the street it would be easy to guess it was me.

I was kind of on a high after I made the solo winter ascent of Denali, and I went to Everest for the first time to guide in 1989. At the time, I was working for Genet Expeditions in Alaska. That was one of the most famous mountaineering guide services in the world. Ray Genet, the Swiss-born mountaineer, had transplanted to Alaska and pioneered guiding on Denali. Genet was the first Alaskan to climb Everest, but he died on the descent in 1979. The company continued on when Anchorage's Harry Johnson took over the business.

There really had not been any attention paid to climbing the Seven Summits until Dick Bass got the idea to target them with his friend Frank Wells. Bass completed the ascent of the Seven Summits when he reached the summit of Everest on April 30, 1985. Bass's book about their adventures, *Seven Summits*, generated a lot of publicity.

Everyone's imagination was on fire about the Seven Summits. But it was Harry Johnson's brilliant idea to offer the chance to climb the Seven Summits with Genet Expeditions on guided climbs. I still remember the brochure. After Bass's book came out everyone wanted to do it.

Naomi Uemura, one of my heroes, who died on Denali trying to become the first to solo winter climb in 1984, had done five of the seven. By the time Harry thought of offering guided climbs, I had been to Denali, Mount Vinson in Antarctica, and Aconcagua in Argentina. On a detour from the Everest trip, I climbed Mount Kosciusko in Australia.

As my first Everest trip approached in 1989, it became clear that Harry Johnson could not go to Nepal. I got bumped up to lead guide. We had four or five clients. At that time, I was not sure I was ready to be an Everest lead guide, particularly organizationally, but there is always a first time.

As it turned out, I was more ready than I thought. Denali is the best training ground for Everest: it is high and cold, has winter storms and conditions, and has crevasses. It has most of the objective dangers Everest has, and all of the subjective hazards of Denali.

Almost all of the good things in my life have flowed from my love of Denali. I had just completed the winter ascent of Denali, and word of that spread my name around. Completing a challenge like that gave me confidence; it was a feather in my cap. It spurred me to think about an international guiding career.

Genet Expeditions was the first company to offer all seven peaks as guided climbs. Until then, only individuals tried to climb the Seven Summits. Genet's advertising was "Come climb the Seven Summits with us." That led to work for me in other countries.

The first time I went to Everest as the lead guide, I reached 28,000 feet, but was forced to stay overnight and slept on the ground after stomping a platform in the snow. If I continued on, I felt I would be risking the loss of fingers and toes to frostbite, or being blown off the mountain because the winds were so high. The second time, the trip was cut short because of a lethal rock-fall on the mountain. There is never a guarantee, even if you have the best guide in the world, that you can make it to the summit. So much can happen, and so much can go wrong.

For my third attempt, I left Anchorage on February 28, 1992, guiding for Alpine Ascents International near Seattle, Washington. By then, I was fully aware of the kind of problems anyone could have on Everest. My eyes were open. Everest had beaten me in the past.

Climbers had been fascinated by Everest for decades, but the British achieved the first ascent in 1953 when Sir Edmund Hillary and Sherpa Tenzing Norgay made it to the summit. A lot of people were beaten by Everest. It took a lot of time, effort, and energy for Everest to be scaled the first time. Ten years later, one of the climbers on the first American expedition to ascend Everest was asked why they were climbing and responded, "Because it is still there."

One climber on my Everest trip was Mike Gordon of Anchorage. Mike was forty-nine at the time and owned Chilkoot Charlie's, the largest and most popular bar in Alaska. Mike always gave it his best shot and was kind of in the same situation I was. Two years earlier, 1990, he was afflicted with bronchitis and he had to turn back before the summit. Mike was nicknamed "Mountain Mike" for his climbing and wanted to be the first Alaskan to reach the top of the Seven Summits. Of course, so did I.

As part of his ongoing desire to climb the Seven Summits, Mike covered one wall of his huge bar with mountaineering pictures and paraphernalia that showed him on various climbs. He was convinced that this time he was going to reach the top of Everest. Mike and I both knew that Ray Genet, who was a tremendously strong climber, had perished on his Everest climb.

The Seven Summits had become a hot topic in the climbing world after the publication of Bass's book. Climbing them all is a geographic challenge, a fitness challenge, and a challenge to the size of your bank account.

Typically, since it is the most difficult and the most expensive to climb, Everest is the last of the Seven Summits approached. In 1992, I believe the climbing fee for Everest was about $50,000 a person. It is around $65,000 now. Much of that stems from permitting fees that must be paid to the Nepalese government and the cost of bottled oxygen. Our group going for the summit in 1992 included me, Mike Gordon, Alpine Ascents owner Todd Burleson, and millionaire Steve Fossett.

From the first organized attempts on Everest, anyone headed to that part of the world understood he would face severe cold, heavy snowfall, whipping winds, hypoxia, and threats from crevasses and avalanches. The biggest danger of all may be the sheer height of the mountain. There are fourteen mountains in the world taller than 8,000 meters, or 26,000 feet. At that height, the air is so thin that it becomes hard to breathe without the use of supplemental oxygen. Being at that altitude clouds one's judgment and makes it so difficult to climb that a body quickly wears down physically. A climber can be afflicted with pulmonary edema filling the lungs with fluid, or cerebral edema putting fluid pressure on the brain. There are many ways to die on Everest.

Harry Johnson recognized the universal climbing itch within the mountaineering world and said people would want to go to Everest "because it's the biggest." He was right. He also said everyone knows Everest. They even saw it mentioned on quiz shows. Practically no one outside of the mountaineering community can name the second-highest mountain in the world, 28,251 foot high K-2 located on the border separating Pakistan and China.

Becoming acclimated to altitude is one of the important intermediate steps between beginning the climb on Everest and going for the summit. Many, many people have turned back because they did not make the adjustment. That is the reason why the 1992 climb began with a long, leisurely paced hike to base camp.

One interesting thing about Everest is that it is in the middle of the tallest mountain range in the world, so it is not easy to see from a distance as trekkers approach from the south. On a clear day in Alaska, Mount McKinley can be seen from downtown Anchorage. It stands out above its landscape. But from the south, Everest is mostly hidden from view until you get fairly close. Lhotse, the world's fourth tallest mountain at 27,890 feet, and Nuptse, at 25,850 feet, block views of large portions of Everest—except for its distinctive pinnacle.

Mount Everest is the tallest mountain on Earth, standing 29,029 feet high

Some of the most fantastic photographic images of Everest are taken at sunset when there is a golden glow on the top of the mountain. You see snow, the rock band, and the sunlight reflecting. Another signature sight of Everest is the so-called plume blowing off the summit. It is frequently very windy at the top, and the wind creates a cloud-like stream of snow blowing horizontally. That is not a good time to be at the summit, though. When the winds scream, climbers cannot advance to the top, and those standing at the top might face being blown off the mountain.

When the hiking began, Mike Gordon, who was accompanied by his wife Shelli as far as Shyangboche at 12,000 feet, turned to Todd Burleson and said, "The adventure begins."

Once the trek finishes, climbers pitch tents. As interest in climbing Everest and the Seven Summits grew, base camp became a bustling international city. It was not as crowded in 1992 as it became in future years, but there were still many groups preparing for assaults on the mountain.

The key obstacle to climbing success is often the Khumbu Icefall. The jumbled-up ice falls 2,000 feet from the Western Cym to the Khumbu Glacier, where base camp is situated. It is a stunning field of crevasses and ice rubble, a danger zone of hanging seracs and unstable footing. The first thing I thought when I saw it was, "Holy smokes! How can a guy go through there?" It is a terribly risky area, and often exacts a price. Many deaths are attributable to problems in the Icefall.

These days on Everest there are many fixed ropes installed for climbs and aluminum ladders extended over crevasses. But the Icefall shifts and changes all the time, so that does not guarantee safety. Sometimes it changes with no warning and huge chunks of ice break free and fall. The Icefall is spread over one-and-a-half miles, and it is nerve-wracking to thread your way through it. Bad things happen there in a split second where there is no taking cover and no way to move out of the way of a fast-rolling avalanche. At different times, the British referred to the Icefall as "Hellfire Alley" and "The Atom Bomb Area." I referred to a particularly broken area of ice as "the popcorn area" because of its tenuous consistency, and it seems to have stuck.

Approaching from the south, there is no way to reach the South Col and the summit without passing through the Khumbu Icefall. A lot of prayers are said as climbers make their way through that area. At the time of the 1992 expedition, there were eleven climbing teams trying to make it to the top from the same side, including groups from America, Russia, New Zealand, India, and Holland.

For decades, climbing Everest had been essentially a solitary wilderness experience. There was only one climbing group on the peak at a time. The human traffic on the mountain has only grown since. The Everest climbing season concludes at the end of May because of the arrival of the monsoon season. You want to clear the mountain—

everybody off—because the snowstorms roll in. Everest is not a place to be during powerful weather like that.

When Hillary and Tenzing climbed Everest, word was sent out to the world by messenger. By 1992, demonstrating the dawning of the age of more sophisticated communication, the Dutch brought a telephone and fax machine to the mountain and charged willing users $26 a minute to send a message to a loved one. Mike Gordon took advantage to send a note to his wife.

Although there were a lot of people on Everest's slopes, it didn't really faze me. This was a case again of my Denali experience helping me because I had been on that mountain when 400 people were on the peak. I thought it was kind of fun to socialize and talk with the people from all over the world who had arrived on Everest at roughly the same time.

One place numbers can be a problem, though, is in the Icefall. Guide Pete Athans and I saw to installing our route for the group through the Icefall to Camp I, at 20,000 feet. While supplies were being ferried ever higher, Sherpas handled the dirty work of placing ropes and ladders across holes capable of swallowing climbers making a simple misstep. That year, worse than the crevasses, were the seracs, huge blocks of ice just hanging above our heads. If the ground shifted without warning, they could crush one of us in an instant. One serac was nicknamed "the Hand of God." because it was up to God if the ice remained stable as people passed beneath. It was a scary, spooky feeling to look up and see that ice overhead. Pete and I had to cross through the Icefall repeatedly. Other climbers only had to cut through a few times. The more frequently you went through it, the higher the odds you would get squished.

I probably passed through the Icefall twelve times. It felt like twelve times too many. Once I got used to the route's idiosyncrasies, I flew through to minimize time in there. Nothing terrible occurred, and Pete and I established Camp II at 21,500 feet. We got very early starts and stopped carrying loads by three p.m. It often snowed in late afternoon, so it was good to be set up early for the night. There were some very high winds, too. By Everest standards—and Denali standards—the cold was not extreme, not dipping below minus-ten.

Steve Fossett dropped back at this point. He had asthma and was fighting too hard to breathe. He said he realized that he could not climb high mountains with his condition and, after that, turned to other adventures. Everest sets limits, one way or another, for all of us. Whether you suffer from asthma or not, Everest can work its way into your lungs.

At Camp III, around 23,000 feet, quite a few people started getting sick. Mike Gordon was one of them, coughing so hard he pulled a muscle in his side. The camps sounded like tuberculosis wards. Mike was far from alone.

Actually, I was worse off than he was. When one of our team members became so sick he had to be evacuated, I volunteered to escort him down through the icefall. The rest of the team was preparing to move up to Camp III in two days. I dropped down to base camp with our ill member and re-climbed back to Camp II to guide team members to Camp III the following day. We spent the night without bottled oxygen to help us acclimate. But with all the extra exertion and without the oxygen, it had the opposite effect on me. The next day, I was in super slow mode. Mike told me I looked sicker than hell, and I felt it. When we returned to base camp, I hiked over to my friend Rob Hall's camp to see his wife Jan Arnold, who was a doctor. She said I had a lung infection and should descend immediately. There was a clinic at Pheriche, at 14,000 feet. Ironically, it had been established by Peter Hackett, the Alaskan doctor and researcher who had preceded me to Everest.

On April 20, nearly two months after I had left Anchorage, I was being looked over by two doctors in Pheriche. They had two stethoscopes pressed against my chest simultaneously and told me to breathe. I said, "I am breathing." They said they couldn't hear me. The diagnosis was double pneumonia, viral and bacterial. I thought that was the end of my Everest climb. Zero-for-three loomed in my face.

For a while, all I did was sleep. I tried fortifying myself at a tea house, eating rice, potatoes, noodles, and eggs. I drank gallons of tea. I also read the book *One* by Richard Bach. Determined to will myself back to health and back onto the mountain, I spent long hours visualizing. I did not allow myself to ponder quitting the climb. I stayed focused and repeatedly visualized the final steps to the summit and (not sure where this came from since I don't drink) celebrating afterwards in a bar. I did this over and over again while taking medicine and sleeping. Nearly two weeks were lost. That is easily enough to doom a climb.

Instead, rather amazingly, after that recuperation, I was rejuvenated and resumed the climb. When we first started moving back up the mountain—rather quickly, actually—I guessed I was at about eighty percent of full strength. I went up high quickly as my body recovered. Mike didn't recover as well. When we got back up to 23,000 feet, he was coughing again, so hard it scared him. He even used bottled oxygen to help, but he turned back at Camp III. The climb was over for Mike.

While I was reading *One*, Mike had been reading *Moby Dick*. It was as if he had been on a quest parallel to Captain Ahab's. I knew it was very hard for him emotionally.

Mike turning back hit me like a ton of bricks. I was disappointed since we had climbed many of the Seven Summits together. This was his second and final attempt on Everest. He honored the commitment he made to his wife to not continue risking his life on Everest. Our first attempt together in 1989 was dogged by horrific winds, yet it only served to enhance Mike's desire to stand on top. We were in the same boat then and made a pact to go back and succeed. He had altered his life drastically to train for the attempt Everest, and now his lungs would not allow it. I was all ripped up inside when it was time for him to depart. All I could do was to hug him and try to hold back tears.

I was still not at peak strength after my illness. At the 26,000-foot camp, I tried to shovel in some nutrition. I ate noodles and threw up. Then I ate a warm fruit cocktail and threw that up. The sky was growing ugly, with big, gray clouds moving in and obscuring the peak. I did not feel well again and slept for three hours on oxygen, which made a difference.

The plan was to awaken the group at eleven p.m. to get ready. I ate a half of a Baby Ruth candy bar and some oatmeal and drank some water. It was time to move for the summit. I was with Skip Horner, another guide from Montana; and Louis Bowen, of Hong Kong. We were bundled up in heavy parkas, thick mitts, and goggles, and climbed with three Sherpas. We started on the trek at one a.m., and I led. I felt renewed.

We topped the South Summit, at 28,750 feet, at nine thirty a.m., and the sun was out. The summit looked like a big vanilla ice cream cone. I started thinking, "It might happen. It might happen." We moved slowly but steadily until we reached the Hillary Step. There was a party of fourteen from New Zealand moving slower in front of us. There is no room to pass another climber on the Step, so we had to wait. We planned to take a short break, but the rest time stretched to an hour-and-a-quarter. We burned oxygen as we waited so we could stay relatively warm.

A human traffic jam near the summit of Mount Everest was unheard of in 1992. There was some irony in going to such an extreme corner of the earth and then standing in line. I think that was the first day there ever was such traffic there.

When it our turn to cross the Hillary Step, our pace was also slowed. It was step, gasp for breath, step again. It was slow-motion progress, but we kept going. The three of us made it to the summit at 11:55 a.m. on May 12. At that time, it was the greatest single summit day in Everest history. The summit is really only about twenty feet long, and there were about twenty people there at the same time. Skip Horner said it was as if we were perched in a row on a wire like crows. Up to that point in time, some 350 people total had climbed Everest since Hillary and Tenzing's day, but on that day alone, thirty-two made it. Todd and his group went up the next day.

I brought a water bottle to the summit and joked that when I opened it, I filled it with summit air. The view was spectacular. I could see Kanchenjunga, the world's third highest mountain, and I took a panoramic view with a video camera. It really felt as if the view extended for hundreds of miles.

The delay in reaching the top, being trapped behind the New Zealand climbers, meant our group had used up considerable oxygen waiting. Skip ran out of oxygen at the Hillary Step, and Louis shared some with him. Then I ran out across the "Death Traverse" below the Hillary Step. I was left gasping for air. A Russian climber I met earlier gave me a bottle. I might have died without it.

We returned to Camp IV at seven p.m., eighteen hours after we began climbing. We were hammered. The next morning I had fresh coughing fits and worried about the pneumonia being back. I staggered as we dropped from Camp IV to Camp II. Once, I was weaving and noticed a nearby 4,000-foot drop. That woke me up. I realized if I didn't straighten myself out, I was going to die on the descent. I thought of Ray Genet because that's how he died. I lost twenty-five pounds on the climb, but I made it.

GROWING UP

It is strange what we recall best from our youth. For a guy whose entire adult life would be devoted to high places, it might be said Vern Tejas did not come to his affinity for tall mountains naturally. Perhaps if he had stuck around his birth place of Portland, Oregon, in the shadow of Mount Hood, it would make perfect sense for him to want to climb magnificent, well-known mountains.

However, most of Tejas's youth was spent in Texas, a very large but generally very flat state. Born in Oregon on March 16, 1953, Tejas does say one of his first childhood memories actually is of Mount Hood, the snow-covered, 11,249-foot-mountain looming near Portland. The mountain is just thirty-seven miles from the city, though the vehicle route takes more than an hour.

The tree line on Hood is at 5,960 feet, and situated there is a building called Timberline Lodge, a National Historic Landmark constructed as a Works Progress Administration effort between 1936 and 1938. The magnificent structure is a tourist attraction drawing some two million people a year, and the outside of the building was used as a body double for The Outlook hotel in the 1980 Jack Nicholson horror movie "The Shining."

Tejas guesses he was three years old when his family took the drive from Portland to admire the mountain and popular stone building.

We lived in the city, but we drove into the country to see Mount Hood from Timberline Lodge. I think that's the imprint on my mind—the mountain. I don't know why I fixated on it. Maybe it was foreshadowing.

The drive was not that long from home, but we did not remain in Portland. My father, Phil Hansel, transferred to a new job in Houston, Texas. It was very different; it was not evergreen or mountainous, just pancake flat. We lived in the city at first, then moved to a suburb. Elementary, junior high, and high school were all in the Houston suburbs. Around there, the only mountain I could see was in the pages of a magazine.

Texas is hot, humid, and flat. There were sugar-cane fields nearby. In fact, we were a stone's throw from Sugarland, Texas. There were rice fields near us, not an Alpine setting as there was near Portland. It was an easy place to live, but I think even at an early age I wanted something more challenging in my life.

My mother Janice was from Canada, near Toronto, and she told stories about how rugged her life was there in the snow, and what the winter storms were like. She loved the outdoors, and that rubbed off on me. We went camping and fishing and I enjoyed those activities.

Even as a little kid, I had a lot of energy that my mother felt I needed to release in a proper activity, so she put me into swimming. I swam competitively for ten years and was strong in the water. My lung capacity and anaerobic threshold were high.

Swimming was a big deal in my family. My father was a prominent swim coach and officiated at the Olympic Games. Ultimately, he became head swim coach of the U.S. Olympic team. My mother was a swimming teacher. My older sister Ginger qualified for the U.S. Nationals. Overall, we were a very physical, very aerobically-oriented family.

We trained with and against some of the best swimmers in the state. Some of them were national-caliber swimmers, and there were even swimmers from around the world. We were held to a pretty high standard of accountability and measurement. I kind of resented it, and I know one younger brother certainly did. I believe that's why he gave up swimming. One sister thrived in that environment, though. We were raised around big-time swimmers and sometimes, if they could not get a room elsewhere, they stayed in the guest house behind our home. Dawn Fraser of Australia, who won eight Olympic medals, including the 100 meter freestyle three times, stayed with us for a while.

I liked swimming when I was doing it, but it wasn't my choice; it was my parents'. Most kids don't necessarily resonate with choices their parents make for them, and I was no exception. I swam through high school until I was seventeen, but I had never asked myself, "Do I like this?" In retrospect, I liked it fine, but I may have liked it for my parents' sake. However, it was probably the best training for high-altitude mountaineering that I could have dreamed up. Still, swimming is a lot of work. The average person has no idea how hard swimmers work. It's also solitary work; you're really in your own head there, in kind of a sensory deprivation environment where everything is warm and sloshy and you can't hear or see well. You can barely breathe well, and yet you're asked to perform at a level of high energy output for a long time. I mean hours. Top swimmers worked out twice a day: an hour-and-a-half before school, and again after school.

The parallel to high-altitude mountaineering is a bit ironic. Swimming long hours is probably the best thing to do to prepare for being a high-altitude mountain slogger. Basically, a mountain climber's breathing is almost the same thing as a swimmer's. Kicking is like walking while leaning on ski poles or an ice axe. Climbing, the whole body is in rhythmic breathing. There is monotonous sensory deprivation, especially high on a mountain when wearing an oxygen mask and hat.

Ed Viesturs, the only American to climb all fourteen of the world's 8,000-meter peaks, was the captain of his college swim team. Several other high-altitude mountaineers I know were swimmers. I know Ed Viesturs's lungs are larger than normal. I had my lungs measured, and they are twenty-five percent bigger than the average person's lungs, meaning I get an extra liter of air when I breathe. The average male's lung capacity is three liters, and I am at four liters. That's significant if you are exposed to a low-oxygen environment.

While swimming was great for building stamina when I was young, getting involved with scouts provided more outdoor time, including hiking. I got involved in scouts early, first Cub Scouts and then Boy Scouts. At thirteen, I went to the famous Philmont Scout Ranch near Cimarron, New Mexico. The ranch was founded in 1938 and owned by the Boy Scouts. I was on the young side—I believe thirteen was the minimum age for acceptance—but my scout master recommended me and maybe even fudged my age. I think he recognized I was searching for something that I wasn't finding, even in a family with five brothers and sisters. I was the second oldest, with one older sister, two younger sisters, and two younger brothers.

Since I was younger than most of the other scouts (only grew to be five feet nine inches anyway), I was the runt of the group. We did some fishing, went through survival school lessons, and then climbed a mountain. Baldy Mountain stands 12,441 feet high and is located on the northwest boundary of the ranch. More accurately, we hiked a mountain. We did not need ropes, ice axes, or crampons. What we did face was an abrupt elevation gain to a respectable altitude that would definitely slow you down if you were not in shape. As we hiked higher and higher on the trail, we had to cope with thinner air. I think the scout leaders believed I was going to be the last one up.

Gradually, as we hiked, I noticed we began losing some of the adults and the older and bigger scouts. As we closed in on the top, I was the only one left: the one in front. I didn't realize it at that time, but that was no doubt due to my swim training.

I did really well and stood out that day. It did set the hook early on for my climbing interest. I found something I was suited for as a side effect of swimming, even though I had never climbed before. I was naturally adaptive to the circumstances, and had good aerobic capacity from my everyday pool cardio training. Climbing to the top before anyone else in my troop left me feeling really stoked. I remember actually running down from the summit and experiencing a certain kind of lightness. It was the joy of discovering I had done really well at something new. I think I was benefiting from my larger lung capacity. I did not think about it for years until I was climbing mountains full-time and had my pulmonary capacity checked.

Baldy may have come easy, but school was rough on me. I had dyslexia and did not socialize well. It wasn't that I was dumb, but I had learning issues. For me, the big challenge was just getting through it at all. When I was about fourteen, my folks enrolled me in a reading course because of my troubles. Once that occurred, I did quite well. I was taught how to read faster. I became a speed reader and was clocked at over 40,000 words a minute. I was burning through pages. I could flash through a paperback book in thirty minutes. I read about things that interested me and learned a lot. It was just zoom, zoom, zoom. I got so good that they put me on TV. I'm not sure the TV part was good; I was not a guy who spoke well, especially in public with cameras on me. It was tough duty for the introverted. Speed reading takes considerable work. I hated working that hard, so it didn't stick. But my comprehension rose from sixty percent to eighty percent.

Even though I was a whiz at reading, I did not like school. Socialization was very painful for me. I knew I wasn't dumb and my teachers figured it out, too, but I floundered in junior high, and was put in advanced placement classes in high school. The speed reading led the school authorities to put me in a gifted class. That was probably not the best thing. Even in English I did poorly. Putting me in a gifted class because of my speed reading was probably a well-intentioned mistake, and I went from being at the top of my class to just being a contender. It mirrored my swimming situation: I went from being someone special to one of a bunch of people labeled special. Really, at that level I was just like everyone else in the class. Somewhere along the way I felt, "Why should I try?" I decided I did not want more competition in my life. So I backed off and my reading slowed down. It took a couple of years before teachers recognized I did not want to be in advanced classes. When they put me back in normal classes, I did OK. I was a lot more comfortable, and before it was all over, I tried to fail my senior year so I could repeat a year of school. I just liked being there.

My parents had chosen our neighborhood based on it being having a good school system. So they were not terribly excited by my attitude towards school. I think it was caused more by social anxiety than anything else. Shyness. It didn't help that I had a bit of a speech impediment. I used to daydream. I was the guy who spent his time looking out the window. I was the guy who wanted to go outdoors, run amongst the trees, play with the frogs, and be left alone. I didn't want to be on sports teams; swimming was enough for me. But I still had all of this energy. My old Alaskan friend Harry Johnson once described me as a Type B personality in a Type A body.

My father bailing out on my mother and the family devastated me and made me quite rebellious. My response was to push authority's limits as far as I could. Basically, I was a good kid. I grew up religious and had a pretty normal upbringing, but I had a feisty streak and wanted to find out where the limits were. I pushed against the teachers, and they didn't like it. School kicked me out, and even had me arrested to get me off school property. I figured out at a pretty early age that I didn't fit in well, but I decided I didn't want to. I had brushes with the law, though nothing big. Mostly, my mother would be called to come get me.

In my junior year at high school, I got sent home for being disruptive. I was wearing a cowboy hat and jeans with holes in them and kissing a girl. Though all very stylish these days, schools back then had rules against such things. To me, it was an attempt to stifle my freedom of expression, so I refused to go. That's when the sheriff arrested me for trespassing and dragged me away in handcuffs.

I wasn't socializing well, and I was not into the same things as my classmates. Houston seemed like a horrible place for a young kid. I kept trying to escape in one way or another. Every time I got the chance, I jumped the back fence and ran off into the woods. We lived close to the Buffalo Bayou, a fifty-two-mile-long slow moving waterway that flows right through the middle of the city. Houston was founded on the Bayou; I just retreated there.

I was going on fifteen when I temporarily ran away from home to the Rocky Mountains, hitchhiking to Colorado. The mountains were an attraction because they seemed to offer solitude. This was in the later sixties, at the beginning of the hippie movement and the theme of back-to-the-land.

Buffalo Bayou, which runs through Houston,
was Vern's getaway in his youth

I discovered that hitchhiking could be an amazing way to get around. It was cheap, I was young enough people weren't afraid of me, and I got rides all of the way to Colorado. Not by accident, I ended up in the San Juan Mountains near the New Mexico border. I was told by a guy that ran an outdoors shop in Houston that the San Juan Mountains are the roughest square fourteen miles in the contiguous United States. Houston wasn't cutting it for me, even though I fished in the Bayou and hand-caught snakes, so I was excited to learn there were places even more adventurous than the solitude of the Bayou. I thought, "I've got to go to the most rugged places." I went alone and took along books telling me how to live in the wilderness. One was *Stalking the Wild Asparagus* by Euell Gibbons; the other was *The Wilderness Cabin* by Calvin Rutstrum. I wanted to learn how to build a log cabin and live in the woods. I took a bow and arrow, axe, sleeping bag, stove, tent, books, tarp, and a whole lot of gumption. I left no forwarding address. My intention was to run away, become a hermit, live off the fat of the land, and hang out in the most rugged fourteen-square-mile part of the United States. I figured I would be a hermit for the rest of my life.

I quickly found out there was not much fat on the land. I lost a lot of weight. Two weeks later, I came out of the woods pretty hungry. I had a few dollars in my pocket so I walked into a café at a truck stop and ate a full meal. It was so good that I began thinking, "I'm not sure if living off the land is what I'm really cut out for. I'm really into pancakes and eggs." It was educational. I found out I loved the mountains, but didn't love trying to live off the land. I could build a cabin, but then I would be stuck in one place. What I really learned was that I enjoyed travel. I enjoyed meeting new people. I actually came out of my shell somewhat when I was not sequestered in suburbia. I could learn from people, learn their stories.

I had a free spirit and fortunately did not get into any major trouble on the road, though I got into a couple of tight jams. I learned the worst animals out there are not the wild ones; they're the human ones. That's what you have to worry about. I survived lots of propositions as a young, long-haired traveler. I got picked up by gay guys and older women, but I was lucky and learned fast. I learned about people and life at a young age. I was only a ninth-grader, but I felt free out there. I could go in any direction I wanted to, at any time. This was all quite novel for someone brought up as a church-going Boy Scout who was a suburban-life dweller. I wanted this bigger, wilder life. After my big, hot meal, I spent a little more time in Colorado and headed back to Texas. I definitely did not want to spend the winter in Colorado's mountains

My mother was beside herself with worry while I was gone, but she also was raising five other kids, and I was the troublemaker. She had many things to focus on like trying to earn a living and maybe find a new boyfriend with my father gone. She didn't want me to run away, but it might have been a blessing for her. I did not even leave a note, but she figured out I ran away when I didn't come to the dinner table for a week.

After that trip, I began awakening to girls, and that's where my main interest was when I returned to school. It didn't bode well for learning much in a classroom setting, but learning about the opposite sex helped me enjoy school a little bit more.

The next year, not running away, I hitchhiked to Colorado with a friend, Michael Mansfield, the nephew of the glamorous actress Jayne Mansfield, who died in a terrible automobile accident. I became more enticed by the 14,000-foot Rocky Mountains on that visit.

My last semester in high school, I planned to flunk out, but the teachers didn't want me back. I picked up what I could from high school, but did not go to college. I can hold my own in a conversation and I can thank my parents for that. We had a great family. We weren't poor, and we weren't wealthy, and although many of the people around us had much more than we did, we had family.

When the school year ended, I was itching to get out of Houston. I felt life was happening out there in the world, not in the suburbs of Houston. The people around me seemed to have a closed mindset. They wanted to tell me how to look, how to think, how to act, how to pray. I mean, it was everything. I was in rambler mode again. I bailed out early and didn't stick around for graduation. My teachers colluded to make sure I wasn't coming back the next year. They didn't want the trouble I represented.

I spent the next two years of my life hitchhiking to every state in the country except Maine and Hawaii. That included visiting Alaska for the first time.

ALASKA AND DENALI WISHES

Even if the idea did not come to Vern Tejas from reading National Geographic, somehow it seemed inevitable that he would make his way north following his sojourns in Colorado. He had been steered to what was allegedly the most rugged corner of the United States's lower forty-eight states, but soon enough he learned there was another part of the country more rugged yet.

Though Colorado was populated by several dozen mountains standing at least 14,000 feet high (not to mention the many more whose altitudes stretched to 13,000-plus feet), Alaska offered more impressive scenery and far more alluring mountains. Alaska seduced wanderers, invited them to a vast territory nicknamed The Last Frontier. Those of free spirit, as Tejas described himself, got hooked easily. They felt they must see it once. Often enough, one peek isn't enough, and they stayed, for years or forever.

The signature geographic feature of the state is Denali, the 20,310-foot high centerpiece of the Alaska Range, a very large bump on the map that stands out in relief because no other mountain close to it is nearly as large. On rare clear days, Denali can be viewed from Anchorage to the south and Fairbanks to the northeast. Denali, called either "The High One" or "The Great One" in native languages, was referred to as Mount McKinley for more than a century in reference to President William McKinley. The mountain is singular as the tallest mountain not only in Alaska or the United States, but North America. Residents of Alaska often casually say, "The mountain is out today," meaning the view is free of obstructing clouds.

Mountaineers come to Alaska each spring seeking to climb Denali and consider reaching the summit one of the great prizes in the sport. Likewise, the fittest and most adventurous of Alaska citizens spend years admiring the snow-covered slopes, and decide they absolutely must climb Denali one day.

Vern Tejas knew none of this background as a nineteen-year-old when, free from school, he headed to Alaska. His early friendship with one of the most remarkable of all Alaskan figures, the venerable Colonel Norman Vaughan, began early during his stay in Alaska.

During the period I spent traveling around the United States, I also dipped into Canada. It was a grand sweep, and I visited most of the largest provinces. I made my way by hitchhiking from Quebec to the Yukon Territory. In Whitehorse, the territory's capital, I hitched a ride with a fellow named Robin Bowen who had just floated the Yukon River from Whitehorse to Circle, in Alaska, and was back to pick up his empty van in Whitehorse. His destination was Circle City to pick up his canoe, so off we went into Alaska, where Robin had lived for about five years.

On my second day in the state, August 2, 1972, we entered Denali National Park, taking the tourist shuttle bus because the road was closed beyond the first fifteen miles. We encountered some mountains, foothills really. We looked at one another and said, "Let's go climb them." Robin was energetic and my age, so we began ascending a 5,000-foot peak. It probably has a name, but we didn't know it. It was just a dot on the map to us. All of the mountains around it were about the same height. There was a little bit of snow on top, and it seemed inviting.

While we climbed, a snowstorm blew in and buried us. There was probably about a foot-and-a-half of snow. I was climbing in a cotton cowboy shirt, jeans, and a straw cowboy hat. Talk about being ill-prepared. We crested the top of the ridge and descended the other side to a valley. By that time I was shivering uncontrollably.

Robin said, "I think you have hypothermia." I didn't have a clue what that was, I just knew I was really cold.

I replied, "I'm so cold I can't stop moving. If I stop moving I'm gonna fall apart."

Anyone with a minimum of knowledge of the outdoors knows how dangerous hypothermia can be. Hypothermia kicks in when a body loses heat faster than it can produce heat. If the normal body temperature is 98.6 degrees, a drop to 95 degrees can threaten your life.

Robin said, "Keep walking, walk around the camp site, and I'll set up the tent and get your sleeping bag out. As soon as I get it set up, I want you to jump in the sleeping bag." I did not know these basics. I stripped off my wet clothes, jumped into the bag still shivering and drank hot tea with sugar until I warmed up. My second day in Alaska, and I nearly died. And that was in summer.

Who could believe I wore a straw cowboy hat to climb a mountain in Denali National Park? Let's just say it was not manufactured by North Face. It was early August, and that is the hottest month in Texas, and yet here in Alaska, I nearly froze to death.

I thought right away, "This place is going to kill me. You're not in Texas anymore. You are in Alaska, and Alaska doesn't care if you die." That's when I realized this level of being rugged was something new, and that hooked me.

A day later, we got back on the bus. We made a stop at a bridge on the Toklat River, a common stopping place for people to use the bathroom or stretch their legs, and there was a bull caribou on a river bar that had been attacked and wounded in the night by a wolf. Its flank was torn open, but it had not died. There were a lot of people around with cameras taking pictures of this otherwise wild scene. All we had left for food was some cereal, and Robin and I retreated into some blueberry bushes to pick some to sprinkle on our meal.

We sat down on a bluff overlooking the river, and Robin said, "Look, there's a bear with cubs." It was a mama grizzly with three cubs.

I thought, "Man, we really are in the wilderness. I am in an area with no bars, just bears." We watched. They followed the blood scent of an animal upstream—the wounded caribou. The caribou was bleeding out, quite vulnerable, and didn't have the strength to run away. The mama bear sensed breakfast for herself and the cubs. It may be a free lunch for a week. She came up on the caribou and charged. The caribou dipped its head, lowering its rack right into the mama's face. The bear backed up, plotting a new strategy, then charged in again and reached a paw between the antlers. With one swat, she smacked the caribou in the head and broke its neck. Down it went, and it was feast time for the bears.

The cameras were clicking, and film cameras were whirring. I am sure I have seen that footage on television three or four times over the years. *Sourdough* was an Alaskan movie that came out about twenty years later. I'm sure I saw that bear-caribou fight in that film, too. It is classic footage of a mama bear knocking out a caribou so her babies can eat. To me, it was like, "OK, there are not only bears here, but there is life and death here." It was part of the same message: the wilderness, the mountains, the snowstorm, the animals. I was in a wild place, the type of wild place where I wanted to make a life, where things are no longer cookie cutter. I was definitely no longer in Houston, where everything was flat and predictable.

I had been in Alaska just a couple of days, and it had already almost killed me. Then I saw Alaska kill something else. We continued on the bus to Wonder Lake and the clouds began to slowly lift as the snow tapered off and stopped. I knew there was supposed to be a great view across the lake. It has often been said that Denali reveals itself gradually, so we looked in the direction of the mountain.

"Whoa!"

All I knew was Denali was the biggest mountain in North America. I knew nothing else about its history or climbing. Up, up, the clouds go, and our eyes were as big as the mountain looking at its humongous size. Then we realized we were just seeing the foothills and barely getting the mountain in focus. What we thought was so huge was just the sub-range in front of Denali. Everything was snow-covered, which made the smaller mountains appear bigger. The big hill was still behind those other hills.

The mountain continued revealing itself very slowly. Twilight sunset on August 2 is just past 11:30 p.m., and sunrise is just past 4:30 a.m., so there is some light in the sky most of the time that time of year. These were really long days. As it approached the end of the evening, the clouds completely disappeared. We watched the mountain become exposed, and we just sat there spellbound. We were making obvious comments like, "I can't believe it's so big." When we glanced around, we saw a bear walking in one direction, and caribou strolling in another area. Looking back at Denali, we saw sunlight forming purples and oranges: alpenglow. We were at lower elevation just looking up. That's when Robin and I both said we were going to climb that mountain someday.

There are a few reasons why Denali has such a stunning presence. It is taller than any other mountain near it by several thousand feet and is extremely wide with a huge mass. So it is common for the mountain to make such a powerful first impression on people the way it did on me. From base to peak, the elevation gain is around 13,000 feet, depending on the manner of approach. That is more than Everest, which from base to peak is 12,000 feet.

Although I never could have imagined it based on my first glimpse, it must be said that Denali is my mountain, my home mountain. Between 1978 and 2017, there were only two calendar years I did not climb Denali. It became the mountain most special to me, most familiar to me. I have climbed it more often than any other person in the world. Some of my greatest personal achievements, my most satisfying memories, and my most horrendous ones are linked to the mountain.

Obtaining my first complete view of the mountain with Robin in 1972, there was no way such things would have entered my brain. Denali was new and fresh and exciting, and, beyond almost paralyzing me with its distinctive natural beauty, I looked at it as a mountaineering challenge and a daring inspiration. Just right away, I had the thought that I must climb it. Certainly the thought was to climb it once, not fifty-seven times.

I did not know how important the mountain was going to become for me. I did know the mountain itself was gigantic; at the time it was the biggest thing I had ever seen. To me, it was like a dinosaur: old and huge. Denali is like being in an IMAX theatre; it paints the whole horizon. It is not as if you are looking at an object, but you are experiencing the immensity. The bigness just overwhelmed me. It was not only larger than anything I had seen, but larger than anything I had imagined. I felt so insignificant next to it. I was motivated by a desire to climb Denali, to see the landscape from the top, to show I was able to reach the summit.

But I put Alaska on pause temporarily. I continued my travels, left the state, and spent the winter working in a commune in Oregon. Around this time, I changed my last name after a big falling out with my father. I told him I would never give him anything to be proud of. In doing so, I hated myself for years until I grew beyond seeking vengeance. Fortunately, we were able to make peace before he passed away. I chose *Tejas* because it means "friend" in Caddo, the language of the original Gulf Coast native Texans. It is actually where Texas gets its name as well. Interestingly, and unbeknownst to me at the time, it also means "roof tile" in Spanish and "brilliant" in Sanskrit.

In 1973, I came to Alaska to live. It was in my mind to climb Denali, but I knew I did not have enough of a mountaineering background to even try. I understood Alaska was a special place. The wildness I had seen on my first trip gripped me. I went to work in Anchorage, the state's largest city, which now has 300,000 people, but back then had about 200,000.

The east side of Anchorage is bordered by the Chugach Mountain Range. Every Alaska resident knows about those mountains, but few people outside the state do. They are not famous, but make up a large portion of Anchorage's horizon. In Colorado, the highest mountains are around 14,000 feet tall. When one looks out from the summit, the surrounding peaks seem to be the same height. In Anchorage, most of the peaks are 4,000 or 5,000 feet. From the summits, they also offer the same perspective. To prepare myself for the day I hoped to climb Denali, I went climbing in the Chugach Range every weekend that I could.

I quickly began meeting interesting Alaskan characters. During my first year of living in Alaska, I got to know Colonel Norman Vaughan, who was not only a wonderful man, but one who never let age interfere with his imagination. Norman was already a senior citizen, and he lived his life by the motto "Dream Big and Dare to Fail." Bankrupt and divorced, Norman moved to Alaska from Massachusetts when he was sixty-eight. It is often said that it is easy for people to get lost in Alaska if they wish to be, and it is a place people go to start over. In Norman's case, he was starting over, but he was too social to remain anonymous. For anyone who cared to look it up, he brought a reputation with him.

In 1928, Norman dropped out of Harvard University to join Admiral Richard Byrd's expedition to Antarctica as a dog handler. On that trip, Byrd named a mountain for Norman. Mount Vaughan is a 10,302-foot peak that Norman vowed to climb one day. Years later, this dream and my connection to Norman became a big part of my life.

In 1932, Norman was part of the Winter Olympics sled-dog exhibition sport. In the 1970s, when he was in his seventies, Norman competed in the 1,000-mile Iditarod Trail Sled Dog Race from Anchorage to Nome, Alaska. I met Norman through a job I held at BJ's Warehouse in Anchorage. I got to know some of the cashiers, and one of their husbands worked as a janitor at Alaska Pacific University across town. He worked with another janitor, an old-timer—Norman.

My buddy Robin was living in a cabin on the outskirts of town, and I lived next door in a five-man tent squatting on the property. I stayed there for two winters. The cashier and her husband came into possession of a large supply of salmon and invited several people over for a big fish dinner. I thought salmon was about as Alaskan as anything out there, so I went with my girlfriend at the time, another cashier.

There was only one Norman Vaughan. He had a forever-young spirit, even though he was way older than all of us, with a white beard that gave him a distinguished look, and he was always looking ahead. Alaskans loved him for that. Some called him Alaska's Grandpa. Right from the beginning, Norman was friendly. This was a short while before he was going to try the Iditarod. Of course he knew quite a bit more than I did about winter travel and gear, but he talked to me as an equal. He asked my opinion about the type of footwear he should choose: the famous white, thick, rubber bunny boots, or mukluks, the Native Alaskan preferred footwear. He asked me because I was spending the winter in a tent. Bunny boots are very heavy when you walk along, but they are waterproof. If you wear mukluks, your feet can get wet. Sure enough, Norman choose the mukluks and ran across some river overflow—water that sometimes works its way through the frozen surface over a river, becoming treacherous—and his feet got wet. He could have frozen to death and was lucky to only suffer frostbite. He did get lost on the trail, though, and had to be rescued. But he returned again and again and raced until he was eighty-four.

Norman, who was later elected to the Alaska Sports Hall of Fame for his accomplishments, made a major first impression on me. He helped juice up my excitement about being in Alaska. The way he honored and respected me in our conversation, I felt an affinity not only for him and what he had done, but for a country that had people like him in it. It cemented a link between me and Alaska. What a great place that had people like Norman living on the edge. Sure, Alaska can kill you and nature is raw, but there are also these amazing people. I met many eclectic people during my first year in the state that made me realize I was home. It was a place I could fit in. I was a social misfit who found a new family there with people like Norman in it.

For a while, I did odd jobs to survive, to pay the few bills I had since I lived very frugally. I was a warehouse man, a construction worker, a carpenter, and a ditch digger. I cleared land, built roads, shoveled snow, whatever it took. Outdoors work was good for me. I joined the Laborers' Union and went to work on the construction of the Alaska Pipeline in the mid-1970s. That was good money. I thought I had it made. We all did. People bought expensive trucks, bought farms, bought all sorts of things. I didn't do all that. I saved. I did not anticipate double-digit inflation following.

I jumped with both feet into the Mountaineering Club of Alaska, the Kayaking Club, and the Alaska Mountain Rescue Group. The rescue group was just starting up, but I learned a lot, and the group evolved into a more elite operation where the people were well-trained to help others who had climbing accidents or were caught up in avalanches. When I joined, it was volunteer work, but I met the old, experienced Alaskans. People like Dick Griffith and Udo Fischer were good mentors. As a German, Udo was conscripted into the Army when he was very young at the end of World War II, but immigrated to the United States and became a survival instructor for the military through the Korean and Vietnam Wars. He sometimes said he lost three wars.

There was a lot of climbing in the near Chugach Range, including the peaks that can be seen from any office window in Anchorage like O'Malley, Flattop, South Suicide, and North Suicide (two mountains not named in friendly fashion), Ptarmigan, The Ramp, The Wedge, and others. Chugach State Park has many more mountains and many taller, but those are right there. When you look out from the tops of those mountains, you see the city. We also made trips to the Kenai Peninsula for other mountains. I learned to ski, although at first it felt like I was trying to learn to fall. I finally got to the point where I could ski downhill without nearly killing myself. Cross-country skiing was easier, and took me into the backcountry to explore. I couldn't afford lift tickets anyway

The Chugach mountain range is visible from Anchorage, Alaska

I was young and full of enthusiasm and energy, and I was drinking in everything about the Alaska outdoors. I didn't have a car back then, so I kept hitchhiking everywhere I went. It was a little awkward when they called out the rescue group, and I showed up after hitching a ride.

They'd ask me, "Where have you been?"

"The rides weren't very good."

Honestly, I got to know a lot of Alaskans by hitchhiking. Some people picked me up several times and I got to know them on a first-name basis. I volunteered for the Mountain Rescue Group for twenty years. Through the Rescue Group, I met Harry Johnson, which was a turning point in my life. The most famous Denali guiding company was operated by Ray Genet. Harry knew Genet and took over the company when Ray died on Mount Everest in 1979. Before that, though, Harry established a survival school for teenagers, and I went to work for him teaching in that program. With that opportunity, I was able to pull together a grub stake so that I could afford the cost of climbing Denali when the day came that I thought I was ready. It took five years from the time I first saw Denali in its splendor until my body, mind, and bank account were prepared for the climb I so desperately wanted to make.

CLIMBING DENALI

The native peoples of Alaska were long aware of the forbidding and mystical mountain in Alaska's Interior. Although the Alaska Gold Rush put the territory on the map for the first time since its purchase from Russia in 1867, for the most part the pursuit of gold focused attention on other areas of the new 586,000-square-mile American property. The earliest excitement over gold strikes in Alaska sent prospectors scurrying through Skagway in Southeast Alaska and over the Chilkoot Pass into Canada and the Yukon Territory. Later, gold was discovered on the beaches of Nome on the western coast of Alaska, which was at the time mainly accessible by steamship. Denali was hundreds of miles from either place and was an unknown hunk of rock to the majority of Americans until prospector William Dickey emerged from the Interior without fulfilling his monetary prospects, yet quite dazzled by the extraordinary mountain he laid eyes on.

William McKinley, who was born in Niles, Ohio, made his home in Canton, Ohio and served as the thirty-ninth governor of the state. In 1896, McKinley was campaigning for the presidency as a Republican, and one of his campaign points was a desire to retain the country's gold standard as a policy. Dickey agreed with this, and his empathy with the program led him to name the colossal mountain after McKinley. McKinley was assassinated in 1901, propelling his vice-president, Theodore Roosevelt, into the White House.

Yellowstone was created as the first national park in 1872, but the Park System steadily expanded. In 1917, the National Park then called McKinley National Park was formed. It eventually expanded to six million acres of landscape and saw the name changed to Denali National Park and Preserve in 1980. However, the McKinley name remained affixed to the mountain until 2015 when, following almost a century's worth of lobbying, President Barack Obama switched the name to Denali. This delighted Alaskans, but disappointed McKinley's longstanding Ohio adherents.

Throughout the long period of pioneering climbs on the mountain, it had been officially named Mount McKinley. For much of that time, as well, the official measurement of the summit was believed to be 20,320 feet. The height was officially changed to 20,310 feet in 2015 after measurement with more modern and sophisticated scientific technology.

Not long after Dickey's naming of McKinley, which officially took place in 1897, the mountain became an object of great curiosity to adventurers who sought the glory that would accrue from becoming the first to stand on the summit. Also, from the start of those attempts, the mountain periodically shrugged off humans, buried them in snow, intimidated them with high winds, and repelled their worthy (and in some cases fraudulent) tries to reach the top.

Mount Denali (McKinley) was successfully climbed for the first time on June 7, 1913 by a small party of Alaskans led by Hudson Stuck, one of the leading figures of the period. Stuck was a native of England, and became an Episcopal priest with the mission of bringing the word of God to Alaska and Canada's Yukon. He delivered his news by dog sled, covering more than 10,000 miles mushing for the Lord. Stuck; Walter Harper, an Alaska native; Harry Karstens; and Robert Tatum were the first people to absorb the view from the top. Harper was the first amongst the first. Tatum famously observed while gazing at the far-reaching landscape that it was like "looking out the windows of heaven."

The time came. Finally, I was going to climb Denali. Mountain Trip was conducting a climb, and there was a cancellation late in the planning. I was offered a half-price deal and I jumped at the chance. The price of taking a guided trip to the mountain, a climb that was scheduled to be three weeks long, has increased steadily over the years, as has everything else in life. In May of 1978 it was much cheaper, although was still expensive for someone who worked odd jobs. Back then it cost $1,100. Now it is about $7,000.

The guides were Jim Hale and Mark Moderow, an Anchorage attorney. Jim had been a guide for Genet Expeditions, but then formed his own company. Ray Genet was hardcore. He understood that his business relied on a good success rate, so his theme was "To the Summit!" For him, it was a sign of failure, not necessarily good judgment, to turn back on a climb. He and Jim Hale had a falling out over that. On one trip, Jim decided avalanche conditions made it too dangerous to continue and turned back his group. Genet reamed him out. The way I recall the story, Genet was pounding his fist on his office desk and yelling, "We don't turn back! We go to the summit! To the summit!"

Jim's response to that was, "You can go to the summit and die if you want to. I'm out of here." Hale took that confrontation as a sign that he was working for someone who believed money was more important than life. So Jim joined with Gary Bocarde, another famous guide, to form a new company, Mountain Trip. I knew Jim from the Mountaineering

Club of Alaska and the Mountain Rescue Group. I had actually been living with Mark; several climbers went in together to keep the cost of apartment rental low.

The scheduled trip included a twelve-man team with the two guides and a very ambitious plan. Not only would we climb the West Buttress route to the summit, but we would make a traverse over the top. The idea was to climb from the south side, landing by plane on the Kahiltna Glacier, climb up and over Kahiltna Pass, and then descend to Wonder Lake. What would normally be a twenty-six-mile trip would have twenty more miles added on. The West Buttress is the most commonly climbed route on the mountain: the path to the top that guided climbs follow. It was pioneered by Dr. Bradford Washburn in 1951. Denali is an exception to the rule in mountaineering. Almost always the biggest mountains are climbed first by the easiest route. When Hudson Stuck's party climbed in 1913, they approached from the north and other groups followed their route. Brad always believed there was a simpler way to make the climb, and because of his expertise as a mountain photographer, he pretty much proved it on paper before making the climb. Turned out he was right all along, and the naysayers of the mountain world who were convinced he would die trying were wrong.

The typical guided group gathers in the community of Talkeetna, which is about 110 miles from Anchorage. A core group of bush pilots established flight services and ferried climbers back and forth to Denali base camp in their small planes, landing on the Kahiltna Glacier. It is a support industry for mountaineers, although they also fly tourists around the mountain, sometimes landing in the same place just for the experience of seeing Denali up close. For a West Buttress climb, the planes carrying climbers and supplies land at about 7,200 feet of elevation on the Kahiltna. That is the jumping off point for mountaineers. For decades during the main Denali climbing season, there has been a full-time base-camp manager who maintains radio contact with the flight services and National Park Service rangers. That's a sign of how much human traffic there can be on the Kahiltna.

One main difference between a guide and a citizen climber—what I was at the time—is experience and mountain knowledge. The guide knows the terrain. The guide has been there before. The guide is trained to handle people. And the guide recognizes the wrong behavior on the peak. The wrong behavior might be a personality problem, or it might be a tendency to make mistakes that could jeopardize an individual's trip or even risk the safety of those around him.

From all of my training in the Chugach Range near Anchorage, I was in pretty good shape. However, I was climbing mountains of 5,000 feet, not 20,000 feet. When you get higher than 10,000 feet, and are not used to the altitude, you can become subject to pulmonary edema, which creates excess fluid in the lungs, or cerebral edema, characterized by excess fluid in the brain. They are both potentially fatal illnesses stemming from lack of oxygen. There are a lot of ways to die in the mountains. At that time, I didn't really know anything about altitude. When I ran away to Colorado, I got sick once and ended up puking, not knowing what caused it. In retrospect, I am sure it was the altitude that got me. I went up too high too fast.

After scraping the money together for my first climb of Denali five years after first seeing the mountain, I was excited to be there, raring to go, and sure I was in terrific shape. I was totally gung-ho, but I did not really understand that it was a totally different animal going up beyond the foothills of 6,000 or 7,000 feet. Our first day on Denali, we were at Kahiltna Glacier, at 7,200 feet, as our starting point. I was not a very big guy; I was five feet nine inches on a good day, and my climbing weight was 160 pounds or so. I picked up a big load to carry to the next camp. I kept thinking, "This was my long-time dream and I am finally going to make it happen." In my enthusiastic state, I grabbed more than my fair share of group gear and lashed it to my sled. I probably had forty-five pounds in a pack and another forty-five pounds on a sled. That's ninety pounds of equipment. It was in the heat of the day, and I took off like a race horse out of the gate.

I'm just zooming along, boom, boom, boom, pulling up a storm. Soon enough, I was just grinding. Given that Denali is always snow covered, everyone thinks it is always freezing on the mountain. Not true. During the long periods of daylight in the summer, it can warm up pretty good. I had my shirt open. My face was getting just totally fried from the sun. I stopped eating. I got dehydrated. We climbed to the next camp, came down, a round-trip of ten miles, and I was exhausted, had diarrhea, and thought I was ruined for the trip.

All of this preparation time and after just one day, I looked at Hale and said, "Jim, I want out of here. Put me on the next flight." I was demoralized.

Jim did a great job in the guide role then. "Vern," he said, "you overdid it. I could have told you that in advance, but you wouldn't have understood." He was right. Given my excited outlook, I wasn't ready to hear it. By the end of the first day, I was ready to hear it.

Jim acted like a coach with superior wisdom. Fortunately, he talked me out of flying out. He said, "Just spend the night. See how you feel in the morning. If you still want to go home you can, but I encourage you to stay in here and take care of yourself. Put the sunscreen on. Drink at every break. Eat every time we make a stop. Don't take on so much weight at one time. We've basically got a month here. Slow down and enjoy it."

I was forced to cool my jets, and the next day I had a better time. We covered only half the distance and we did not make a round-trip. I didn't carry as much weight, and perhaps more importantly, I started taking care of myself. I drank and ate every hour and applied gobs of sun cream. I was able to take a step back and take a deep breath. I started to just enjoy being in the mountains and not thinking of the climb as this big challenge where I had to throw everything at it every minute.

That was a very big lesson for me, and what Jim said to me I still apply and say to my climbers today. It is more about taking one step at a time and one day at a time. The more I approached the trip that way that first time on Denali, the easier the climbing became, and the more enjoyable the journey became. I ended up having a great time and developed lifetime friendships with some of the people on that climb. Once I got acclimated, everything came much easier. It turned out I was someone who acclimates slowly. I got stronger the higher we went, and at high camps when others were tired, I was eager.

My enthusiasm returned, although I had to learn to temper it. I even had to hold myself back and keep a steady pace. Our high camp was at about 18,200 feet, higher than most people set up because we were going to do more than just go for the South Summit, the highest point. Having our camp higher than usual allowed us to be in position for traversing the mountain and a potential double-header. The South Summit is where the 20,310-foot absolute top of Denali is located, but there is also a North Summit, which few people go to. It is a little bit shorter at 19,470 feet, so most people don't bother with it and are satisfied with only the South Summit.

Reaching the top of Denali was a special moment. I put on my cowboy hat and played "Old Susanna" on my harmonica. It was my first of many times on top, absorbing the view, and I loved it, but the day was not over.

Jim said he wanted to see what the North Summit looked like. He had never been there; very few people do both, much less in one day. Jim asked if anybody else was up for it. I immediately sprang up: "Yeah, I'll go!" I was the only one. The other guys went to sleep while Jim and I went off and climbed the North Summit, un-roped, unsafe in retrospect: one of the foolhardy things people can do and somehow get away with.

The most intriguing Denali tale of the two summits relates to the so-called "Sourdough" climb of 1910. By then, a few expeditions had come to Alaska to climb Denali hoping to be the first to knock off the summit. They failed, although one inappropriately took credit for the first ascent, enraging some Fairbanks residents. Sitting around in a bar (many Alaskan grand challenges owe their origins to the creative thinking of drinkers) one day, a group of old-timers boasted they could make the climb. They set out to prove it, hauling along a tall wooden post they intended to plant on the summit as a signal to their friends back home.

Making good on their optimism, the Sourdoughs climbed Denali, installed the pole at the top, and returned to Fairbanks, having conquered difficult conditions with primitive equipment. Only they climbed the wrong peak, the North Summit. It was still a very big achievement, but their mistake left the way open for Hudson Stuck's expedition as the first to the true summit.

Jim and I got to the edge of the Wickersham Wall, the huge face of Denali I had first seen five years earlier. We wanted to look down that wall, but we were not sure if the snow cornice would hold us if we walked on it. We debated whether or not we would fall to our deaths if we stepped out upon it. We compromised with the mountain and I crawled out on the cornice while Jim held my feet, then Jim crawled out on the cornice while I held his feet. As if we could have saved one another if the snow had given way.

The view was beautiful. There was nothing protruding in the way, so we could look down this immense mountain face that drops between 13,000 and 14,000 feet. We were totally in awe and had a wonderful summit day. It was much more than I could have expected five years earlier when I first looked at it, or even more than I could have expected five minutes earlier. I had no idea if we were going to die or see the most spectacular sight on earth. Fortunately, it was the latter.

As we walked back to camp, I just felt heroic. I had climbed both peaks of Denali. And I had climbed them with a very excellent climber who had good judgment and knew how to deal with people. I was enthralled with the mountain. I was enthralled with the man. I was enthralled with the moment.

It got even better. We trekked out to Wonder Lake, caught the Park bus and made our way to the train depot inside the Park. We were all starving, so we jammed into the dining car. When we told the tourists what we had just done, they treated us like heroes and bought us food and beverages. We were mountaineers, people who had climbed the mountain they merely looked at from afar. Climbing Denali was not as commonly done nearly forty years ago. It was very special that we had done it. It was just an amazing response. We intended to celebrate with our own cash, but they wouldn't let us pay. "You want another hamburger?" "Yeah, I'll take two." We were chowing down. The train ride was actually one of the big highlights of the trip.

There was a special glow about that trip for me, but I didn't have much time to savor it. Almost immediately when we got back to Anchorage, Jim Hale asked me and another climber from the trip, J.D., if we wanted to go right back to Denali and guide a client. There were supposed to be others on the trip, but they cancelled. Jim was still committed to one client, and that wasn't worth his time, so he deputized us. I had just paid half price for a climb, and now I could go back and do it again for free. The trip was set for two weeks later, so in the space of three weeks of climbing, I went from novice Denali climber to Denali guide. It was an accelerated education.

J.D. and I went right back to the mountain. The client was Dave Walsh, an Anchorage guy who later ran for mayor. He got two novice guides. We got him to the top, but we rushed it along. I think we summited on the eleventh day. In the process, I think we hurt him pretty good. He was not happy on summit day. He had altitude issues and wasn't walking straight. This was not a good thing. I learned that if you run your clients too hard, you could kill them, and if you run them too fast, they can kill you just as easily.

Just below Denali Pass, high on the mountain, there is a stretch between 18,000 and 17,000 feet called "The Autobahn." It is called that because some German climbers fell and dropped 1,000 feet at high speed. It can be a dangerous place on the peak. As we descended, Dave kept slipping off the trail there, and J.D., who is about six foot two and a lean, mean fighting machine, was in front. Each time Dave slipped, I'd yell, "Falling!" to give J.D. a heads-up there was going to be a big pull on the rope, so he wouldn't get pulled off the mountain. It became very unnerving when Dave kept slipping.

Finally, J.D., who believed he was going to get dragged to his death, stomped back to Dave, seventy-five feet behind him on the rope, and picked him up by the collar. He said, "If you do that again, I'm going to kill you!" He looked right into Dave's eyes as he said it, and it cut through the high-altitude fog in his brain. Dave realized the precarious nature of the situation. He also figured J.D. was just as much a threat to his life as the mountain. He managed his footing better after that. He got his act together and negotiated The Autobahn with no more slips.

Dave needed our help, and I learned what to do in the future. Normally, if a climber is getting loopy on our way down from the summit through The Autobahn, I give a little speech. I tell people, "This is the most dangerous part of the mountain. More people have come to grief here than in any other place. Eat, drink, breathe, and stay focused." But in Dave's case I didn't know enough to say that then, or to make him eat and drink before we went down. I was very harsh with him. I actually said he was so weak that I would never vote for him. In retrospect, Dave was probably one of the better candidates. He had a heart. He had a conscience. He made the summit of Denali. Hey, how many politicians go climbing? He probably limped for a month afterwards because we worked him so hard. And I did vote for him when he ran for mayor.

That was my initiation into the world of guiding. I learned and modeled myself after Jim Hale. He was excellent; he had charisma, good people skills, a sense of humor, and a real *joie de vivre*. He loved being outdoors. He really wanted to share the mountains because he loved being in them. We were about the same age and he implanted in me the feeling that not only were mountains challenging to climb, but they could be a fun place to be. So, as a guide, that has been one of my primary drives: to bring the joy out instead of employing a tough-guy act. I tried to soften the experience, tried to make it as comfortable and easy as it could be. Poor Dave. It's still tough, a very tough enterprise, to climb Denali, but it's tough enough on its own. Why scare people away? Why make it an ego trip? We were hard guys with Dave, but it did not take long to realize the better way to lead a climb is to enjoy it. After that, I've always made an effort to create the best mood possible for my people.

There are going to be times the weather is intense, where you are pounded by snow and wind, and you are fatigued and all you want to do is crawl into your tent for the night. The challenges of Denali should never be underestimated. But early on, I decided to inject some fun aspects. I became known as the harmonica-playing guide. Climbers don't want to carry any more weight in their gear to high altitude, but a harmonica? It fits in the pocket quite readily. When we were at camp and had some bad weather, I'd break out the harmonica and make music. Then I moved on to the fiddle and, ultimately, a guitar, which was a little more complicated. A guitar can't be too big or heavy, and you don't want a valuable, marvelous instrument subjected to vicious elements. So I made my own fiddle from scratch or brought along skeletal guitars that could handle the extremes. I began carrying both a mouth harp and guitar just to hear the echo off the mountain.

In 2016, after the season's climbing group finished and were hanging out at the bar at the Fairview Inn in Talkeetna, we talked the barmaid into letting us entertain. We had been practicing at 14,000 feet, and when we took the stage, we had the place stomping. One of the climbers was Ben Barron, an excellent guitar and banjo player. He made some good tip money that night.

Climbers head up the West Buttress of Denali
with Mount Hunter behind them

Shutterstock / Nobusuke Oki

49

When I arrived in Alaska, I wanted to climb Denali. I never imagined there was a career out there for me as a guide who could make his living in the mountains. I was a laborer who suddenly became a professional mountaineer, a Denali specialist. By following my passion, I was having the time of my life.

DENALI BECOMES A
CLIMBING HOME

Man has always possessed the innate desire to explore his surroundings. The first areas of inquiry were the immediate neighborhood. Then, as knowledge expanded and travelers appeared from afar, those who could plotted journeys to other parts of the world. They wanted to see what was out there.

The major prosperous European countries did so by sail. Whether or not Columbus really discovered America in 1492, he did at the least make a harrowing voyage from Europe to North America. Many others, representing various nations, did so as well. Gradually, curiosity shrunk the world and people wanted to better understand what was in their own backyard, as well as across the ocean.

By the twentieth century, the areas of the world that seemed to be of the most intrigue were the poles, North and South, and other frigid areas too cold to be hospitable. In those early days of the 1400s, 1500s and beyond, explorations were authorized by heads of state with the aim of expanding territory. Once an agent of the country planted a flag, theoretically it belonged to the king or queen of somewhere. By 1900, there seemed to be a lot of individual glory attached to leading a band of intrepid adventurers to an unknown place. One could become world famous by being the first to reach the North or South Pole. It is quite clear that there were also faked claims being perpetrated by such well-known individuals as Dr. Frederick Cook.

American explorer Robert Peary is generally credited with being the first to the North Pole in 1909. Dr. Cook announced that he beat Peary to the North Pole by a year. It took a long time to get the word out to the world in those days. He was later discredited. This was relevant because Cook also claimed to be the first to climb Denali.

In May of 1903, Fairbanks Judge James Wickersham, appropriately enough appointed to his federal position by President McKinley, sought to climb Denali. Accompanied by four other men and two mules, Wickersham's group made the first recorded ascent attempt, but failed. In 1906, Cook announced he had accomplished the first ascent. Although there are those who still believe him, Dr. Bradford Washburn—perhaps the most important and influential figure to focus on Denali geology, history, and climbing—

spent decades amassing evidence proving Cook had not succeeded. Cook's alleged summit photo later became known as Fake Peak because it was proven to be at only 5,338 feet of elevation.

The Alaska Sourdoughs gave it their best shot in 1910. In 1912, attempting for the third time to reach the top of Denali, Belmore Browne, a renowned landscape painter, and his partners, including Herschel Parker, got within 300 yards of the summit before being turned back by a wicked storm. Browne and others retreated, and just as they reached the base, a massive earthquake struck. If they had lingered any longer to make another push to the summit, they likely all would have perished.

Once Hudson Stuck's party reached the top in 1913, glory staked, history made, activity virtually ceased on the mountain. Periodically, climbs were made for the adventure—and Denali's reputation grew only more fearsome as casualties accrued. The first two recorded deaths on the mountain occurred on a 1932 climb. Allen Carpe and Theodore Koven died. A New York Times headline on May 18, 1932 reporting the incident read, "Carpe, Koven Died in a Feat of Daring." In early 1967, a team of Alaskans, including Ray Genet, Dave Johnston, and Art Davidson, undertook the particularly daunting task of climbing Denali in winter. In the end, the party succeeded, but not before suffering one death on the trip from a crevasse fall, and courting death themselves in weather so extreme that when Davidson chronicled the adventure, he titled his book *Minus 148*, representing the wind chill factor they endured. Later in 1967, in what was at times referred to as a "superstorm," though surely not an official weather service phrase, swept across the mountain, killing seven young members of the Wilcox Party.

This place of such deadly beauty became Vern Tejas's seasonal office. He did not escape the nearness of death or disaster on the mountain's flanks, and as the code of the wild dictates, also selflessly contributed to against-the-odds-rescues.

I never planned to become a professional mountain guide. My first forays into the outdoors were really about escaping from people and the claustrophobia of suburbia on the outskirts of Houston. There was a lot to learn before I became an accomplished guide. I learned a lot from Jim Hale, but I also learned from experience. Gary Bocarde and Jim Hale of Mountain Trip were connected with Mountain Travel, a much bigger company that had a huge list of people in a data bank wanting to take adventures. Gary hired me and Nick Parker of Anchorage to be guides on a Denali trip in 1979. I knew Nick from the climbing community and we actually became housemates. I was twenty-six years old and younger than anybody else in the twelve-man climbing team.

This was my second commercial trip. Otherwise, I had been working menial jobs; I was a dig-a-ditch, build-a-house kind of guy. Guiding was more fun. On the trip with Dave Walsh, J.D. and I had felt we were practically stealing. We had a free flight to the mountain, free food. This time I really had to be a leader. It was an opportunity. The door opened, and I walked through and started guiding.

At that point in my life, I called Alaska home and liked the crazy people that lived there. It was starting to work out for me, and I'd been getting offered jobs, although most of them were jobs I didn't want. When Gary asked if I wanted to guide a trip on Denali, I said, "Sure. Love to." I didn't negotiate the fine points.

It was as simple as him saying, "Do you want to do it?" and me saying, "Yeah."

I didn't even know how much money I was making until two days before the trip. I asked, "So, you're gonna pay me, right?"

He said, "Yeah."

"How much?"

"$1,100."

That's not really very much for three weeks. For a two-week trip, that's not bad. For three weeks, it's like OK. But you know what? I wanted to be there. I don't do it because the money is great. I do it because that's where my heart is, and, in this case, it was another way for me to get back into the mountains and particularly to Denali. That's what sucked me in. I had that great experience with Jim doing the double summit. I went from thinking I was a failure at the beginning of that trip to being the strongest climber in the group. That really went back to when I was thirteen at the Philmont Ranch. It was something I excelled at. I didn't know why the altitude favored me, but it did. I wasn't a money grabber, and I got a lot of experience quick.

On this trip, I was improvising, making it up as I went along. This is when I truly began modeling myself after Jim's lessons interacting with people. I tried to do things as he did and keep the same good attitude. I wasn't as charismatic or experienced with leadership skills, but we pulled together a reasonably successful trip.

The National Park Service supervises climbing on Denali, and it also controls a limited number of concessionaire permits for commercial guide companies. There are not very many and the season has a limited window when the weather is not consistently too brutal to climb. Soon, I was running three trips a season, each planned for three weeks, May-June-July, May-June-July. At some point in there, I became an advocate for serving better food because I was eating climbing food for three months of my year. Everybody else was only putting up with bad food for a month. It was crappy, but that was the norm for all the companies. No one had given much thought to providing food that tasted good. Most of the meals were packaged, boiled in hot water, and processed. It didn't go down well, and ramen and tuna only go so far.

By then, I was working for Harry Johnson. I got to know Harry through the Mountain Rescue Group. When Ray Genet died on Mount Everest in 1979, Harry bought Genet Expeditions, and I went to work guiding regularly for him. He was able to obtain the concession from the Park Service to guide on Denali. I wonder how different my life would have been if I had been able to get in on ownership. There was always a big fight over getting permits; it would have been a very good move for me to snag one. I would have made some money instead of being a guide in my sixties. But it has actually worked out to my advantage; I don't need much money. Maybe that will change when I am in my eighties. Ultimately, I decided I would rather do what I love on a small salary than be well off doing something I didn't like.

Guiding on Denali for Harry, I used my influence to upgrade the food. I said, "This is not the place to skimp. You get us good food, and you'll see that it sells. You're not doing yourself any good if the quality of food is low. Climbers won't eat it, and they won't make the summit, and they'll tell other people. You'll ruin your success rate by saving $10 here and there on food. It's not worth it. You might have a mutiny." I made sure there was plenty of good quality food. People knew if they climbed with Vern Tejas, they would eat well.

Early on, probably my fourth trip on Denali, I was asked to lead a group of Boy Scouts on a climb. They had a team leader who had to withdraw for work-related reasons and I was asked to fill in. Their team leader said, "I've got some Boy Scouts who really want to climb that mountain. Can you take them? We can't pay you anything." Well, I was a Boy Scout and had enjoyed it, so I said I would do my best. They were fifteen- through eighteen-year-old Explorer scouts with a couple of adult leaders. It was unusual to have a group that young on the mountain.

For some reason, the trip was scheduled for an April 9 departure. I don't ever go in April because April is cold, cold, cold. You don't get credit for a winter ascent, but it might as well be one because it can be minus-thirty or minus-forty. If the temperature is in that range and you have a storm, the climbing can turn deadly. Denali brings sufficient risk at any time, but you are inviting more trouble if you are there when the thermometer bottoms out. As a group, despite their youthfulness, the scouts and explorers fared surprisingly well on the mountain. Ultimately, the cold was just too much and we had to descend, but we returned with all of our fingers and toes.

The average person who is not familiar with climbing may not realize the mountain itself sets the terms of the climb. It contains more power than humans. Snow, ice, wind, cold, and objective conditions such as open crevasses all factor in to the progress a climber can make. They can terminate a climb because it is simply too much to overcome. A guide's top priority is to keep people safe, not to make it to the top. Guides are being paid to shepherd others to the top and return them safely to sea level. Of course, every guide on a big mountain wants to reach the summit, but their desires are secondary to the clients' needs. The clients count on the guide. As much as anyone else improves with time in their profession, I became a better guide the more I did it. I became wiser at recognizing clients' needs. I also became a better guide with more experience for all mountains, not just on Denali.

Vern Tejas

Tejas's first summit of Denali filled him with an enthusiasm for mountain climbing that has lasted all of his life

There is a law of the jungle that if someone gets into trouble on Denali, or on any big mountain, whether they are in your group or another, if you are able, you lend a hand. You drop what you are doing to help out. Sometimes that makes the difference between life and death for someone. The more I guided on Denali, the better known I became to the Park Rangers, mountain company owners, and guides for other companies.

Although the vast majority of groups are guided, there are some big teams that come to Alaska from other countries that travel together, climb together, and work together. They represent their nations. Denali became a popular place for Japanese mountaineers (perhaps because of adventurer Naomi Uemura's connection to the mountain) and South Koreans came in large numbers. In the early 1980s, there was a bit of a communication gap with some of those climbers. They might have been seasoned mountaineers, but it is very easy to underestimate Denali. Denali does not have the altitude of Himalayan peaks, but the weather can be just as nasty as it gets on Mount Everest. Also, because there are not many very technical areas on Denali's West Buttress, it sometimes has had a reputation as a "walk-up" mountain. Sometimes people do not give Denali the respect it deserves which can foster an attitude of carelessness, or a belief that it is not very hard to climb it. Some climbers do not think they need to acclimate as much, and they can be ill-prepared, at least psychologically. I always remember how I pushed it so hard coming on to the Kahiltna Glacier on my first trip. You could say I was also fooled, but did not suffer consequences beyond first-day fatigue and embarrassment—and I learned from my mistake.

In the summer of 1986, late in the season, I had just finished guiding a group to the summit and was still on the Kahiltna. My group was scheduled to fly back to Talkeetna the next morning, so we were just hanging out. Two Korean climbers appeared, running up Heartbreak Hill nearby and chattering excitedly in their language. I went, "What's going on?" You could sense something was wrong. There was panic in their faces. They were flailing their hands and talking fast. We tried to figure out what they were saying.

"Slow down, guys." I cleared off some snow from the surface, took out a wand and used it to write in the snow. "Denali?"

They go, "Denali, Denali."

I asked which route and they said Cassin. I drew a picture of the mountain in the snow and made a map up to the Cassin Ridge. They pointed, indicating there were two people high up on the mountain, but not on the top.

The Cassin Ridge is a difficult route to the summit, first climbed in 1961 by a group led by Riccardo Cassin of the Italian Alpine Club, and, according to Brad Washburn, it was the first real mountaineering climb of the mountain. The Koreans were trying to tell us two more members of their expedition still were up there and needed help. The radio operator at base camp was in contact with the Park Service in Talkeetna, and it turned out the rangers had been trying to decode some kind of CB radio message for days, which had been fading in and out, and were aware a Korean group was overdue. The transmission had seemed like an SOS, and now these guys were from that late group.

Ultimately, after the rangers found a Korean interpreter, it was determined someone on the mountain was trying to talk and was broadcasting an SOS in such a heavy accent it did not sound like English. We had already put the story together through sign language and snow diagrams before the interpreter confirmed it. It became clear the leader of the expedition was suffering from cerebral edema, and one of the stronger members of the party stayed with him. Then the batteries on their radio died. The climber had been sick for a while, and the friend was pinned down with him. We knew we had an emergency rescue on our hands.

The Park Service said it was flying in a helicopter with some fit rescuers, and I was asked if I could join them. I had just had a very exhausting day with my group, but I was acclimated. My climbers were just waiting for a flight, so I could go. There was another fit guy who had been working 14,200, helping organize things at that camp, and he had been on the mountain for a while. He had just descended, so he was acclimated as high as 14,000. The rangers were looking for other volunteers. A well-known, powerful English climber named Joe Brown was in Talkeetna, and they thought he was going. An Austrian named Wolfgang Wipler, a very strong climber, volunteered, but was told he wasn't needed because they had Joe Brown lined up. When the Park Service went to get Joe Brown, though, they found he was drunk and in no condition to climb. At 8 a.m., the Park Service went looking for Wipler again, and he had a colossal headache from staying up all night drinking and partying. They apologized and said he was needed now. He was pretty groggy. A helicopter swooped in to the Kahiltna and picked me up, which made four of us including the pilot.

The pilot zoomed up to 20,000 feet, and we looked down at the mountain, trying to pinpoint the Korean climbers. The pilot fought over the ridge, but it was so windy it was difficult and there was nowhere nearby to set down. We didn't see anything. We spent thirty minutes hovering and never saw any sign of human movement. It turned out the people were in a tent that was buried in snow so it blended in. They did not know we were coming so they had made no effort to clear the top. They may have been so deeply asleep that they never heard us.

The helicopter descended to 19,500 feet, to what we now call the Football Field, a moniker I bestowed on the area in the early 1980s. It is a flat area that is often the last stop for climbers before they head to the summit ridge. The wind was still gusting. We couldn't land there either. We tried to land at normal high camp at 17,200 feet, but it was also too windy. The pilot was not going to land and let people out; it was too sketchy for him. He finally landed at 14,200 feet. So we were almost 6,000 feet below the Koreans and on the other side of the mountain. Plus, we didn't even know exactly where the sick guy was. It was a long climb to the Cassin Ridge. Almost right away we lost the ranger. He just peeled off, probably not acclimated, or acclimated enough considering how fast we were trying to go. The Australian guy who had been working at 14,200 feet made it to 17,200 feet and said that was it for today.

We believed this was an urgent situation. We didn't really know how badly off this guy was, but the indications were that his life was at risk. At high camp, 17,200 feet, I picked up 600 feet of rope, and Wolfgang grabbed a bottle of oxygen and a supply sled in case we had to transport the Korean. By this time, it was getting late in the day, going on evening. We got to 18,200, Denali Pass, at about six p.m. Wolfgang and I bumped into another climbing group, led by Gary Bocarde, at Denali Pass. The climbers were camping in the midst of a traverse. We told them we were on a rescue mission, and Gary said he had heard it on his radio. Wolfgang said he was really trashed. He looked beat. He had been up all night and said he just had to take a nap, an hour's worth of sleep, and dove into one of Gary's tents. I was the only one still on the rescue.

I had a radio, and every once in a while I communicated with the Park Service. The rangers checked in. They asked how we were doing, where we were, and I said, 'Uh, basically, right now, it's me."

"What do you mean?" I explained where the other three were, and the ranger said, "Let's get this straight. The rescue team is one person?" They began trying to talk me out of it because, really, a one-man rescue is not very practical. But heck, I had just spent the entire day going up high, like a vertical mile, and I wasn't going to stop.

I made like my batteries were dying, although they weren't, and kept saying, "You are breaking up. I'm losing you," so that they wouldn't make me turn around.

I had a lot going through my mind, as well. In 1984, I had lost my lady friend, and I had taken her ashes to the top in 1985. She died from an aneurysm, not common in a thirty-five-year old woman. She was also one of the earliest kidney transplant patients and lived a good fifteen years longer than she would have without that kidney. She was taking immunosuppressants to keep from rejecting the transplant. She was very special to me, and I was pretty emotional, no doubt because of the circumstances and fatigue, too, but I was thinking about her. We had traveled the world together and eaten in some weird places. She caught typhoid fever and, because of the drugs she took, she could not get rid of it; her immune system couldn't fight it. The doctors found the aneurysm and were scheduled to operate the next day. That night, it blew up and killed her. The rescue in 1986 was the first time I had been high on the mountain again alone. She had a great spirit and was a great person. I very much missed her when I was crossing the Football Field and approaching the spot where her ashes resided. I miss her still.

I was by myself, pushing hard. Lack of oxygen makes you less cerebral and more emotional. Sometimes it benefits the self to grieve. I was pretty sad, and the rangers were trying to talk to me. By then, they were telling me to come down. But I was pretty close to the summit where her ashes were. I had frozen tears collecting in my beard. The rangers said, "Vern, can you hear us? You need to come down." You couldn't blame them because it wasn't very safe for me.

"I can't hear you guys. You're breaking up." I just didn't want to pull out at that point. Physically, I was hell-bent to see what was happening with the Koreans. So I just turned the radio off and continued to climb.

I reached Pig Hill, which is at the top of the Cassin Ridge, looked down and couldn't see jackshit. All I had were two pickets, the rope, and the radio, which was no longer a helpful tool. I wondered how I could find these Korean guys, then it hit me. Everyone who knew me back then knew I was a hot-shot yodeler. Besides making music with a harmonica, fiddle, or guitar, I yodeled. I figured everybody knew that yodeling was a signal for an Alpine mountain guide, so I yodeled. I thought I heard a very weak response, so I yodeled again, and damned if I didn't hear yelling back. They knew somebody was there.

I saw snow pop off the top of a tent and two heads pop out. They were waving 650 feet below me. Holy moley. They had made a camp on a little bench. Using the rope, which I anchored with the two pickets, I rappelled down to within fifty feet of them. The slope gentled out, and I was able to climb down the rest. All I had with me was a bottle of water, a sandwich, and some Decadron to help fight cerebral edema. I shared it with them.

The healthy guy who had stayed with his buddy was ecstatic to see me. His reaction was like, "Yes, it's the cavalry!" The other guy was woozy. He was not in good shape. I gave him Decadron. I gave the other guy Decadron. I gave me some Decadron. We all drank water and split the sandwich. We were at an elevation that people should not be for too long, and they had been there for a long time.

Did I mention how wonderful Decadron is? It's my go-to emergency drug on a climb. It began working on the guy with cerebral edema. It has been well-tested and used by the Army. I use it when people are in trouble mentally. I could see his cognition returning. It is not a drug you take for any length of time, but, in small amounts for a limited time in high altitude, it can be very helpful. Sometimes I justify giving it to a climber because I think it can be the difference between him having the strength to get down safely or not. Other times, I have given it to someone to transform him from comatose to ambulatory. It is a big deal if it helps saves someone's life. When a guy is laid out and suffering and can't make sense, and it helps get him to the point where he can tie his own shoes and start walking, that's a big deal. I saw that kind of reaction in this guy. His eyes brightened up and understood me speaking English, with a combination of sign language.

I directed him to the rope, to climb the fifty feet over the snow and start climbing up. He went over to the rope, but what he didn't understand was that he had to ascend the rope. These guys finally realized that I was all they had. There was no cavalry; it was just me. I couldn't carry them on my back. This sick guy especially hoped two other guys were going to appear and carry him up the 600 feet.

It was time for me to stop being subtle. I said, "No, it's not quite that good. You're actually going to have to climb up." While his friend collapsed the tent and packed up the gear, I started climbing next to him as he used his ascenders on the rope—one for each hand—to grip it. His friend was pretty OK. He was hungry and dehydrated, but he was ambulatory. We wanted to take the gear because I thought we might still need it later. We didn't know what was going to happen, and it was possible we were going to have to make another survival camp.

On the rope, I kept cajoling this guy. I was breathing with him. "Slide your ascender up. Slide your other ascender up. Let's go. Up the hill we go," I was sing-songing. I was talking to him, although I'm sure most of what I was saying was incomprehensible to him. He was trying to figure out why there were not more rescuers involved. The Decadron revived him, but when at last we reached the top of the 600 feet and he saw the two pickets and nobody else there, he gave out. He looked at me and lay down. That was it, the extent of his energy. That was the last time I saw him up.

I was getting pretty demoralized myself. We were still very high on Denali, on a ridge just forty minutes from the summit. We had a whole big mountain to descend with a guy who was basically comatose again with just two of us to help him. That's a bad combination. I did not know what we were going to do. I glanced around while I was thinking, trying to drum up an idea to save us, and twenty-five feet below the ridge, I saw a big, orange plastic sled heading our way. It was sticking out of Wolfgang's pack. He really did only sleep for a short while! That sucker blew my mind. He appeared right when I needed him. I got the oxygen bottle from Wolfgang, put the weakened Korean climber in a sleeping bag and lashed him to the sled and turned on the O_2.

We quickly formed a descent plan. I unfurled the 600 feet of rope again. I gave Wolfgang a picket, and he stayed next to the sled to steer and brake. The other Korean had his hands full carrying both his pack and his buddy's. The guy hadn't moved for a week, so he was still getting the blood flow going in his legs. I stayed behind, made an anchor out of the picket, belayed the rope, and attached it to the sled, banged in a picket, and belayed the rope again, little by little lowering the sled. Going down wasn't difficult, just repetitious. I lowered the sled 600 feet at a time, removed the picket, and ran down to where Wolfgang was holding the sled with the other picket. Then we did it all over again.

We got back down to the Football Field. It was flat there, so we did not have gravity working for us. The Korean, Wolfgang, and I pulled the sled, with our patient on it, behind Archdeacon's Tower, where there was a snow drift about forty feet high. It was not easy getting over it, but everything else was downhill. When we got to Denali Pass, Gary's team was still there. We just pushed the sled into a tent and said, "Take care of this guy." Then Wolfgang and I quickly dropped to 17,200. We had been out twenty-four hours straight, working hard, doing manly things to save this guy's life, and were pretty darn exhausted. Radio contact was made with the Park Service, and the rangers said Gary's team was going to lower the sick Korean on ropes to where we were, and then a pilot would try to fly in a helicopter to take him to a hospital in Anchorage the following day.

I pretty much passed out. I slept in an igloo that night, and Gary's climbers got him lowered. The ranger and the Australian who had been working at 14,000 came up and we all dragged the sled across the flats to the pickup area at high camp. A helicopter swooped in and took the Korean off. His friend came over to me and gave me a $20 tip. It wasn't a lot of money, but it was symbolic.

He said, "It is from the bottom of my heart. Would you please accept it?" I did.

The Park Service wrote up that I saved two people myself, but it was really only one because the Korean friend could move on his own. Maybe one-and-a-half since he was trapped with the guy with cerebral edema.

Actually, right after I got to 14,000 feet, the Park Service flew in a big Chinook helicopter to dismantle the camp there for the season. The military guys asked if I wanted a ride, and I said, "Hell, yeah. Get me out of here."

I could say that I saved that $20 bill forever, as a remembrance of a life-saving trip, but that would not be true. I spent it on lunch.

WINTER ON MOUNT LOGAN AND MOUNT HUNTER

Mount Logan is the tallest mountain in Canada at 19,551 feet and the second tallest mountain in North America. Located in the St. Elias Mountain Range, which also stretches into Alaska, Logan is contained within the Yukon Territory.

It is nearly as tall as Denali, and the peak is more remote and has the weather to match Denali. If anything, Logan carries the potential for more dangerous weather than Denali because it is regularly bombarded by storms forming in the Gulf of Alaska. On May 26, 1991, a temperature of -106.6 F was recorded at high altitude on the peak.

This mountain is not climbed as frequently as Denali because Denali is the biggest peak on the continent and gets more attention from that status. Mt. Logan was named in 1890 by I. C. Russell, a member of the United States Geological Survey studying the St. Elias Mountains. Russell chose Logan as the name after Sir William Edmond Logan, who founded the Geological Survey of Canada in 1842. Logan passed away in 1875.

The first ascent of Logan was recorded on June 23, 1925 by a six-man party made up of mountaineers from Canada, the U.S., and England that included Allen Carpe, who later perished on Denali in 1932. In 1987, Vern Tejas helped jump-start an all-Alaska expedition organized with the goal of making the first winter ascent of this incredibly cold mountain. He joined John Bauman, Willy Hersman, Steve Koslow, George Rooney, and Todd Frankiewicz for the climb that began on March 1 and culminated at the summit on March 16, Tejas's birthday. To be classified as a winter climb, it had to be completed before March 20, the Equinox.

Several of us were talking about climbing one day and recognized no one had ever made a winter ascent of Mount Logan. Logan was the other great big mountain in the neighborhood. A few of us had climbed together on other major Alaska peaks, and Logan loomed as a challenge.

Four of us came up with the idea, but then we heard a rumor that a couple of other guys were planning to go. We were surprised. I mean, nobody had gone there in the winter, and we found out another climb was being planned. We tracked them down and asked them what was up, as if they had heard about our climb and were trying to beat us. They said, "No, we came up with the idea on our own."

"You know what? Why don't we just join forces?" I said. We had a great time climbing Logan. It may not be fun for everybody with that extreme weather, but it was for me.

The reason why Logan's weather, which in general is similar to Denali's, can be worse is that it is so close to the coast. We were fortunate. We did not have horrible weather. But it was winter, so we were not going to camp out in tents. Before leaving, we practiced building shelters in the snow. They were modified ranger trenches, built to suit our needs, designed to be dug so the snow never fell in and we could move a lot of gear in and out quickly. Seen from above, the trenches were T-shaped. We dug down four feet and belled it out, putting snow blocks loosely over it. The snow blocks were a lid. We made a little hallway at the bottom of the T. With six guys digging, you had a shelter in an hour or an hour-and-a-half, depending on the quality of the snow. We got down out of the wind pretty quickly as we were shielded by the walls we were building. When you throw the snow over the top, the snow blocks soon set up like an igloo. After a few hours of living inside, the whole roof freezes together so strongly it will easily hold the weight of a man on top.

Snow is good insulation. It easily got up to the freezing point in our snow trenches. We didn't want it to get any warmer than that because then the entire structure could start melting. The trouble is not that it gets too warm for you, the trouble is that if the walls start melting, they become glazed with ice and there is no breathability. Ventilation becomes super important once inside. We cooked in the hallway near the entrance-exit to avoid poisonous fumes and excess heat. We did not want either too close to our sleeping quarters.

We took a helicopter to the 9,600-foot level on Logan on the western end of the mountain, landing near an area called King Trench. Actually, just getting there was an adventure. We had hired a Canadian pilot by the name of Andy Williams, but on the day we were scheduled to fly, February 26, he said, "Can't fly today, boys. It's too cold." It was minus forty. Then February 27 and 28 go by, and we were into March. Our time frame for completing the climb in winter was ticking away. He kept delaying, and finally we hired a helicopter pilot from a different air service.

We made our base camp shelter at the King Trench. There were tons of snow there, but we had to be careful about the placement of the camp because of avalanche danger.

The climbing on Logan, as compared to Denali, is less technical. There are no fixed ropes put in each season like on Denali on the Headwall. It is steep, but less dangerous. There are fewer crevasses, though I did worry quite a bit about avalanches. To watch for avalanche danger in certain areas, we employed a technique I learned in an avalanche class from Jim Hale.

He asked, "So, you want to go from here to there. But there's a gully full of snow in-between. What are you going to do?" He made us think about the problem. You think maybe you can tip-toe across this area, but it can still go and then you die. Ski patrol people throw charges of dynamite into suspect areas. But what if we didn't have dynamite? He said that you could find a good-sized rock or throw your pack. See what happens.

On our way down Logan, we came to a steep slope with a foot-and-a-half of new snow on it. Our body weight could easily trigger an avalanche. We were above it and thinking, "I don't want to go down that. I'm scared. If it goes, we'll be buried forever. They'd never find us." Since we had to get back to base camp and the way looked like treacherous territory, I got the idea to try and set it off. We cut through the surface of the snow and created a big wheel with our shovels and saw and propped it up at the top of the slope. It was quite wide and weighed about 400 pounds. Then we rolled it down the slope in front of us. As the ice wheel gained momentum, it also gained more mass, turning into a gigantic snow roller. It thundered down the slope and didn't set off an avalanche. If the ice wheel didn't, me, weighing 165 pounds, and the others shouldn't either. We took turns walking right down the slope in the rut the ice wheel created. That solved the problem. It took us a little while to think up a solution and it took a little longer to make progress, but for forty minutes of futzing around, we relieved the stress and didn't die.

Sometime later, in 1989, I was on Everest for Genet Expeditions with some climbers; Todd Burleson, who ran Alpine Ascents International; and a guy with him who wanted to ski down the North East Ridge that linked up with us. During our attempt, we came across the same kind of situation and I thought about the ice wheel.

At the time, we were descending from the North Col for a rest. I started down the fixed line and noticed the right side of the slope was a foot-and-a-half deep with fluffy new snow. The other side was hard-packed with old snow. I paused and asked myself why they were different. "This is ripe for an avalanche! This is probably ready." I ascended back up and told Todd we had a situation. I told him the wall we were going down had conditions underneath ripe to avalanche. Not only our weight could set it off, but just about anything could set it off. We could wait for it to trigger naturally, we could initiate it ourselves, or we could set it off by other means. The texture of the snow was different than it was on Logan, so we could not make an ice wheel. Instead, we made a giant round snow ball. When we pushed it over the edge, everything broke loose.

It was not just below us, but one hundred feet above us, too. We both dove for the fixed line and held on. When the snow settled, we were each half-buried. The right side of the bench we lay on was buried under four feet of new snow. We dug ourselves out with our left hands, holding on to the fixed line with our rights.

Once free from the snow, I jumped up and yelled, "Yippee!" I was full of adrenaline. I was so stoked that it had worked and we had cheated death. Todd looked at me and said, "You know, my company is looking for a man like you."

I went on to work for Todd and Alpine Ascents, and a few months later, he called me up and hired me to guide on Aconcagua in Argentina. Save a man's life, get a job.

The magic snow wheel helped us out on Logan, and we all made the summit. John Bauman wrote up a little story on the climb for the *American Alpine Journal,* and in it he said my snow shelters were instrumental in our success. Two years later, I refined this survival technique and used a smaller one on my solo winter ascent of Denali.

Budgeting three weeks to make the top of Logan, we had put in several days as a cushion in case of storms, but we lost them at the beginning of the climb due to cold weather. We did it in less than two weeks, which was fast for a winter expedition. When it wasn't storming, we gained a thousand feet of elevation a day. We were pushing our parameters pretty hard. When we got back to base camp, we radioed our original pilot on a single-side band radio. The weather was clear, and it was no longer minus-forty, so we thought he could come pick us up. We radioed for three more days and still got no ride or response.

Our food was starting to get a little low when somebody said, "Screw it. He didn't fly us in. We don't even know if he's out there. He's not answering the radio."

Our message was, "Weather is clear. Need to be taken out. We're ready to go. Please come get us." We did that every two hours. Nothing. The radio could be broken. He might not be listening. A few of the guys had to get out and get back to work. Todd, Willy, and George hung in there, but John, Steve, and I decided to ski out. It was a 120-mile trip to the Alaska Highway over three glaciers. Our plan was to ski ten miles a day pulling heavy sleds.

Only an hour-and-a-half after we skied away from base camp, I was in a crevasse yelling, "Get me out of here!" Steve was the better skier and was in front. I was in the middle, and John was behind me. I fell in a crevasse going downhill. We were roped, but even skiing exactly where Steve did, I went poof. It was a trap door. My first thought was "Oh shit," and that I was a dead man. When the rope caught and halted the fall, I thought, "I'm alive!" But I was in a hole surrounded by snow, and it was cold and black below.

I probably dropped ten or fifteen feet. It was not too far, but far enough. I didn't want to be there. Fortunately, John kept the rope pretty snug behind me, so he felt the bulk of the weight. Steve was able to retrace his tracks back to the crack I was in. I was yelling, "Get me out of here! Can you guys hear me?" I couldn't see anything but white above. I couldn't hear much either.

Steve stuck his head over the hole and hollered, "Vern! Vern! You OK?" With the snow sucking up the sound of our voices, we had yelled at the top of our lungs, though we were right next to each other. Looking back, it was humorous. We did a quick extraction. I was able to take my pack off and pass it up first, then my sled. Then I was finally able to climb out. It was the first big crevasse I had ever fallen into. A few years earlier, I fell into a smaller one on Mount Dickey in Alaska, a quick in and out. But that time I was at the rear on the rope and was able to muscle my way out before anyone even noticed.

In all of my years climbing on glaciated mountains, I have fallen into just two crevasses over my head, and that was the biggest one. It was completely spooky. I am lucky, but I'm also very cautious around cracks. When I am on a glacier, I tend to look around for crevasses all of the time. I never want my epitaph to read, "Fell into a crevasse." I got out of that hole, and we continued skiing to the road at Kluane Lake. About that time, we heard a plane go overhead. The rest of our guys were going to be back in civilization in an hour-and-a-half. We had five days to go, but we had a great time.

We dug other shelters on the way out and had a tarp that we used as part of the covering. Later, a tail wind came up, and we turned the tarp into a sail in the middle of our trio of skiers. We figured that we might lose a little control, and if one of us fell in a crevasse while blowing along, the others could help. We flew along at almost ten miles per hour for five hours. We were moving right along. Sailing was the highlight of what was a great trip. Somewhere, they've got our names written down in the record books as the first winter ascenders of Mount Logan.

Mount Logan is a technically difficult mountain and the largest mountain in Canada

Gerald Holdsworth Courtesy of the National Oceanic and Atmospheric Administration

It was pretty special to be associated with the first winter ascent of Mount Logan—or really any ascent of Mount Logan given that is a true brute of a mountain—however that was not the first winter ascent for me.

Logan got more attention because of its size and stature within Canada, but in 1982, I was on the first winter ascent of Mount Hunter in Alaska. Like Denali, Mount Hunter is also located in the Alaska Range. It stands 14,573 feet and is what you would call a mountaineer's mountain. This is not a mountain that is close to being the tallest in the state, but it is far more technically difficult than Denali. The average Alaskan has probably heard of Hunter, but knows little or nothing about it. Only serious climbers entertain the idea of climbing it by any route at any time of year.

I joined up with Gary Bocarde and Paul Denkewalter of Anchorage for Hunter. Logan, by the route we took, was not technical. We could have taken a harder route, but we knew better. Our planned line on Hunter was much more hardcore. It was called the Lowe-Kennedy Route, after George Lowe and Michael Kennedy who first climbed it. Hunter itself was first climbed in 1954 by Heinrich Harrer, Fred Beckey, and Henry Meybohm.

Climbing Hunter in winter might be the most heroic thing I ever do. Hunter is a very cold mountain. The route we chose faces north and is usually in shadow. It is technically challenging and can be avalanche prone on the approach. One of the stories of my life was going through an avalanche gully at 7,000 feet with a huge, hanging glacier above our heads at 12,000 feet. It was like a two- or three-story building, 200 feet across. Our route was right there under it. We were halfway through when a house-sized hunk of snow came roaring down the chute. I was in the middle position, Gary wanted to run this way and Paul wanted to run that way, each to his own perceived safe spot. We were roped together; I was in limbo in the middle of a deadly tug-of-war game. I had the thought that Hunter was so tough that we couldn't even get to the route without getting killed.

When I saw what was going on, I unclipped from the rope, thinking, "Well, you guys can fight it out." I only had seconds to do something, and I was really motivated. I just dove behind an old ice block. Gary won, I think, and Paul went running across his way, but by that time, stuff was just flying by me. I am guessing it fell from 12,000 feet to 7,000 feet, so covering a vertical mile with it coming at 100 miles per hour probably only took seconds.

The avalanche created such a loud roar that it seemed as if some giant had picked up a building and thrown it at us. The visual when an avalanche is rushing down a slope at you is pretty exciting. It's a white wall coming at you, but this was like a tsunami of debris in a deadly cloud. There were thick chunks of ice that could kill you. I was scared I was going to be ground to death or buried. It all took maybe fifteen or twenty seconds to reach us. Real projectiles zoomed past my head, stuff that was heavy and would leave a mark.

The mountain was saying, "Here boys, time to quit playing around." But when the avalanche cleared, we were all still there. It took several minutes of coughing to remove pulverized ice dust from our throats. As climbers, though, we played down that stuff. I said, "Oh, that was close."

Gary said, "Yeah."

Paul said, "Let's keep moving."

I don't remember us pausing for long. We went right to our route on the Northwest Buttress. OK, it's a hard-guy route. We didn't want to worry about little things on the approach, not that you can truly forget a close call like that. The route started up in earnest, a ridgy thing, and there were several crevasses and seracs to negotiate. We had to keep the rope tight to get to the bottom of the triangular face. We dug in, built a snow cave, and went to sleep. That was our last camp; the rest of our five nights were spent in open bivouacs. The face nearby was ice.

A little more than halfway up on the sixty-five-degree ice face, there was a big sloping rock, about the size of an easy chair. It is still there; I saw it not long ago, frozen in. The other guys bivouacked on one side of it and I bivied on another spot that was a steeper slope. It was a hanging bivouac. We were roped and hanging off of ice screws in harnesses with our sleeping bags draped around us.

I kept slipping off the steep rock all night long. When I woke up in the morning, I saw the rope had been rubbing against the sharp rock because of the constant slippage. It was super strong nylon and it was frayed part-way through to its core. It had not been a very restful night; my body was slipping off and bouncing. The rope was frayed to the point if I just jerked on the line, it would fail. If anything had happened, I would have gone a long way, and it wouldn't have been fun. That would be your high-speed descent. In the morning, I just cut off a short piece of rope. Whew, Hunter could kill you in your sleep.

We had actually begun that trip in February with grand ambitions. We planned to climb Hunter, then move on to Mount Foraker. Foraker is 17,402 feet high and the second tallest mountain the Alaska Range. After that, we planned to move on to Denali. It was a planned triple-header. We were going to do all three on the same trip in winter. We had all kinds of food at base camp, and we found some vegetables left behind by other climbers. They were sponsored by the Carrs grocery store chain in Alaska that was eventually bought out by Safeway. The climbers had to cut the trip short and left behind cases of vegetables. They were frozen. They would have still been good, except ravens got into most of them and feasted. All that was left was Brussels sprouts. The birds left them because they were too big to swallow. So we had a month's worth of

Brussels sprouts. I ate a lot of them. To this day, I still never want to see another Brussels sprout.

We had about eight hours of daylight to work with. It took us so long to make progress with all of us carrying gear. We thought we would get up the face in one day and it took two. As we climbed higher on the triangular face, we encountered fluting, bands of rotten snow and water ice that had to be painstakingly traversed. Once we got to the ridge, there were snow cornices sticking out in both directions. The snow was like whipped cream on a ripsaw blade. It was difficult to forge a good line across the ridge, and ultimately we rappelled off and pendulumed along under the chaotic cornices. We thought it would take us hours, but it took us days. Ah, the joy of winter mountaineering.

Our plan called for taking eight days to reach the top and, while we had plenty of food, especially those Brussels sprouts, upward movement was slow. There was no good place to camp on the airy, double-corniced ridge. It made for very disjunctive climbing. So we decided to camp right at the beginning of the traverse before tackling the horrendous arête. We chopped out a long platform with ice axes and ice hammers. For ice, my North Wall hammer was sweet, yet the hammer proved not so handy in soft, sugar snow. I resorted to inserting my hammer lengthwise into the crappy snow, then turning it sideways and pulling on it. I prayed it would hold. In my other hand, I wielded a normal ice axe, until the ice turned to non-cohesive snow, then I switched to a climbing picket, stabbing it into the sugar snow and hoping it would hold my weight because it had a larger surface area. It was all very tenuous. We were not sure if the sugar snow was deep. We feared our tools might run straight through the precarious placements.

The hanging glacier that nearly buried us earlier was right at the edge of this ridge, and it calved and avalanched two or three times a night. Every time it happened, we thought we were going to die. We were only a couple of hundred feet away from the active face. It was as if a train had run off a cliff. We were soundly passed out in our sleeping bags when a gunshot boom sounded. A hundred tons of ice calved off, shaking the ground and the very air we were breathing. We could feel the vibrations in our bones. We practically crapped in our pants every time it happened. Although we were in a safety zone and knew it wouldn't get us, psychologically we were not calm. It was a complete physical and mental rumble, rumble, rumble.

We spent three-quarters of a day working our way across the ridge before Gary came up with the idea to lower a rope and pendulum below the hazards like Tarzan in the jungle. We hooked up a rope, swung across, and climbed up past the end of the ridge. The rope trick worked and we were able to establish our camp on the upper mountain. We climbed to the summit from there the following morning. It was only 2,500 more vertical feet, pretty straight-forward going. We arrived on the peak in a storm, as a bonus.

Gary promptly said, "That's it! Let's go!"

Only I said, "I can see something higher behind you." Sure enough, the real summit was fifty feet higher. We could almost not see it in the mist. The reason I could see it was because I had Gary as a reference point. We were all wearing goggles and practically fogged out. The first guy is almost always blind in conditions like that. It's easier for the second guy to see. We almost went through all of that and turned back without reaching the true summit.

We did not stay on top long. Our view from the summit was pretty much a white sheet over our heads. We were in a hurry to get out of there. I was leading off the summit and came across a pretty big crevasse. It might have been eight feet wide, but I was coming from a higher slope. I had pulled up what I thought was enough rope. I tried to jump across, but when I hit the other side, I bounced and rolled and in the process I pulled Paul off his feet and he pulled Gary off his feet. I realized I yanked them off their feet when I heard, "Aaagghh!" I dug in, making a self-arrest with my ice axe and crampons. In retrospect, I should have made more slack in the rope. I also think I caught them off guard. It was poor communication from me, although it's not always easy to communicate in a blowing storm.

Those guys were pulled so abruptly off their feet that they went flying over the crevasse and past me to the other side. They were below me and I felt a huge tug on the rope. I waited for a second tug, but there wasn't a second pull. I thought they must have stopped. Gary did stop, but Paul came off the rope. He was no longer hooked in. He came free, still sliding way below, but fortunately it was in soft snow. We don't know how he came unclipped. Paul popped to his feet and shouted, "It was locked. It was locked." He said his carabiner somehow came loose. To this day, I climb with two carabiners clipped on a rope. Paul was lucky. He fell another 200 or 300 feet without injury. We were able to descend and pick him up.

At no other time on my climbs have I ever again seen a rope come out of a locked carabiner. It either was not locked as he thought, or a screw gate came loose and opened, which is possible. That is why I use two. It is not likely to happen twice on one rope. That experience will shake you up. We climbed down and camped at the end of the ridge. The next day was spent rappelling down and swinging across, climbing back up and scooting across to the other side of the ridge.

Before we made it back across, we had one more teensy little problem. In the process of traversing back across the whipped cream ridge, we used a horizontal rappel. That helped ensure safety as we shuttled loads under the cornices. Then all we had to do was pull on the double rope for it to slide through the anchor and back to us. That was the theory. Only, after hauling in about half the line, the rope got stuck. We figured it was frozen. The rope could create friction and melt ice as it was pulled, but it was easy enough for the ice to re-freeze at twenty degrees below. Paul and I pulled and pulled, but it did not budge. We arranged a three-to-one pulley system like that used in crevasse rescue. This probably created 600 pounds worth of pulling power, and the rope still did not move. Only one piece of it was stuck, and we didn't know what it was stuck on.

Someone had to climb back along the heinous ridge to free the rope. I was the low man on the totem pole on this climb, so I said I would do it. I did say, "Tell Nancy I love her." She was my girlfriend of the time. That's how unsure we were about this. If the rope came free, I was going to swing big-time and I was going to get hurt or worse. There were rocks below us on a seventy degree face. I put another ice screw in. Gary was on the triangular face below our position trying to find other screws we had left on the ascent, but it had snowed while we were up high. It was taking a long time to find them, but we needed them to rappel off the mountain.

The ropes were designed to slip through, but the rope was tied in a beautiful knot. We didn't have a clue how it happened, but I saw it was complicated as I untied it. We called it the "Thank God Knot," because if it had not formed, we would have been on rappel and could not have advanced. We would have had to hang there all night. We returned to our old ice-shelf camp and listened to the avalanches thunder again. We were able to find the ice screws in the daylight. In the dark, searching would have been a disaster.

At the time, I was cussing the knot, but it probably saved our lives. The climb felt like a hard effort, with a good result. It was a great accomplishment to climb that mountain in the winter time. But that was going to be the last time I tackled such a hard route in winter. We did not go on to climb Foraker and Denali that trip. We were spent.

A lot of my friends have died in the mountains doing crazy stuff like that, and I'm still here, which is pretty phenomenal. I've lost several buddies in airplane and motor vehicle accidents, too. I suppose if you are unwise or unlucky, you check out early. If you are lucky and last long enough, you may ultimately lose all of your friends. For life to be good, I must keep making younger friends.

I once asked older friend Brad Washburn how he got so famous. He said, "That's pretty easy. Do something difficult when you're young and then relax a bit and don't get yourself killed. Live to a ripe old age and people will respect you. The whole trick is not to die after you have been to the edge. Then you get to hear about your successes for years."

Brad was almost ninety-six when he died in 2007. He lived a good life.

WINTER SOLO ON DENALI

In 1984, Japanese adventurer Naomi Uemura set out to make the first solo winter ascent of Denali. Uemura was flown to the Kahiltna Glacier, and, among others, the Japanese press tried to keep track of him on the mountain. Uemura, whom Vern Tejas considers a personal hero, was the first person to climb Denali alone during the normal summer climbing months. He did so in eight days round-trip in 1970.

Naomi was a busy guy; he was always chasing adventure and the physical and exploratory challenges that stretched a man's capabilities. He made a solo trip to the North Pole. On that journey, he had to shoot a polar bear that was menacing him. He also floated the Amazon River. At various times, Uemura also made solo ascents of Mount Kilimanjaro, Mount Aconcagua, Mont Blanc, and the Matterhorn. Uemura wrote best-selling books about his adventures, and there is a museum named after him in Japan. It was natural that he would want to book-end his pioneering Denali solo with a winter solo. It was right up his alley—mountain climbing and cold weather.

Climbing by one's self, one has the advantage of setting the pace without anyone else being consulted. However, you are by yourself with no assistance at hand if something goes wrong. Solo climbing calls for tremendous self-reliance and good judgment, especially in a precarious environment. Between the limited hours of daylight, crevasses, forbidding temperatures, powerful winds, and snowstorms, winter climbing can be dangerous.

The first climb of Denali in winter was accomplished by a group of Alaskan climbers. Three members of the party—Ray Genet, Art Davidson, and Dave Johnston—reached the top. While successful, their journey was an ordeal as they ran short of food and became trapped high on the mountain by storms. But they lived to tell the story, and Davidson published a marvelously written book called *Minus-148*.

More recently, Minnesota polar adventurer Lonnie Dupre, from Grand Marais, completed a solo climb in January of 2015. Any winter climb of Denali is notable (there have not been many), and any solo climb during that season multiplies the risks and difficulties. Lonnie's climb differed from Vern's and others because he summited in January when there is less daylight and colder temperatures. To illustrate how complex the ascent can be, the successful climb was Dupre's fourth try. Dupre's success merits special note; during an earlier era, Dupre would have been vying to seize the prize of making the first-ever winter solo, but he was too late. Uemura, to the degree he succeeded, and Tejas had come along years before.

On his 1984 trip, Uemura communicated to the world by radio that on February 12, he had successfully reached the summit of Denali and was beginning his descent. He perhaps worked his way down to 18,000 feet or 17,200 feet. Some suggest he slipped on the Autobahn and tumbled into a crevasse or was buried by drifting snow. But he was never heard from again, and his body was never found. Many people believe he had sought shelter from a storm in a snow cave, but then something went wrong. The official date of his death is given as February 13, 1984.

When Vern Tejas set out to follow the same West Buttress route four years later, he and the rest of the mountaineering world viewed the solo winter ascent of the mountain as a task uncompleted.

When climbing is thought of as a sport, the biggest prize, first place or the gold medal, is awarded to someone who makes the first ascent of a peak. In most cases, due to the accident of birth, those prizes are claimed by others who came before you. Next, climbers seek to put up new routes, ones never tried or completed. But again, depending on when you were born, all of that may have been accomplished on a certain mountain by others who came along earlier. This was virtually all true on Denali. The chief major challenge remaining for an accomplished climber was to solo the mountain in winter and live to talk about it. In 1984, the Japanese adventurer Naomi Uemura set out to make the first solo winter ascent of Denali and died trying.

Four years later, I set out to try to become the first person to complete the solo winter ascent. The definition of winter is built around the calendar. As long as you are finished before the first day of spring in late March, it counts as winter. A big ingredient for climbing in Alaska is how much daylight you have. That far north, in the heart of winter around December 21, there is very little daylight. So you don't catch many people trying a solo then. March can be friendlier because you have much more light. The weather may be just as awful, but at least you can see. My departure date was February 15. I had just returned from guiding a climb on Aconcagua in Argentina, going above 22,000 feet. I was in a hurry to get going because I was acclimated from the South American climb. I actually wanted to leave on February 12, but pilot Lowell Thomas Jr. was still on a trip to Hawaii.

Shutterstock / Romi22

A ladder similar to this helped ensure that Tejas
would be safe while crossing crevasses

A big danger to a solo climber on Denali stems from crevasses, cracks on glaciers or ice sheets, usually disguised by a thin layer of snow. They are hard to see, and even the most experienced climber can be trapped unawares. When you climb in a group where such gaping holes form in the snow, you are all roped together. If the ground suddenly shifts and drops you down, you can be readily hauled out. If you are by yourself, there is no one to rely on. A key part of my strategy was to design self-protection. I utilized an aluminum ladder that could expand and contract. I could slip it over my head and attach it to my harness horizontally as I walked across glacial terrain on Denali. It vastly expanded my footprint to catch both sides of a crevasse and prevent me from tumbling down to an abyss. I could contract it so it was easier to carry, and then park it in an area above base camp for lighter travel later in non-crevasse zones. I bought my ladder at the Pay N' Pack store in Anchorage. It was a sixteen-foot-long extension ladder which could collapse to eight feet for travel on a plane. I brought it home to the garage, fully extended it on blocks and jumped on it in the middle to see if it was going to be strong enough to hold my weight. It bent. So I turned it around, jumped again, and bent it back into shape. Then I shortened it to twelve feet, overlapping the steps, reinforcing it by making it double. I then lashed two aluminum pickets to it, too, for more strength. For the same purpose, Naomi used bamboo poles long enough to keep him from falling into crevasses. He set them up in two different directions and attached himself to the middle of the X.

The winter climb was my fourteenth time on Denali, though all of the others were, of course, during the normal climbing season, not in winter. I was well aware of the areas where crevasses could be bothersome, where the steepest and most exposed parts were, where the wind was likely to blow hardest, and how much a person could reasonably expect to gain in altitude in a given day. Deeper snow, stronger winds, and colder temperatures were likely to diminish the pace that I might set during a guided climb. However, I did not have to look after other climbers; I was only looking after myself.

One night, in a snow cave at around 18,000 feet, completely enveloped by darkness, I felt a presence. I believe it was the spirit of Naomi Uemura. I did not see a ghost. I did not hear anything except the wind, which was unique because I was deep inside a snow cave, but I felt it was him. In fact, I let out "Good morning!" in Japanese. It was a one-time thing, but that moment has always stayed with me. I don't know if I interpreted it as being Uemura's blessing, but I would like to think his spirit remained there. After all, it was likely his snow cave from four years earlier.

On the way down, a storm blew in and the winds roared and I had to pause in another snow cave. Despite my impatience to get down and off the mountain, I had to wait things out. Many of the worst climbing accidents occur because people rush on the descent when they are very tired, and the euphoria and determination of reaching the summit has worn off. The wind was so loud at times that I inserted ear plugs to block the noise. And because I was delayed, I had to ratchet my food intake down. Ironic for a guy who pushed for better menus on guided trips. Ideally, at altitude on a climb of Denali, I think the proper caloric level is 5,000 a day. I had hoped to be off the mountain sooner than the twenty-nine days it took me. I only took sixteen days' worth of rations, so I had to conserve towards the end. I didn't know if the storm would fade after one day or five; I was on a crash diet. When food is short, my rule is to never eat more than half of what I have with me.

Pilot Lowell Thomas Jr. was trying to keep track of me with flyovers in his small plane, and the news media asked him about my progress. I was wearing a bright red snowsuit, which contrasted sharply against white snow, but there were several days when Lowell had to tell people that he saw no sign of me on the peak which created a definite uneasiness amongst my loved ones, friends, and the public at large. This was only four years after Uemura had been to the top and vanished and that type of thing was certainly on people's minds. A lot of people were praying for me, hoping the same thing did not happen again. Most assuredly, I did not want to die trying. I was thirty-five years old and hoped I still had a lot of years still ahead of me.

After the successful winter ascent of Hunter, I thought this might be my thing, dealing better with cold weather climbing than most people. This was different because I was on my own which needed a tremendous amount of preparation, but by 1988, I had also gained a large amount of climbing and survival experience.

I think the biggest difference between being out there with a bunch of people in summer and doing it solo in the winter time is not that the environment is much harsher, but that you have to be more psyched up for it. You have to know that you are going to survive. It has to be innate that you know you can handle all of the challenges. It is self-reliance and knowledge that I could protect myself from crevasses in two or three different ways, that I could navigate four or five ways. I carried a map, a compass, wands, and could follow the wind direction. I knew I could employ different methods and use them as checks for each other.

Concentration is also very big. You're in the moment every step, but you cannot be so focused that you can't absorb the big picture. You're hearing things; you're smelling things; you're feeling things. When it comes to figuring out where a crevasse is, you use all of your sensory input. You try to see it, hear where the wind is coming from, and feel the little swells in the snow when you're walking.

I know of climbers who have gone in solo and been so freaked out when they realize they were truly alone there, aware of what can kill them, that they turn back on day one. Crevasses, frostbite, avalanches, and hypothermia are threats. Those are the four big killers in winter, so steeling the psyche is imperative. A winter climber must recognize that, if anything happens, there is no one to help. Climbers have to believe in their own ability to deal with whatever situation comes your way.

Overall, physical preparation did not take much longer for me than it did for a summer climb. The difference was that I was carrying more protection for the cold. Instead of just taking one sleeping bag, I took two sleeping bags. Instead of taking a stove, I took two stoves because if one malfunctioned, I was dead. Anything and everything can go wrong. I had to have backup.

Guided trips are planned for twenty-one days, but I thought I could make the climb in twelve. There was a limit to how much my equipment could weigh, including food. I packed sixteen days' worth of rations, estimating that would give me a four-day cushion. My total carrying weight for the solo was about 150 pounds. I planned on two carries per move up in altitude, split each time between my pack and a sled I pulled. Especially in the winter, though, I did not want to get separated from my food and fuel too much. I made the carries shorter because of that.

If a climber is not with his food and fuel when a storm hits, he has a very marginal amount of time that he can hang out. If he runs out of fuel, he will dehydrate and die. Instead of making a three- or four-mile carry and then turning back, I did multiple shuttles of a mile. There were about eight hours of light to work with. As I moved, I stayed in snow caves, or snow trenches I dug, shielding me from the wind. Inside, the shelters stayed at the freezing level, thirty-two degrees. One time, around 12,500 feet, the snow wasn't right for building, but I had to make do with what I had. I almost got blown out during the night. Working by the glow of my head light, I was crawling on my hands and knees with my crampons on and ice axe in my hand to cut blocks for repairs. I fought the wind until I finally made large enough snow blocks to hold everything down. It's cold enough in April during the regular climbing season; it was plenty cold in February.

At my 16,200 camp, I was running low on food and found some left-behind food supplies. There was a duffel bag full of freeze-dried sweet-and-sour pork. I ate so much of it that I still cannot eat it now. At 17,200 feet, there was already a snow cave in place, and I used that for shelter. Then the weather deteriorated, and I was essentially stuck. The wind was too furious to move up. When that happens, all a climber can do is wait it out and be patient. When the weather got so extreme that I was pinned down, I had to sit still until it abated. I hoped it would be over in hours. Whether it went on for ten days or two months, either way I was screwed. I just wondered, "What will it take for me to be able to move out?"

Being trapped in a storm can be boring. When I packed, there was no wiggle room for anything considered to be excess, non-survival weight. I did not bring a copy of *War and Peace* with me, but I did bring a radio. I am a fan of public radio and had just become a subscriber to KSKA in Anchorage. For signing up, I was given a transistor radio with earphones. It was small and lightweight, and I could hang it from the ceiling of my snow cave. I was very fond of a program called "Radio Reader" and got reception in the snow cave because I was so high on the mountain. Another handy thing about listening to public radio was hearing sister stations from around the state give weather reports. This gave me access to weather news: telling me if a storm was blowing in from the east or the west, if it was minus-fifty where I was, and how cold it was somewhere else. It made me feel as if I was in harmony with the rest of the state. If it was cold and stormy everywhere, it was actually a psychological boost because it meant it was not just me feeling miserable. I could also figure out, based on the wind reports, whether or not it might soon be reasonable to move up. That little radio was quite precious to me on the trip.

The day I wanted to go to the summit, the weather report seemed OK. I made it to the top on March 7, but I didn't stick around very long. I was there about three minutes and snapped two pictures. The first was of the Japanese flag I brought in homage to Naomi. The flag photo went to Jim Wickwire, the first American to summit the second tallest mountain in the world, K-2. He was a good friend of Naomi's and, when Wickwire traveled to Japan for a talk, he showed the flag photo to Naomi's wife. I got a nice reply from her and a copy of a book about Naomi's life. The other photo was a joke picture for the Anchorage singer-showman Mr. Whitekeys who always cracked wise about Spam. I took a picture of a Spam can on the summit and he used it in his show.

In all, I spent twenty-nine days on the mountain. Lowell flew me off the Kahiltna Glacier into Anchorage, and I had a marvelous reunion with family and friends. It was good to be with people again. A solo winter climb is a lonely experience, and I had long before determined I was a social person.

After all of my jobs in extreme weather places, climbing the coldest of mountains like Denali and Mount Everest, everybody believes I have a fabulous cold tolerance. Actually, I hate being cold. I'm a big baby, really, and I do not like cold toes. I am not innately in tune with the cold; I have to think about it. I have to consciously make decisions that keep me warm, or, if that fails, to plan for rapid re-warming.

The trick is to learn how not to be cold in tough conditions. Being underground is the number one technique for staying warm. The Eskimos do it. They understand the insulating qualities of snow. You want to get off the surface and out of the moving air. Convection and conduction can be hypothermia's best friend.

There was quite a hullabaloo when I returned to Anchorage. People were happy to see me, glad that I did not disappear or die on the mountain. Then they celebrated the achievement, treating me as a hero. These were Alaskans who love the mountain, and they understood better than most the hardships that might be faced in winter on this gigantic, ice-shrouded rock. It was a grand welcome back to civilization.

NEW OPPORTUNITIES

Alaska is such a special place and Denali is such a special mountain that someone who enjoys climbing and challenges, but has a full-time career in a city such as Anchorage, might be content to never seek to climb any other big mountains, or with merely taking the periodic vacation.

There are many Alaskans who fit that description. However, as illustrated earlier in his life, Vern Tejas was often struck by wanderlust and a desire to visit new and exotic lands. By establishing a reputation as both a renowned and experienced guide on Denali, and enhancing it with his solo winter ascent of that mountain, Tejas became a guide in demand. He was not someone who had deep pockets and could afford to simply fly anywhere in the world he chose. For Tejas to undertake world travels and take advantage of invitations, he had to be paid. He was not a wealthy citizen-adventurer, but a professional.

What he accomplished by succeeding at the winter solo on Denali was to make himself into a hot commodity.

Making the first solo winter ascent of Denali changed my life. It put my name out there in the field. People who never knew my name before now associated it with an important climb, and when they went shopping for a guide, they thought of me.

The actual first thing that happens after such an adventure, doing something difficult, is that your confidence level changes, your self-image changes, internal stuff. The external stuff changes when people begin to invite you to do things. My solo opened doors. I fell in love with Denali, and she blessed me multiple times throughout my life. Gradually, I came to believe that my calling was to meet the challenges where the most difficult conditions could be found. It's not that I was the hottest climber in the mountaineering world—actually, I was probably the coldest—but I was willing to challenge myself in the harshest conditions. I was not the greatest of climbers, but I could withstand really harsh environments. Working on the North Slope of Alaska in the winter helped me get my chops together on how to stay warm.

My friend Dave Johnston, who was on the first team winter climb in 1967, tried a solo of Denali. In fact, he started skiing from his cabin near Talkeetna and made it up to 12,000 feet, but he ran into a brutal

storm and turned around. If it hadn't been for that, he probably would
have succeeded, but there are so many ifs involved with Denali in winter.
In the main season, there are people around, even if you are climbing
solo. You may be doing all of the work yourself, but you can't avoid the
company. Yet if you fall in a crevasse and can't get out, you're still just
as dead.

In most ways, 1988 was a special year for me: I got invited to climb
on Mount Vinson in Antarctica. The Denali climb jump-started it all;
that got the ball rolling for me. Up until then, I never thought of climbing
mountains like Everest. Mostly, I was happy to climb in Alaska. I lived
in Alaska, and Alaska had plenty of mountains. It was not as if I grew
up dreaming of becoming a mountain guide. Even after I began doing it,
I did not plan on it becoming my career. It was obvious nobody got rich
being a full-time guide. However, I eventually made a conscious decision
that I wanted to stick with it. To me, having the opportunities to travel
the world and live a life of adventure out-weighed staying home and
making more money. People started asking me to lead trips to countries
I otherwise never would have visited. I went to Iran to climb the highest
mountain there. How would I have ever gotten to get to Iran otherwise
without becoming an oil executive?

One job I did off-and-on for quite some time, about twelve winters,
was helping build and maintain telecommunications towers on the North
Slope of Alaska. That is the coldest job in the world. I climbed towers
when it was minus-forty degrees out and the wind was blowing twenty
or thirty knots; forty knots was my limit. I don't think anybody can say
there is a colder job than that. At the end of each project, I was paid a
big chunk of cash and sent home. Some people compare it to mountain
climbing, which is probably why they thought I would be the perfect fit.
It paid good money, but that was not full-time, year-round work, either.
When I was done, it was "Goodbye. Thanks a lot. Here's your big bucks.
Go home, kid." The appreciation was there monetarily, but I would rather
have somebody notice, "Hey, you're really good at this. You're the best
guide I've ever met for doing high altitude work." People appreciated me
for that, and I wanted to go where I was appreciated.

Now my job description as a guide is to go to the most beautiful
places in the world with very interesting people and have fun. There
is nothing not to like about a job like that. Climbing has taken me to
Bolivia, Kenya, Chile, Argentina, India, Indonesia, Iceland, South
Georgia Island, Borneo, Peru, Tibet, Switzerland, Japan, Bhutan, France,
Greenland, and Fiji—places most people in the U.S. don't ever see. It is
an exciting way to live: a current passport always in your pocket, visiting

different corners of the world, getting to know people from different cultures you would never otherwise meet.

I will also admit that living that lifestyle did not make me the best father or husband. My son Cayman, named for the islands, who is twenty-seven years old, grew up mostly with his mother Gail. She was my partner at the time of the Denali winter solo and for many years afterwards. I figured I would slow down and help raise him, but all of these opportunities were coming my way and I could not say no. I did not settle down. I learned from trying to raise my son that a mountaineering lifestyle is hard on family relationships. It's great work. It's fun. We're out there climbing and skiing, but here's the deal, it's rewarding on certain levels and not very rewarding on other levels. If you want to have many exciting experiences and not much money in the bank, it might be your cup of tea. Do you want to have a wife? A home? A car? Kids? Forget it.

I know from raising my son as poorly as I did that it is hard on families. He turned out quite well, but that was mainly due to his mother. In retrospect, I wasn't such a great father because being a mountain guide is pretty selfish. There is a responsibility people should have for raising a kid well. Fortunately, I had a great partner and she was a very good mother. She probably overcompensated for me not being there. We did things together when I was there, but I wasn't there much. I was doing three Denali climbs a season, and in the winter I was on the North Slope.

I have long been in demand for guiding on Denali, but that only filled four months of the year tops. The 1988 solo led to invitations to make trips to the North Pole and the South Pole, Mount Everest and to Greenland. It opened the gateway for me to become a full-time guide with a major company. Also, once clients began taking regularly scheduled trips with me to such places as Mount Kilimanjaro, Mount Elbrus and others, they started approaching me to guide them on trips around the world that are not standard guide service offerings.

Becoming a guide is a process. It is not just about gaining experience. There is a rigorous certification process that can now cost a young guide between $30,000 and $40,000 and take three or four years. You might as well go to college and become a lawyer, make more money and spend it hiring a guide to take you on trips. I know guides that make only $20,000 a year working year-round. People only climb Denali between April and July, but working there only four months of the year, you cannot make a living.

Vern Tejas

Sunrise from the Roof of Africa

I have been in demand as a guide for Denali for decades, especially after the solo winter climb. I would like to think that it is more than just ego; I could not see me in a city in an office all of the time. Yes, I would have been home more frequently, but I felt a little bit of me would have died inside if I was not developing the best of me, not pushing my abilities. Ego is involved, but I would rather say there is a big because-it's-there drive within me, part of the definition of who I am as a person, that keeps me doing these adventurous things.

New Opportunities

One example of leading a climb to a rarely visited spot was being asked by four guys from New York to guide them in Iran. I know a lot of Americans don't want to visit because of all the troubles there and throughout the Middle East, but I jumped at the opportunity. In the late 1990s, we were in a little period of détente with Iran.

Mount Damavand is 18,406 feet tall, a substantial mountain. Mount Damavand is as big as Mount Elbrus in Russia, one of the Seven Summits, and maybe a little taller by some measurements. If it was located a few hundred miles north, it would have been the second-highest mountain in Europe, but it is in Asia instead, so it is out-classed by all of the Himalayan peaks. It is Asia's highest volcano, and the route was pretty straightforward. Being farther south, it did not have much snow on it. Actually, as we got higher and I saw white spots on the mountain, I thought they were snow patches, but as we got closer, I realized they were sheep. We thought the sheep would run away as we approached, but they couldn't; they were dead. These were the bodies of sheep that had been walked up there and sacrificed to the God of Abraham. I thought, "How Biblical. Things don't change much here in 2000 years."

Just because bombs weren't going off did not mean that Americans were particularly welcome. We weren't having a war, but some of the people still hated America. There was still the "Death to America" feeling, and that was the government's daily opening line on broadcasts. But we had free reign to travel all over the country, except for entering mosques. I squelched that idea pretty quickly since my climbers were Jewish and that could have set off a riot. I did not particularly want to go in one anyway, though my climbers did.

THE WORST MOMENT

Mountain climbers die. That is one of the risks of the sport. Many of them are ill-prepared, overrating their fitness, or underrating the danger of climbing to high altitude. There is a body count for many peaks. As of 2016, about 120 people had died while climbing Denali. A magazine article of a few years ago estimated that Mont Blanc, which saw its first recorded climb in 1786, has seen between 6,000 and 8,000 deaths, with dozens of people perishing each year. Located in the Alps, the French peak has attracted thousands upon thousands of would-be climbers from all over the world for ages.

New Hampshire's Mount Washington—the place where the highest recorded wind velocity on the planet, 231 miles per hour, was measured in 1934—stands just 6,288 feet high, but has experienced more deaths than the typical 26,000-foot peak in the Himalayas. The first recorded climb of Mount Washington took place in 1642, meaning some Pilgrim probably took a hike to the top. Since 1849, when officials began recording such things, about 150 people have died on the peak. Altitude is not the reason so many people die on Mount Washington. Wild weather, temperatures recorded deep in the negatives, and super high winds conspire to pin down climbers and cause fatalities. The message from these fearsome statistics is that mountaineering is not for the faint-hearted.

Guides who are hired to lead citizen adventurers to the top make a basic assumption that a client has some kind of climbing background, has trained hard for the journey, and will listen to the best advice offered. Sometimes that is true and sometimes it is not. Vern Tejas, an inexperienced trip leader in the 1970s, had learned much by the time he completed the first solo winter ascent of Denali. The accomplishment only enhanced his reputation. He was a far more seasoned guide, but as circumstances proved, sometimes it doesn't matter how much effort is put into careful planning or how closely the weather is monitored, nature rules and can overpower the best-made itineraries.

Unfortunately, if someone guides as long as Tejas has—more than thirty-nine years—the odds are that something awful will happen on a climb.

Yes, 1988 was a special year for me, but in one very significant way, it was terrible. A terrible thing happened on a guided trip of Denali only months after I completed the winter solo.

Even a well-prepared climber can fall victim to Denali's many dangers

As a guide, I think of myself as a caregiver, a shepherd, someone who takes care of my people. We build a rapport. Above all, it is safety first. And yet, on my very next climb of Denali, I lost a client. It is a big scar on my life. It is a blemish on my guiding career. There is a hole in my heart where I failed one of the people who was paying for my services and my services were not good enough. It is not something I like to talk about. It's one of the worst chapters of my life.

Lynne Salerno was a climber with a really high threshold for pain and discomfort on a nine-person Genet Expeditions trip. There are many ways to die in the mountains: being battered by storms, covered by avalanches, falling into a crevasse, falling down a ridge, running out of food, freezing, or contracting illnesses such as pulmonary or cerebral edema. Some climbers are so focused and determined to reach the summit that they put themselves at risk. Although a guide cannot read clients' minds, it is his responsibility to monitor their condition and step in if he believes a climber is overdoing it and has misplaced judgment. We are the eyes and ears. Sometimes, it is difficult to tell if climbers are simply performing admirably and applying all they've got to make the top, or if they are straining their body too much.

The Worst Moment

Lynne, who was thirty-one at the time, was super-motivated to reach the 20,310-foot summit. I learned later, by talking to her family, that she had a learning disability, but pushed herself through school with tenacity and hard work. Damning the torpedoes and full-speed ahead, she got through school and apparently applied that determination to reach the top of the mountain. Chief climbing ranger Bob Seibert interviewed Lynne's brother and father. They told him Lynne had suffered an illness as a child that affected her speech, writing ability, and part of her brain. She did not learn to talk until she was six years old, and the illness left her with dyslexia, but she was a very determined woman who, once fixated on a goal, worked hard to achieve it. Another side effect of Salerno's illness was a high tolerance for pain and ability to absorb cold.

One might think her innate pluck and will to keep going would be beneficial in high-altitude climbing, but that is not always the case. Often, those can be good assets in the mountains, but she didn't know when to stop. Dr. Peter Hackett, the high-altitude specialist on Denali who ran a medical study at the 14,000-foot camp, was the physician who did the inquest into her death and the autopsy. He concluded that she died of exhaustion-hypothermia. She ran her tank dry and died. I didn't catch it in time, and she didn't give me any clues either. Basically, I let her commit suicide. I want that lesson to stay in my mind forever when I'm dealing with other people.

I am an enabler; that is my coaching instinct. I want to give clients every chance to reach their goals. The trick is to know how much is too much, and that's the hard part. I sensed Lynne was having some difficulty, so I sent others in the group to the top with an assistant guide.

She kept saying to me, "I'm fine. Let's go."

I said, "No, we're going to stay here and wait for everybody else to come down." The others in the party were moving much faster. I wanted her to rest more before descending. "Lynne, I'm going to let the other guys go. We're going to wait here a little while."

She said, "Yeah, but I'm getting cold. What I need to do is move, so we can just climb up, and we'll go down with them." Lynne could work her way through stuff a lot of people couldn't, but I didn't know that then. She talked me into leading her to the summit.

Although Lynne did not have experience at high altitude, she had taken mountaineering courses through Alaska Pacific University and climbed in the Chugach Mountains next to Anchorage. It had been a winter course, so she had been out in harsh, cold conditions and passed. Nobody else on the team had that kind of background. They had climbed a few mountains before trying Denali, but they hadn't gone through Alaskan winter instruction like that. In that sense, she was the most experienced cold-weather climber besides the guides.

She said, "I'm good. I'm good. Let's go. I want to get there so badly." She ran out of fuel getting to the top, and I let her do that. I didn't see it. She did it, though. She got there. But she collapsed on the summit, melted into my arms, and I immediately began trying to get her to a lower altitude. We glissaded on our butts down to the Football Field. Unbeknownst to me, some others in the group who had descended earlier were courting frostbite and other injuries, as well.

The Football Field is at roughly 19,500 feet of elevation, not far below the summit, but a long way to high camp. She was beyond exhausted. We were high on the mountain, but we couldn't stop trying. There were two other guys with us and we had to carry her across the Football Field. It was there that I realized she was comatose. She was not going to be able to help herself. She was a heavy lady, and we were all too tired to carry her up Archdeacon Hill. Worse, there was now a lot of wind and snow and we really shouldn't even have been there. We had to help her, but that was a bad place to be as the weather deteriorated. The three of us were in danger, too. I slipped my hand up inside Lynne's jacket and shirt and felt that her belly was frozen with no pulse or sign of breathing. She was gone. Lynne died on May 18, 1988 and we couldn't do anything more for her. We had to get out of there for our own safety.

It was concluded that the cause of Lynne's death was hypothermia and exhaustion to which other circumstances contributed. My judgment of her fitness failed, and I should not have allowed her to talk me into taking her up the final approach to the summit. When the weather rolled in, trapping us up high, it precluded calling in a helicopter rescue. The only other climbers around at the time were those from our team who had to evacuate the high point quickly. There were no other groups nearby to help. It was never completely clear whether any other kind of immediate assistance would have made a difference. It was suspected, but not definitively stated, that Lynne's youthful illness contributed to her death. I have been haunted by Lynne's death all of these years. Lynne Salerno is the only climber who ever died on one of my trips, and I hope to God such a thing never happens again. I have never forgotten her and hope that my experience on that climb was a terrible lesson that has helped me help others in high places.

I had worked with the Alaska Mountain Rescue Group, but those were almost all body recovery trips from airplane crashes, drunken

fishermen who fell overboard, or avalanche victims. Once or twice a
year, we rushed in looking for a live body, and those all had good results.
Once we had thirty people combing the woods for a lost child. It was
damp and he would have become hypothermic if he stayed out alone
all night. We found him. On avalanches, by the time the group gets to
the scene, it is usually too late. You have about thirty minutes to rescue
someone under the snow. Thirty minutes is your golden window.

More than once on high mountains, however, there have been
other close calls. Five years ago, I guided a seventeen-year-old girl on
Aconcagua in South America who began breathing funny. She did not
know how to take care of herself and was not interested in learning how.
She would not eat enough because she wanted to lose weight. She would
not drink enough because she did not want to have to pee. She was not
interested in learning my pressure breathing method because it was too
much work.

I told her, "Don't pant like a dog. You'll die like a dog." I sometimes
use that phrase to wake people up, but this girl almost did die. She came
close, very close. She eventually passed out, and we carried her down.
With more oxygen and some medicine, she came to and was able to
descend with help.

Pressure breathing is a key element in my plan to help climbers get
the most from themselves as they ascend to high altitude. I am probably
the biggest proponent of pressure breathing in the world. Also known
as positive pressure breathing, pressure breathing is simply exhaling
forcefully enough against resistance that it momentarily increases the air
pressure inside the lungs.

By increasing the pressure in our lungs, we can drive O_2 into our
bodies. The pressure simulates being situated at lower altitude and
allows us to gain more oxygen. Done correctly, pressure breathing can
provide up to fifteen percent more oxygen than normal breathing. That
fifteen percent can make the difference in getting a headache or not,
making the summit or not, but you have to work at it.

First, blow out hard through pursed lips. The harder you blow,
the greater the pressure in your lungs and the more oxygen will enter
your bloodstream. Puff your cheeks out hard like Louis Armstrong
on the trumpet. It's like blowing out candles or blowing a kiss. Doing
it properly makes noise and looks uncool. That's why some people
give up on it, and that can be their undoing. After nearly forty years of
guiding experience, I know it works, though. I did a sub-three-hour race
in the Honolulu Marathon using this technique and my nickname was

"Choo-Choo" because I sounded like a steam locomotive as I passed the competition.

The next year on Aconcagua, we had a man who wouldn't take good care of himself. His tent-mate, a medic on the team, declared him hypothermic. We stripped off the man's clothes and both jumped in a sleeping bag with him to warm up his core body temperature. The following day, another guide led the other people up to the next camp while I walked this guy down to lower altitudes. It was not in the cards for him. I couldn't have him not taking care of himself. I didn't blame him, but to get him to turn around I said, "Hypothermia will *kill* you, man." This guy apparently had a mental issue from cracking his head open in a car accident. He was intelligent as hell, but not wise at self-tending. He was doing things that were not beneficial for his survival. His lack of self-preservation put an end to his climb. He returned the next year for another attempt and nearly died from dehydration.

Many times on Denali, I have assisted in bringing down someone from another climbing group who was suffering from altitude sickness. Often, I had good experiences giving them Decadron. Soon enough, the climber ties his own boots on and walks down. The important thing in those situations is to get the guy down as fast as possible. Most of the time, if he drops to a lower altitude, the edema goes away.

Physical carries are really the last resort, but I have done it. If you have to make a litter, you need a lot of people to help balance it on the descent and take turns. Eight people will suffice, but you really need twelve so there is some relief.

I probably have a half-dozen saves to my credit. The only time I tried mouth-to-mouth, which isn't easy to do, was on Lynne Salerno, but to no avail. I have friends who gave mouth-to-mouth resuscitation for an hour to a corpse. When we left Lynne Salerno behind at the Football Field, I knew she was dead. I didn't want anyone else to get killed in that storm, so I led the other two guys down from there. One was already frostbitten, so I had to leave or the tragedy would have been worse. Of all of the joy I have experienced in the mountains, watching Lynne Salerno die on my watch represents the single saddest moment of my nearly four decades guiding on big mountains.

In 1990, the Mountaineering Club of Alaska established a Lynne Salerno Climbing Wall. It was constructed in the basement of the Atwood Center on the campus of Alaska Pacific University, the same school where she took her mountaineering course before climbing Denali, for use by students and faculty.

THE SEVEN SUMMITS

Businessman Dick Bass changed mountaineering. Until Bass completed his climbs of the tallest mountains on each of seven continents, no guiding outfit and virtually no other climbers had thought of sweeping through the Seven Summits and labeling it an achievement. After Bass, an oilman who ran a Utah ski resort, finished the Seven Summits and wrote a popular book about it, climbers by the thousands became intrigued with the idea of replicating his feat. Born in 1929, Bass moved to Texas, where he later ran an oil company and a family ranch. Searching for an interesting physical challenge in the 1980s, Bass essentially coined the term Seven Summits. The mountains were always there, but no one had ever packaged them before.

Setting out with his friend, Frank Wells, the president of the Disney Company, Bass culminated his quest on April 30, 1985 by summiting Mount Everest. At the time, he was the oldest person to stand on top of the world's tallest peak at fifty-five. Wells climbed six of the mountains, but Bass completed the circuit without him.

By conceiving of this adventure, achieving this tour de force of climbing, then writing a popular book about the challenge, Bass revolutionized commercial guiding of mountains around the world. Matching the tallest mountains with the continents provided a special appeal. Not only were accomplished mountaineers interested in having such a glittering deed on their resumes, but average adventurers, some with no climbing backgrounds, believed they could also take on the dare. They figured if a middle-aged man like Bass could do the Seven Summits with a minimal background in the mountains, they could, too. Outdoor adventure companies quickly began offering guided trips to parts of the world they barely knew how to locate on a map. Established guide services with experience on Denali and Mount Everest had a head start. Those firms were already in business with guides on staff. Suddenly, there was more work available than they anticipated. New markets opened for climbers who wished to go to Europe's Mount Elbrus, Africa's Mount Kilimanjaro, Australia's Kosciuszko, Antarctica's Mount Vinson, and South America's Aconcagua.

Those who already guided the toughest mountains on the list, Denali and Everest, were ahead of others. When climb shoppers turned to the internet, they found a handful of guide companies listed. If the companies did not adapt and start offering trips to the other peaks, they would be left behind. They might not even hold on to Denali and Everest climbers. The new breed of citizen-adventure mountaineer tended to imprint with brand loyalty. If the climber had a good experience on Kilimanjaro, and especially if he bonded with a particular guide, he leaned towards sticking with the company that got him to the summit of one mountain.

In the space of a few years following Bass's completion of the Seven Summits and the release of his 1986 book, engagingly written with climber-author Rick Ridgeway, interest in mountaineering exploded. Demand to climb the Seven Summits skyrocketed. It was a very good time to be a savvy mountain guide who had been around the right mountains.

Vern Tejas was just blossoming as a guide, making a reputation on Denali, and traveling to more places around the world first with Genet Expeditions, and then with Alpine Ascents. He never imagined he would spend most of his career guiding trips on the Seven Summits.

Until 1986, I was primarily a Denali guide. However, Genet owner Harry Johnson wanted to grow the business and was already receiving requests to guide 22,841-foot Aconcagua in Argentina. Harry thought of the idea of guiding the Seven Summits in 1986. Nobody else was doing it yet. Harry read Dick Bass's book and right away said, "This is what we've got to do." I don't know exactly how he figured out there was a demand for it, but there certainly was. So we started doing Aconcagua, then we expanded to include climbs of Mount Kilimanjaro, the Roof of Africa, at 19,341 feet. Things snowballed, and climbing and guiding the Seven Summits gradually gained momentum. Todd Burleson with Alpine Ascents in Seattle took a page out of Harry's playbook by 1989 and got on the bandwagon. Rob Hall and Adventure Consultants in New Zealand also got into the game. No company was offering all Seven Summits, and it wasn't until 1989, when Genet started offering Everest as a commercial climb, that it became possible for the public to hire guides to do all seven.

In the meantime, Pat Morrow, a Canadian, was also entranced by the Seven Summits. However, his version of the Seven Summits included Carstensz Pyramid instead of Kosciuszko. That is because the British Commonwealth doesn't view Australia as a stand-alone continent. In Canada, they teach that the seventh continent is Austral-Asia, or Oceania, not Australia. When Morrow completed his Seven Summits in 1986, it differed from Dick Bass's Seven Summits, but Morrow will tell you that he had no other option really. He had to come up with an alternative to top Bass. If you ask somebody from Australia, Australia is a continent. In the United States, Australia is considered a continent, but in the British Commonwealth, they think of Oceania as the seventh continent. To some degree, Pat Morrow's climb threw the entire Seven Summits concept into disarray and really formed it into Eight Summits. If you don't want to have somebody question your accomplishment, you have to do eight summits to get seven summits indisputably.

Certainly, Carstensz is a very good challenge, much more challenging than Kosciuszko. You could call that the highest point in Austral-Asia, if Austral-Asia is a continent. Every continent seems to have some exception to the continental terminology. Is a continent surrounded by water? Antarctica is. We call that a continent. So if that's the definition you're looking at, someone could counter and say North America is attached to South America by land. It's not completely surrounded by water, so it's not really a continent on its own. Then look at Asia and Europe; in Russia there is no water in-between at all. They're hammered straight together. There's no two ways about that. So it becomes a dispute over terminology, and you have to talk to cartographers, geologists, and people studying plate tectonics to come up with a clear definition. It's still fuzzy. I think both Bass and Morrow took advantage of the fuzziness and said, "This is it." Because Carstensz is a tougher climb, that stuck as the seventh summit for some, so to satisfy all critics, you have to do it. I made sure I did all eight.

In the mid-to-late 1980s, the housing market collapsed in Alaska due to an oil recession. In addition to owning Genet Expeditions, Harry Johnson owned a title company. Business was bad, and when the opportunity first came about in 1989 for Genet to take a group to Mount Everest, he wanted to lead it. I was going along, too.

However, the real estate situation became more complicated. Harry realized that if he worked at it and was creative, he could buy out all of his competitors and be riding high when things bounced back. He couldn't spend three months on Everest. He said, "Vern, if you're not going forward, you're going backwards." I could not relate to giving up the chance to climb Everest, but he said, "This is more important. I've got a family. I've got this opportunity." The circumstances provided opportunity for both of us.

So he withdrew from the climb, and I moved up in the pecking order. Since we already had a concession on Denali and great programs on Aconcagua and Mount Kilimanjaro, being allowed to jump in on Everest from the China side was big-time. That meant Genet Expeditions guided the four toughest mountains in the Seven Summits group, and that same recession in Alaska was opening doors for Mount Elbrus in Russia.

I almost lost a toe on Everest on my first climb in '89. I prefer to keep all of my fingers and toes and still be able to count to twenty on them. Let's just say I am very attached to them, but it was a close call.

Originally, for that first trip, Harry was going to be the climbing leader and I was going to be the main guide, but I got bumped to climbing leader when Harry got bogged down with business. The Alaskan economy was changing, and he had to be on top of it. At the same time, the guiding world was changing, and Genet had to be on top of that. I had never climbed in the Himalayas, and all of a sudden, I'm a Himalayan guide. I had fourteen ascents of Denali, though; a half-dozen climbs on Aconcagua; been to the top of Vinson; and knocked off Elbrus. I had five of the seven summits under my belt. That's not bad.

When I said I was going to Everest, people said, "Oh, cool." I was not pushing my accomplishments. I was pretty modest, pretty humble, but people were figuring out I was close to climbing the Seven Summits. When the Everest opportunity came along, naturally I said yes!

Being climbing leader didn't pay me any more money, but it did give me more responsibility. We had some good, experienced people. The base camp manager helped facilitate setting up. We had four very large bottles of liquid oxygen that we shipped out during the summer for our fall climb. They were loaded on a truck and, unfortunately, somewhere along the way twenty-five percent of it vanished. No explanation, no rebate, no nothing. When we got to base camp, there were only three bottles. That damaged our chances of everyone getting to the summit.

On the climb, things happened. There was bad weather and delays. The wind came up. I was high on the mountain with a deaf climber named Ken, who was very strong. He did not want to turn back. He was very motivated to show the world deafness was not a handicap. He wanted to stay on the mountain as long as it took to get a shot at the summit. There was really only one shot left, if that. Then, in late October, the wind died down when Ken and I were at Camp Three at about 23,000 feet. It was like camping on the top of Aconcagua for a month, really. We were acclimated, but were enfeebled by the lack of oxygen. It was the beginning of the day, and we were positioned on the North Col, fairly low on Everest, but above base camp and advanced base camp. There was also an interim Camp IV. We had been shuttling up loads of supplies so that we would be ready for a weather window. We had spent three weeks waiting for something to change, and it finally did.

Tejas breaks out his travel guitar for a world-top guitar solo

We had food and fuel and two bottles of compressed oxygen. We knew it would not be enough O_2, but it was all we had. Liquid oxygen is in the bottle at -140 degrees, but once you bottle it, you have no control and it starts to warm up. You can either use it, which is great for sleeping, or it's going to go away without being used. Since we had lost one bottle, we were low to start with. We had been using it up as we worked and waited. We were severely low that late in the season because we never expected to be there that long. The liquid oxygen stocks were almost all gone, so we only took compressed oxygen. We had them as part of our emergency medical stock, but we decided to use it for climbing.

At Camp IV, we knew how little oxygen we had, so we only took periodic small hits and turned it off. We knew we would need it more higher up. We pushed upward to 27,500 feet. We knew a tent from a French group was left there, and it was a goal for us. It looked like a mushroom sticking up. The winds blew everything else away, but there was a pillar of packed snow about two or three feet high left with a tent on top. We could see it, cocked at a rakish angle because of snow deformation, but it was a shelter we did not have to carry. The tent was our goal for the day, but we did not make it. We were still climbing when darkness fell. We were close, so we slowly crawled upwards in our hypoxic haze. Then Ken fell and his headlight went out as he slid down the North Face. I turned and called his name futilely into the darkness below. We were in a very dangerous area. This was the same face where a well-known climber named Marty Hoey disappeared on a Dick Bass trip, and where George Mallory disappeared back in 1924 on the first attempt to climb Everest. I was searching for Ken's light and yelling, "Ken! Ken! Where are you?"

Of course, since he was deaf and mute, he couldn't hear me or yell back. I was like, "Oh, my god, I've lost my client." Thoughts of Lynne Salerno flooded my clouded mind. I dreaded the thought. I kept yelling hopelessly for Ken. Then, remarkably, he responded. About fifty feet down the hill from me, a light went on. He had slipped, and it slowly took him fifteen minutes to climb back up, but he was getting there. I started digging a platform in the snow to stay there until we could see what we were doing. This was too dangerous. So we made a bivouac at 27,300 feet. We did not make it to that tent. We called it a night, dug in, and flattened a place where we could lay our sleeping bags.

We had sleeping bags rated to minus-forty degrees, but it was so bitterly cold we could barely sleep. Ken slept some, but he got frost nipped in his sleeping bag where his hands were touching the zipper. His fingers had several black spots. Our communications were basically in sign language or written down. I still have some of the notes and they take me right back to the moment.

In one, I asked him, "What do you want for breakfast?"

"I was thinking bacon, eggs, some steak on the side."

"How about granola?"

"Great, thanks." We were parched, and I was trying to make water. Mt. Everest is one of the driest places on earth, but maybe the South Pole is drier. We're dying of thirst, but couldn't make water quickly on the stove because there was no oxygen to make the flames go. It took hours and hours with me staying up a good part of the night to melt snow for water. I woke up Ken and gave him some water. I was up most of the night, nodding off here and there while the stove was going. I woke to make him drink, and he went back to sleep, and I started melting more snow.

Morning finally came and we were exhausted, but we could see the tent above us. The tent was so lopsided that I decided to level it from the inside out. We shoveled snow inside the tent and then flattened it. Feeling hypothermic and hypoxic, we crawled inside for the next night. Anything above 26,000 feet is called the Death Zone and climbers do not want to spend too much time there. Climbers especially do not want to spend unnecessary extra nights. We were at around 27,500 feet and thought we could stay there and sleep indoors. It was probably negative ten degrees inside.

We had radio contact with the rest of the team. Call times were designated twelve hours apart, at 8 a.m. and 8 p.m. Some team members were coming up to support us. They were at Camp III, and we were at Camp V. At 3 a.m., Ken and I drank some water and ate granola bars. We threw a liter of water into our packs and were out the door by 4 a.m. going for the top.

We progressed and reached the first step. There, you can get to the ridge itself and look down across the Kangshung Face, the east face of Everest. It is a huge and amazing wall of ice. It was bitterly cold, but our heads were above the ridge and hot because of the brutal sunshine. Due to the steepness of the ridge's incline, our lower bodies were in its shadow which was negative fifty degrees Fahrenheit. We were freezing hot; it was a terrible paradox. I cannot ever remember being colder than that. My metabolism was shutting down. We did not have much food, we were cold, and we were dehydrated. We started traversing below the ridge to where the Chinese Ladder is. I was so dehydrated, I felt I was swallowing via a leather throat. My throat was crisp and raw, and I felt as if it was breaking apart. I had to have water. I reached into my pack and pulled out the bottle and the water was frozen. It was as solid as a rock. I felt like throwing it away—it was no good to me then—but I knew I would need it later.

I looked at Ken and took stock of myself. The big toe on my right foot had been cold for hours and hours. I was dehydrated and feared I was going to be frostbitten. I had tried to warm up the toe by slipping a hand warmer in my boot, but it had slid around and was inhibiting circulation. Ken reached the Chinese Ladder, slipped his pack off, and actually got a drink. With my frozen fingers doing the talking, I told him he was strong enough to go for it, but as his guide, with the wind returning, it would be unwise. We were probably only 700 feet below the summit. At the speed we were going, and it being late morning, it might have taken another five hours. It would be either late afternoon or night before we got to the top. I told him I was going down and that I thought he should, too. He looked up and looked back. I could hear the wind roaring. He was stronger than me at that time, but he decided to go down. He got way ahead of me, and I was so dehydrated that I ended up crawling. Our goal was to get down to the camp at 23,000 feet, to the others, and below the Death Zone. I needed some help and crawled into the night. It was probably 10:30 p.m. when I saw team members coming out of camp waving flashlights. I was trying to save power in my headlamp, so it was off. Also, I knew if I ran totally out of gas, being able to turn on the headlamp was the only way they could find me.

The classic sign of dehydration is that you can't hold water. It's paradoxical, but true. Upon crawling into camp, the others gave me a cup of water, and I puked. I was so cold and dehydrated that I would drink water and throw up. Ken has a wicked sense of humor and handed me a plastic bag like I was on an airplane. The third time I threw up, he gave me a bag with a hole in it, so when I tossed, the vomit ran down into my suit and my sleeping bag. He was laughing so hard. I was so pissed off, but I was too weak to retaliate. I slept fitfully as my frozen body slowly warmed up. The next morning, somewhat recovered from the ordeal, I realized I had a frostbitten toe, yet was able to descend to base camp. Our doctor at base camp told me to take an aspirin, and it would make everything OK.

Ken could also effectively communicate a temper or sense of outrage. Before our summit push, at that 23,000 camp, Mike McDowell, our base camp team manager was cooking. He wanted to get higher on the mountain for a potential shot at the top. Mike was sharing a tent with Ken. I was outside when this happened, but it was kind of hard not to notice the fireball. Mike ran out of gas in the stove. Your fuel bottle is empty so you don't think about turning the stove off. You screw on another bottle and the stove is on full. There was another stove burning next to it. WHOOSH! Half the tent vestibule went up in flames, just disappeared in a flash fire. Ken flipped out. He started cussing out Mike in sign language, waving his arms making very rude gestures. It was very humorous to watch. For a guy unable to be vocal, Ken was pretty expressive.

The next meal, Ken took over the cooking and the gas ran out. When he changed the bottle, the same thing happened. Ken looked dumbfounded because he had repeated Mike's mistake. Mike repeated all of the same gesticulations back at him, angst, anger, in sign language. I was rolling on the ground laughing. That will stick with me forever.

We retreated from the mountain and traveled by truck to the Nepal border, leaving Tibet, or China. We drove straight to Kathmandu, but I didn't even go into town. I got dropped off at the airport and took the first plane out. Within seventy-two hours, I was in Anchorage visiting with the late Dr. William Mills, the frostbite expert, about my big toe. I had met him at mountaineering meetings, but I had never been a patient. He was one of those grandfatherly figures in the climbing community. Dr. Mills had also come to rescue group meetings from time to time. We consulted him on frostbite issues. I told people he wrote the book on frostbite and that is literally true. More than that, he wrote the encyclopedia.

He could be pretty funny. When I went to see him he said, "So, you're a climber." I said, "Yeah." "That means you probably don't have much money." I said, "Yeah." Then he said, "You probably want to be one of my study guinea pigs." I said, "Yeah." "OK, that means the government is paying for your treatment."

He gave me a Silvadene antibiotic, which is really expensive, some circulation meds, and a portable whirlpool bath. Then he told me to stay off of my toe. I followed the instructions to a T and, to my dismay and delight, about a month later, the whole end of my toe, from the knuckle on down, calved off. Inside, underneath where it slid off, there was a little, itsy, bitsy pinky toe about half the size of my big toe. That was the core that was saved that includes the bone, and, for some reason, the toenail. I don't know how that happened, but my toe not only regenerated itself, the toenail came back even though it was black back to the knuckle and should have died. It all came back, and today I have a normal looking toe.

I must be part star fish. I can still dance and run and do all of those good things. It is because I went to the best frostbite doctor in the world as soon as possible and followed his rules perfectly. All of my toes are cold all of the time, but that's just from too much cold exposure.

Ken and I probably got within 700 feet of the summit of Mount Everest and turned back. But we lived to tell the tale. Discretion became really important. You have to make good decisions based on the information available. The information was that the wind was back in a big way and the two of us were almost dead already. If we continued, it seemed all it would do was prolong the misery, and we would be likely to die later that night on the way down. That was versus going down then and believing we might live to climb another day. We lived.

My first time on Everest was not a lot of fun. It was a heck of a challenge. I felt very close to dying as I was crawling along. I made the decision to turn back when I thought I would never get back to Everest and have another chance. Before going to Everest, Gail had gone into labor with Cayman. I had a newborn son waiting for me at home.

I was still going to guide on Denali and Aconcagua, but then Todd Burleson asked me if I wanted to go back to Everest for Alpine Ascents. I was back in the saddle, ready to rock and roll after the frostbite healed.

For my second trip to Everest, I worked with two European guides and another American guide. I met Willie Prittie, who was co-founder of Alpine Ascents with Todd. Todd was the marketing brains, and Willie was the engine. Todd was the mastermind in the company, but Willie made sure things worked smoothly on the mountain.

One of the guides was Peter Habeler, the Austrian who was one of the most famous climbers in the world. Along with Reinhold Messner, he was the first to climb Everest without oxygen in 1978. That achievement was thought to be impossible at the time. He was a big deal in the climbing world. I found out Alpine Ascents was paying Peter a lot of money, and I was making like zero. Todd knew he was a big draw and his weight was considerable. He had super mountain cred. We also had Martin Zamuletta, the first Spanish mountaineer to climb Everest. So we had some well-known guides whose reputations helped fill the trip.

On our way to the mountain, we took a flight out of Beijing. We were in our seats and one of our climbers sitting next to me started bumping me and pointing out the window. We were starting to taxi, and this guy realized our luggage was still on the runway, a whole cart full. So I stood up. The flight attendant came running down the aisle to tell me I had to be seated. I said, "Our baggage is on the runway. We're not going anywhere without our baggage." She ran up front and told the pilot. He stopped while the leftovers were loaded on.

The whole trip got a little bit wacky. Our two high-cost guides from Europe went over the bottom of the route, and they said the rock fall was too dangerous to pass through. The group wasn't climbing it. I'm going, "What the heck?" There was a different route Habeler was interested in, and he asked the Chinese if it was OK if we switched. They said it was alright with them, but there was another group on it and we needed permission because it was paid for. The other "group" was a European soloist with his girlfriend. Peter had a lot of prestige, and this guy who knew he was.

The guy was not happy about having a bunch of Americans on his route. If Peter or Martin wanted to climb there, no problem, but we might as well go home because they're supposed to be working for us. This debate went back and forth for days, and stretched into a couple of weeks. He kept waffling back and forth, "Yes you can, no you can't." We tried to cut deals like saying we would build the camps and he could take the first shot at the top. Ultimately, Peter took a fall on the top of the West Ridge and that, combined with an impasse on the route, spooked him, and he went home.

I still wanted a shot. We were on the mountain for close to two months, and at the end of it, I was very frustrated about how the European guides acted. They didn't interact with the clients at all and spent very little time with the Sherpas. It just seemed as if these guides were more there for themselves than the clients, taking Todd's money. My payoff was getting another shot at the top. That's why I wasn't making a salary. I asked Todd to give me a stove, food, and permission, and he said he couldn't do it. At that point, no one had been hurt, so he considered it a successful expedition. He was afraid I would go up alone and die, and it would reflect badly on him and the expedition.

He offered me a deal to come back in 1992 from Nepal working for him. The chances of success are better from the south side than the north side. I stifled my ambition and agreed. I was hoping my third time on Everest would result in a summit climb, and it did.

ACONCAGUA

One of the Seven Summits is Aconcagua, located in Argentina. At 22,841 feet of elevation, it makes the list for being the highest peak in South America. It is also the tallest mountain in both the Southern Hemisphere and the Western Hemisphere, and claims the title of being the tallest mountain in the world not situated in Asia.

The more literal location of Aconcagua somewhat resembles Denali in that it is located inside Aconcagua Provincial Park. Nearby is the city of Mendoza, Argentina, which was founded in 1561. The city is the capital of the province where it is located and its population is just over one million. A prominent wine-producing region, beef, as is true throughout much of that country, is a popular side dish to eat while imbibing.

Mendoza is the jumping off place for those who wish to climb Aconcagua. The community cultivates the image of an outdoor center beyond mountaineering. People visit for hiking, horseback riding, rafting and skiing, as well.

Although Aconcagua receives its share of snow, its objective dangers are nowhere as risky as those on Denali, which is about 2,500 feet shorter. The normal route on Argentina compares to the West Buttress on Denali, but does not require the use of ropes on the path to the top. The altitude is an obstacle to overcome, but its terrain on the normal route is graded non-technical by the best climbers.

Temperatures are not to be underestimated, and people caught in storms and ill-prepared for the altitude have been killed on Aconcagua. The government does not keep precise track of the success rate of those attempting to reach the top, but it does note that seventy-five percent of those who try are foreigners.

The first recorded climb of Aconcagua came in 1897. The European team of mountaineers was led by British climber Edward FitzGerald who attempted to reach the summit eight times over a two-year period. However, it was someone else in his group, Matthias Zurbriggen, who was the first to stand on the summit on January 14 of that year.

By the time Vern Tejas began guiding all of the Seven Summits, he was an old hand on Aconcagua. As one of his longest gigs, Tejas had been to the summit of Aconcagua thirty-four times by the end of 2016.

Aconcagua is not my favorite mountain to climb, but Mendoza is my favorite place to hang out. I'll do a climb there and stay around Mendoza for a month. I might go early, do the climb, and stay late. It's a great place to be during the Alaskan winter. I used to have a wonderful girlfriend there, but that was a long while ago.

Even if you're not a big meat eater, you should try the steak there because it is just that good. You can just go to a corner café and get a steak for $6. It could be the best you've ever had in your life. It is easy to get a very good steak for less than $10.

Aconcagua is a challenging mountain and includes a trek to base camp. As the guide, it is one of the hardest peaks to pack for because the trek, base camp, and the climb each can involve special preparations. A Denali guided trip is based on a three-week adventure. An Aconcagua trek is four days, three days in and one day out, wrapped around the climb.

It is a desert environment, so it is dusty and mules are carrying the supplies. It takes careful packaging of the supplies because they are going to be bouncing around on the backs of mules. Things are loaded into barrels, but you don't want them shaken up inside the barrels. If a can is touching another can on the mule ride, it will wear a hole in one. If a fuel bottle is touching another bottle, it's going to be empty by the time you get there because it is going to vibrate a billion times as the mules trot. That's why I say everything has to be mule proof. It makes for my most challenging preparation trip in the mountains.

Base camp supplies and food are separate. They have to be readily available. Once you reach base camp, you are going to be hanging out there for three or four days. You have a different set of supplies. Most of the trekking food you pretty much eat on the fly. The base camp food is richer and more nutritious. Then you have the high mountain food for when you are climbing. There are ten-to-twelve days of those supplies and they need to be lightweight and easy to cook and clean up. There is always a fair amount of carbohydrates in the meal plan.

On the mountain itself, you don't want to spend too much time cooking, so it is simple, processed food: instant mashed potatoes, instant rice, instant noodles. That's the quick-cook stuff. You don't want that on your trek or you will become burned out by the time you get to Day Twenty-Two. Plus, all of your shopping is done in Spanish. It all calls for pretty intense planning beforehand.

Aconcagua

On Denali, it is a one-hour approach to the Kahiltna Glacier. On Aconcagua, it is the three-day, dusty approach. Since Aconcagua is so high, you have to watch the clients on their acclimating process. You really have to preach careful breathing. There are a couple of camp sites on the way in on the trek. Base camp is at 14,340 feet, Plaza de Argentina, but it is not your typical base camp. It includes meal tents, showers, and even internet access. The Park Service actually has a medical team in place, and there is mandatory screening of climbers to determine if they are in good enough shape to go higher.

Aconcagua being in the Southern Hemisphere, climbers think it will not be that cold. It is definitely going to be warmer than Denali or Everest most of the time, but if they believe it is not going to be stormy, they are wrong. It is one of the windiest places around. You've got a big pressure differential between the Pacific and the Atlantic Oceans, and I have seen the wind scream in from the west. The whole west side is devoid of snow because it is blown off. The opposite side is loaded with snow and glaciers. For all of that, some 10,000 people a year try to climb Aconcagua.

Aconcagua is the tallest non-Asian mountain in the world,
but is only the 189th tallest mountain on Earth

A lot of people grabbed hold of the Seven Summits idea. It was an amazing creation by Dick Bass. It was pretty easily defined as seven continents, seven high points and anyone who embraces the concept gets to see diverse cultures all over the world. You get to pretty much see the whole world and have the trophies of climbing to the highest mountains on each continent. There are also a lot of people who just want to take a great trip to a place and climb one great mountain. If only one percent of those 10,000 people coming to Aconcagua per year also went to Everest in the same year, can you imagine what base camp would be like? There are a lot of people intrigued and motivated to take a three-week vacation on a big mountain. Some people only have two weeks off from work to try it and they get spanked. That happens a lot. Most of the health problems that climbers face are altitude-related due to climbing too fast.

Based on all my years of experience on high mountains, including Denali, Everest, and Aconcagua (which is actually the second tallest of the Seven Summits after Everest), I always teach my climbers about pressure breathing. I feel very strongly about it. You need oxygen. Oxygen is good. More is better. The best way you get more into your bloodstream is by pressure breathing. You can get upwards of fifteen percent more in a lungful by pressure breathing. It is not a free lunch, though. You have to concentrate on breathing. You breathe out intensely. Your cheeks expand. On Everest, you start training climbers very early, on the approach, so it becomes natural later when they need it and they are hurting and distracted. You can hear climbers when they breathe. That's what tells you they are exhaling correctly. You must start early to build up the breathing muscles and increasing the number of functioning alveoli, the little air sacs in the lungs. It is not natural. If you are sitting around or walking around at sea level, you just breathe the way you always have. We are trying to increase your expiratory pressure ability so that it will be naturally occurring when you are at high altitude and in thinner air.

I also caution people not to go too fast. I learned that lesson the first time I was on Denali. I tell clients to watch their pace. I tell them my main job is to keep them from hurting themselves. One way is to prevent them from stepping too fast early in the climb. I know they are super trained. They've been working out. They've been working in the gym, but their bodies have not adapted to altitude yet. So take it easy. Take lots of pictures. Let's laugh and listen to music. I might whip out the harmonica, fiddle, or guitar. I suggest we just enjoy being in the mountains. Go fast, you won't last. Go slow, to the top you'll go.

If I choose to let someone else lead, they tend to dwell on what everybody in the group thinks about them. They don't want people looking at them and saying, "What's wrong with him? He's so slow." He thinks he's got to pick up the pace and he goes too fast. Pretty soon they're running. I'm going, "Whoa. Take it easy." I get back out front and put the pace in slow mo. I hope the climbers notice we're going slow and know I am doing this intentionally because I know what works.

It is slow. It is steady. You build a better foundation and, when they are going for the summit in two weeks, they'll be so much better off. The climbers may get bored, but when they finish and think everything was easy, I will say, "Great!" That's what I want. I want it to be easy. I don't want it to be life and death and high drama. I want it to be predictable, mundane, steady Eddie, the tortoise beating the hare every time. We are there to get to the top with the least possible strain and maximum enjoyment. We can't control the weather, but we can control our own bodies to a large extent.

That is another thing I harp on. I ask everyone to take care of themselves. Oxygen is primary. Water is the next most important thing. According to the Survivor's Rule of Three, you can go three minutes without air, three days without water, and three weeks without food. Everything is worse on the mountain; you can probably die within a week without food. Ignoring any of these even for a short time can have dire consequences.

When you are at sea level, you don't even think about it much. You're pretty unconscious in what you do. If you are thirsty you go get a drink. If you are hungry you go eat lunch. The problem with altitude is that it fools you. It works against your sensory input because everything is oxygen related, and without the normal amount, all systems are negatively impacted. When you get hypoxic, your drive to eat is diminished because you might not have enough oxygen to digest it. Your stomach doesn't feel like eating. That last peanut butter sandwich is still there.

Many times, I have forced myself to eat by taking a small bite and chewing it well. I push it down. You must eat because you need the fuel. I set up my feedbag for the day before setting out. If I plan to climb for eight hours, that means I schedule eight breaks. One break every hour, and I will have a something to eat at each break.

If, at the end of the day, my energy bars are still there, then I am not taking care of myself. You are working very hard, so eating a Mars bar or a Snickers bar every hour is nothing. If you do not eat regularly, you will become hypoglycemic. You are not going to feel like yourself. You are not going to make good decisions. You are going to be irritable. A lot of things hinge on keeping your blood sugar at the right level. Water is even more important. High altitude is usually associated with cold, and that's a diuretic. As we get cold, our blood vessels contract, and our bodies decant liquid as our pressure increases. Cold also inhibits our drive to drink because cold liquids can lower our body temperature.

Then there is water loss due to increased respiration at altitude. The gist of this is we take on less water just when we need more.

I know I need to drink a cup of water each hour when I am working. I measure it out, and if I make a stop and I have too much in the bottle, it means I am getting dehydrated. These things are the bedrock of my guided climbs. Drink up! Even the drive to breathe is diminished at altitude. Humans' primary drive to breathe is actually to rid our bodies of carbon dioxide. With the lower pressure found at altitude, CO_2 easily escapes from our lungs. When it does, we have only one reason to breathe, and that's to avoid suffocation from the lack of O_2. The alarm will eventually go off, and we will be left gasping since that means we have been hypoxic for some time already. Our normal, basic drives are diminished, and we must consciously make our bodies do what they should do. This is huge. If you don't get it, you will have a tough time up high.

It took me years of guiding to recognize these basic, important principles. However, when you have a sample of 1,000 climbers, experience tells you what the right thing to do is.

The wind certainly turns people back on Aconcagua, even if they are prepared. Mostly, though, if you are acclimated and follow a good nutritional plan, you can get to the top. The three weeks gives you time to cope with the winds, but it also helps your altitude adjustment. If you try to climb it in two weeks, you are not going to be sufficiently adapted.

My friend Daniel in Mendoza has told me that he has seen the wind send rocks flying through the air on the mountain. If you get it in the head with one of those, you're out. That's life-threatening, or at the least paralyzing. Any wind stronger than sixty miles per hour will stagger you. You can't walk at a normal pace when you are being thrown around. If you are wearing a pack, fifty miles per hour will knock you over. If it is higher—and it gets to above 100 miles per hour sometimes—you're going to get thrown to the ground. You can get hurt. I've been bounced. If you land on the snow, it's not a big deal. If you land on sharp rocks or boulders, it's a big deal.

If we are in one place and I am not actively guiding, I will stand up. I've been up when the wind has reached the point of picking me up and throwing me down. There is one area on Aconcagua that is called The Ridge of the Wind. It is like Windy Corner on Denali. It is a very short section to cross, but it howls there. I have actually climbed up there and been spun around. I have been on the ground crawling with my goggles pulled tight over my eyes and still had the goggles fill with snow.

When the wind comes in that strong, it is too much of a fight to make progress climbing. We don't typically guide when the wind is more than thirty miles per hour. I would never take a group out in those high-wind conditions. As for myself, I did a speed solo to the top, and I was forty-eight hours into it from the road before climbing season began. I was not going to be easily persuaded to turn back. Yet the wind was so powerful I was getting totally disoriented. I was beat up, slam dunked, and rolled around. The third time it occurred, I went, "OK, this climb is not happening."

I had two choices. I could wait it out or go home. That time I went home. I said, "Screw this. I'll come back another time when she wants to be climbed. She doesn't want to be climbed right now." That is the central spot for the wind on that ridge. If you advance 200 yards beyond that, if you can crawl past that area, you will be out of the worst of the wind. Wind just screams across the ridge right there. But there are those times when you just can't get over the ridge.

On that trip, I tried it three times. I wanted to get through the venturi. Three times I steeled myself for the hurricane. Three times, I bravely crawled up to the shrieking storm. And each time I got clobbered. I was totally beat up and disoriented by the time I retreated.

I wanted to get it over with and go climb another mountain. But the mountain had other ideas. When the weather says no, you don't go.

Someday, I am going to stop climbing Aconcagua, but boy I am going to miss that beef. Argentinian beef is the best in the world, and when I am there, I eat a steak at least every other day. I know I won't be able to have it that good again for a long time.

The river is fed by Aconcagua, and from the river comes the irrigation. But they are losing the snow cover there. Global warming is apparently the cause. The glaciers are going away. Right now, the city seems to be at the height of its glory, but I can see that it could dry up and go away some day. There is a lot of sunshine, and there is that nearby desert environment. They probably have the most productive vineyards in the world. The Malbec wine is from a purple grape and is world class. It was once an Old World strain of wine that was decimated by blight in Europe. So now Mendoza is known as the Malbec capital of the world. But they also have many other tasty varieties.

Wine aficionados come from all over the world, the way the mountaineers do. However, they stay at the vineyards, and when they leave, they bring cases of the wine back to their home countries. *Vendimia*, the National Grape Festival, is a big holiday. Besides

Christmas, the biggest day of the year there is when the grapes come in. There is a huge parade. The town fills up with tourists from all over. They have a queen contest. It is a big party. Mendoza is a sun-loving, fun-loving, beautiful place. I fell in love with my Spanish teacher, my professor. She taught me first, and then we got romantically involved. I ended up learning to speak Spanish, and she ended up learning to speak English. We were a couple for three years or so. I almost became Argentinian. And the town was only a three-hour drive from Aconcagua. It is the jumping off town.

I love the culture there. I see it with people who come to climb Denali, and they are swept up by the beauty of Alaska and the Alaskan culture. I, too, once was one of them, and I still am. I came to Alaska and was overwhelmed by the sights and amazed by the eclectic mix of humanity there. I think, when climbers come to Alaska, they have been watching things on TV like *Ice Road Truckers* and *Deadliest Catch*. They are fans of those shows and are looking for the Last Frontier. They show up in Talkeetna and pretty much find it. It is a tourist trap for sure now, but it is still one of the last great little towns there. Visitors still have that old vision from the TV show *Northern Exposure*. Talkeetna is that kind of place, and that is where mountaineers start their climb.

The locals have long used the phrase "Beautiful Downtown Talkeetna" as a motto, even though the entire town is only a couple of blocks long. Now that Alaska has legalized marijuana, beautiful downtown Talkeetna has a marijuana dispensary at one end of town. But the landmark Fairview Inn and the bar are still there. For people who stop there after climbing—I spent time there in 2016 after our team summited—they have a great time. I lived in Talkeetna for a while before I became a citizen of the world. I always enjoyed being in the bar even though I don't drink. I think Alaskan culture is very vibrant in Talkeetna.

There are some colorful people there. The guy that owned the Fairview Inn had a seven-story house built around an old radio tower. I moved to Talkeetna because it felt more like Alaska to me than Anchorage. There is no international airport. You're not right next to the mountains, but you can get there. It is on the Talkeetna River, so you've got rafters and fishermen coming in. The flight services that go to Denali have their headquarters there. It is kind of a package town for the mountain. There is even a zip line there now.

Talkeetna and Mendoza are about as different as you can imagine.

MOUNT VINSON

To most people, Antarctica is the most exotic and forbidding of lands. The Antarctic continent is both huge and virtually empty. There are very few people considered to be permanent residents. However, at any given time 1,000 to 5,000 scientists and workers are performing duties there, but there are no cities.

The continent, the land, is not a colony or property of a single nation. In 1959, a dozen countries which had been active in scientific projects signed the Antarctic Treaty, pledging cooperation and essentially agreeing to keep the continent open to all signatories. Since then, forty-one additional countries have signed on to the treaty.

Antarctica is a vast ice sheet that is home to scientific researchers representing many countries. It is difficult and expensive to reach and so cold that much of the time only a small number of hardy tourists and adventurers with large bank accounts even consider traveling there.

Antarctica is the southernmost of the world's continents, and while the bottom layer of the continent is land, it is almost (ninety-eight percent) completely covered in ice and snow. It is 5.4 million square miles and the geographic South Pole is located there.

Strangely, although it was centuries after explorers reached distant continents by ship from Europe and Asia, Antarctica was first sighted in 1820 by a Russian ship.

The first thing twenty-first century humans have in mind when thinking about Antarctica is of the fantastic cold. The lowest recorded temperature on the continent (-128.6 Fahrenheit) is difficult to fathom.

During the annals of exploration, Antarctica was the last great puzzle to be solved. Many famed adventurers sought to make their reputations by racing to the South Pole, and in ensuing decades trying to find new routes across the ice, new ways to traverse it and new ways to explain it.

English seaman Captain James Cook sailed within seventy-five miles of the coast in 1773. Nearly seventy years later, James Clark Ross discovered and named the Ross Ice Shelf. In 1935, Lincoln Ellsworth discovered the highest mountains in Antarctica and the mountain range is named after him. The tallest peak in the Ellsworths, part of the Sentinel Range—and the highest on the continent, making it one of the Seven Summits—is Vinson Massif or Mount Vinson. Vinson stands 16,050 feet above sea level and is located 600 miles from the South Pole.

Nicholas Clinch, who died in 2016 at eighty-five, led the first ascent of Vinson in 1966 as part of a ten-man American Alpine Club group. Clinch also led the only American first ascent of an 8,000-meter peak, the 26,500-foot Hidden Peak in Pakistan. His team reached the top of the world's eleventh tallest mountain, Gasherbrum I, in 1958.

Vern Tejas, who has climbed Mount Vinson thirty-nine times, made the first solo ascent of the peak in 1988. Tejas has had dozens of adventures in Antarctica and on Vinson. It is possible he has spent more time on the continent than all of those famous explorers put together.

As of early 2017, the cost of a commercially guided trip to Mount Vinson was $41,000. The climbing season is between November and February, which is the Southern Hemisphere's summer. However, temperatures of minus-thirty degrees, or colder, are common on the climbs. Not nearly as time-consuming as an Everest or Denali trip, it is expected that the summit can be reached in between five and nine days from base camp. The view from the top is of snow and ice as far as the eye can see.

My first trip to climb Mount Vinson was in 1988, a few months after I completed the winter solo of Denali.

Two climbers from Hong Kong that I guided up Denali wanted to do more climbs. We had a great time on Denali and they wanted me to guide them. I'm all about having fun and being safe, and they appreciated that. First, they wanted to go to Mount Elbrus in Russia. They were not paying a guide fee, but my expenses were covered, and I cut a deal where I would be able to paraglide off the summit.

I was into paragliding off the tops of mountains at that time, and they said sure. One of those guys was a photographer, and he took pictures of me doing it and wrote a magazine story. It was in Cathay Pacific in-flight magazine, and there is me flying through the air over Europe. We all had a good time doing Elbrus, and then they said, "We'd like to do Vinson."

We made the same deal where I would guide them and then paraglide off. It was a guide-to-glide program. Everything went smoothly. We made the summit with no problems. In fact, I have never been skunked on Vinson. Every time I have climbed on the mountain I have reached the top.

Mount Vinson

On this trip I got to climb Vinson twice. After summiting, those guys went to sleep at base camp and I told them I was going to take a walk. I didn't say what I was planning to do, but I got the idea to make a solo climb of the peak. When Robert Falcon Scott was leading the British team that tried to become the first to reach the South Pole, his expedition ran out of food and was trapped by storms on the way back. Captain Lawrence Oates, a member of the team who was weakening, sacrificed himself by excusing himself from the dinner in hopes it would aid those remaining. He announced, "I am going outside and may be some time." It was a suicide statement. But the others all died, too.

I quoted Oates in a melodramatic way, although I had no intention of walking to my death. So the others went to sleep and I went climbing again, moving as quickly as I could on my own without any responsibility to take care of anyone else.

Everything was fine at base camp and I zoomed up the mountain and back in something like fifteen hours. This is the acknowledged first solo of Vinson, although there was a rumor, never confirmed, that a Russian geologist may have snuck up there. He was in the area. He could have made it or faked it. No one knows for sure.

I was definitely a driven young man at the time. I had just come off the first solo winter ascent of Denali and I was enjoying the opportunities it afforded me. Since I was quick at acclimating and I was already acclimated from the climb with the boys, it seemed as if it was a good time to give it a try.

Never was I going to be the fastest climber in the world, but I could go and go for a long time. I had endurance. For me it was just a big marathon. All I did was tag the summit and run down.

Vinson was not a very crowded mountain at the time. The wide appeal of the Seven Summits hadn't kicked in yet. It was only 1988. The concept of more citizen adventurers trying it had not quite taken root yet. It was the cusp of the boom. I think only five other people went up that season. A couple of people had climbed it a little earlier and the flight that brought us out took them in.

Transportation is the big issue in getting to Antarctica. It was even more challenging then. Most people who wanted to climb Vinson flew in from Punto Arenas, Chile. Flights were rare and expensive and had to be specially arranged. Since then, more people go to climb Vinson, but also the South Pole has been opened up commercially with adventure groups booking people to ski the last sixty miles to the Pole. The continent became a little bit more approachable. Now there are dozens of flights per season.

Being Antarctica, it can get quite cold on Vinson. It's the luck of the draw, same as Denali or Mount Everest. It can be colder in those places than on Vinson. It can get warm on Vinson, too. When I say warm, I mean only minus-thirty degrees. I know that not many people use that kind of temperature and the word "warm" in the same sentence. But I do have a nude photo of myself from the summit of Vinson. I have been asked what possessed me to do that at minus-thirty, but the sun was out and there was no wind.

It took some effort to peel off all of my clothes, but it was worth it. I did it, uh, because I could? I was on a guided climb, and you do sweat when you work at climbing, even in what we would call cold temperatures. I think I said, "It's so hot out I could take off my clothes." I was guiding a team of three or four. The climbers looked at me kind of strangely, but then they began egging me on.

All of a sudden, it was, "Go for it!" "Yeah, dude!" "What happened to your weasel? It's gone." I said, "It's cold guys. What do you expect? He's gone into hibernation."

I know people cannot identify with minus-anything as warm, but we had been working hard to reach the top and you still have residual body heat. When you get up in the morning, you've got like fifteen minutes

As the tallest mountain in Antarctica at 16,050 feet, Mount Vinson is also the second most expensive to climb due in large part to its location

when your body actually stays warm from being in bed. You can do crazy things in that time. The nude shot was not a selfie. I have the pictures, so there is no threat of blackmail. I was only out of my clothes for about five minutes.

Almost all of the tallest mountains in Antarctica are bunched closely together. One of the other biggest, Mount Shinn at 15,292 feet, is only a day-trip climb from high camp on Vinson. We were able to zip over and do it. I did it another time with a woman who was a strong climber on a Vinson trip.

Danielle Fisher was a young girl with lots of energy, always chomping at the bit. I kept telling her, "Slow down, slow down, slow down." She said, "Why?" I told her if she did not slow down and work with the team, I was not going to allow her to go to the summit. She said, "I want to get to the summit. And I want to go over and do Shinn."

I made her a promise. "Here's the deal," I said. "Cool your jets. Climb with the team. We'll go to Shinn afterwards." She was practically jumping up and down with excitement. When we got to the top, she was still very strong and still wanted to climb Shinn. I felt compelled to allow the co-guide to take the others down, and she and I went over and zipped up Shinn and back down in about three hours and caught up with the team.

Danielle was the real deal. She was born in 1985, and in 2005 she became the youngest climber to complete the Seven Summits. The Vinson trip was in January of 2005, and later that year, when she reached the top of Everest, she finished her seven. Most of her climbs were guided by our company, Alpine Ascents.

Actually, when I got it into my head that I wanted to set a record for climbing the Seven Summits twice in one year, I did another Vinson solo. I had no guided climbs that year, so I paid money out of my own pocket for the flight. At the mountain, I was with another team and that group did not make the top. One guy said he wanted to try again, and I said I would climb with him.

We did it, and that provided a scouting mission for me. I could get acclimated and examine the ground to see how the route was lined up. A couple of days later, I went back up to do another solo and to climb Vinson twice within a week.

I was originally going to South America to do Aconcagua twice, but detoured to Antarctica first to do Vinson twice. So I did two doubles in one trip to that area of the world.

My goal, which no one else had done, or even thought about, was to climb the Seven Summits twice within 365 days. It was not a calendar year. The year began and ended with a summit of Everest. It was May 24, and the climbs were determined by the seasons after that.

However, I just missed, completing the circuit in 367 days. Then I tried again and it took 372 days. The first time when I failed to complete it, I thought, "Oh, damn. So close." The weather was a factor, but you also can't tell your clients to climb faster because you are on this particular mission. Two days! Damn! Sure, it's going through my head, "I wish you would hurry up." But you can't say that. So I have climbed the Seven Summits on three different occasions in less than 372 days.

The third time, when I completed it, it was darned close, too. It was 363 days. I'm goal-oriented. I grew up competitively. By then, I thought I just had to get it done. No one else in the world seemed to have that goal at that time. I was competitive with me, pushing myself.

It was a goal I had selected in my head. I thought, "I can do this. Let's see if I can do this." The third time was the charm. I've never gone back since to see if I could do it faster. You could say, let's see if I can do it within 300 days, but a year, 365 days, seemed to make sense.

My second solo of Vinson only took me about eleven hours. That's ascending from 7,000 feet to just over 16,000 feet. It's moving along. I never run, but there are people who do run on speed climbs.

I intended to ski down off the summit, but it was too icy, so I couldn't do it. I had to carry the skis back down to 9,000 feet and then put them on. Carrying the skis was a waste of time. I could have cut thirty minutes off the eleven hours by not bringing them, but really, who cares?

Vinson had a base camp manager at the time, and officials frowned on going solo. I said to him, "You know, if someone were to go solo, would it be a big deal? This guy said, "Not if I never heard about it."

I pushed very hard, enjoyed it, had a great time, and skied back into camp. He said, "How long did it take to do something I never heard of?" I said, "Eleven hours, twenty minutes." He went, "Whoa!"

A funny thing happened during the summer of 2016. That same guy posted a picture of me from that ascent on Facebook. He remembers me, the guy who did the climb he never heard of.

It really is amazing how many times I have been to Vinson and to Antarctica, also for other reasons. Unlike Aconcagua, where you can hang out and drink wine and eat steak in Mendoza, you do not get attracted by those types of bonus features. Antarctica is about snow and ice and beautiful wide vistas of snow and ice. But I have had several things that have drawn me there over the last decades.

And they were dramatically different adventures from Vinson and its connection to the Seven Summits.

NORMAN VAUGHAN AND MOUNT VAUGHAN

Norman Vaughan was born in 1905 in Salem, Massachusetts and retained his Boston accent for his 100 years on earth. His family was well-off, making its money in the manufacturing world. But Vaughan was blessed with an adventurous spirit that refused to let him be tied to a desk.

In particular, in his quest for adventures, Vaughan became quite attached and impressed by the working sled dog. On the fast track to a good education, Vaughan dropped out of Harvard University to become a dog handler for Admiral Richard Byrd's 1928 expedition to the South Pole.

Vaughan spent the years from 1928 to 1930 with Byrd on the ice. To recognize his contributions, Byrd named a 10,302-foot Antarctic peak "Mount Vaughan" in Norman's honor.

Over the decades, Vaughan participated in the exhibition dog-mushing category at the 1932 Winter Olympics in Lake Placid, New York; ran a dog-team search and rescue unit during World War II and was, for most of the rest of his life afterwards, called Colonel Vaughan by many; participated in three presidential inaugural parades while mushing dog teams; and in his seventies, and raced in the Iditarod Trail Sled Dog Race.

Vern Tejas met Norman Vaughan not long after the young climber moved to Alaska and they remained close. When Vaughan adopted the slogan "Dream Big and Dare to Fail," he contemplated at long last returning to Antarctica to climb the peak Byrd named for him. He was approaching his eighty-ninth birthday.

Many thought Vaughan foolhardy, many were inspired by him, and Tejas promised his assistance to make the indomitable senior citizen's dream come true.

In the end, against strong odds, Vaughan did stand on the top of his own mountain. It was a feat that garnered nationwide attention and made him a hero across Alaska, where he was beloved and came to be known as "Alaska's Grandpa."

While touching many with his gumption and commitment, Vaughan unveiled a fresh quest. He wished to return to the summit of his mountain for his 100th birthday. A teetotaler, Vaughan schemed to gain the sponsorship of a French champagne company. He envisioned popping the cork on the summit above 10,000 feet and proclaiming, "I've waited 100 years for this!"

Alas, Vaughan celebrated his 100th birthday, December 19, 2005, with a party in an Anchorage hospital and passed away only four days later.

———————

Norman was one of the first people that I met in Alaska and certainly one of the most impressive people I ever met in my life. Norman was the kind of guy who had a story for every occasion, and I loved listening to his stories. The man had stories. He wasn't making them up. They were all based in reality, and it was a very large reality. I was won over by his charisma and his experience.

He had done everything. He had been in the war, worked in top-secret conditions destroying the Norden bombsights in Greenland so the Nazis couldn't get them. He tried to rescue fallen soldiers in the Battle of the Bulge. He taught the Pope how to dog mush. He rode a snowmobile from Anchorage to Boston. You can't make up stuff like this.

At the age of sixty or so, he was booted out of the house by his wife, or something like that, and came to Alaska with just pocket change. He became the grandfather figure for most Alaskans.

He took me under his wing at an early age and took me into his confidence. One day he would say, "Do you want to ski from Kotzebue to Nome?" That is a ski trip of more than 300 miles.

"Sure. Love to." I'd reply.

Or, "Let's go dog mushing."

And I'd say, "Yeah, I would love to."

I bumped into him in various places or just went to listen to his little talks. The first time I remember him mentioning Mount Vaughan was when he came to one of my book signings, my story of the first solo winter ascent of Denali. He said, "Hey, Vern, ever thinking of going back to Antarctica? I'm going." And I said, "I'm volunteering my services."

Many people thought he was rash to announce he was going to climb that mountain at his age. I was rash enough to say, "I'll be your guide." Boom, it was done. Later, I lost a little bit of appreciation for it when we had delays for weeks and weeks, and I was on my own nickel and almost went broke from it.

It was not easy to get permission to take this kind of trip to Antarctica. It was a long, long process. We needed the help of the late U.S. Senator Ted Stevens to make it happen. God rest his soul. We put together a team. Besides me and Norman, there was Carolyn Muegge-Vaughan, Norman's wife; Ken Zafren, an Anchorage doctor; Brian Horner, a survivalist specialist and former medic in the military; and Dolly Lefever. Dolly was an Anchorage nurse-midwife whom I had guided with occasionally. Dolly had recently climbed Everest, and in 1995 became the first American woman to climb the Seven Summits.

Ironically, Dolly's last summit was Kosciuszko in Australia, the easiest one, and she and the friend she was with got caught in a surprise thunderstorm and basically became hypothermic. Even the smaller mountains can cause big trouble for you.

Carolyn was the spark-plug. She got Norman there. There was also a veterinarian from Wisconsin named Jerry Vanek, a dog handler named Larry Grout, and a pilot out of Canada named Bruce Alkhorn. George Menard from Trapper Creek, Alaska was the radio operator.

We set out to do the climb for Norman's eighty-eighth birthday in December of 1993, but the whole thing began to fall apart early on.

We were in Chile waiting for word we could go, and that took much of October and November. We finally got the OK on Thanksgiving Day. While waiting for approval, we began by staying in a hotel, then kept downgrading because of the cost to a motel, a lodge, and then a hostel. Finally I was camping out with the dogs.

The holdup was that the National Science Foundation did not want tourism there. And an eighty-eight-year-old guy does not sound like a good bet. That sounded like a rescue to them. It sounded like a heart attack. That sounded like somebody dying, a horrible scenario, so they kept saying no way.

Norman had a lot of old influential Army buddies, and he called in a lot of favors, but they couldn't budge the Science Foundation either. We mustered a public outcry in Alaska. Finally, when we talked to Senator Ted Stevens, he said, "I wish you had told me this months ago. I could have helped in some way. Let me see what I can do now."

The next day, we received a Telex, a telegram, and a telephone call granting us permission. Boom, boom, boom. We knew Senator Stevens had done something. I found out later he flexed a lot of muscle. At the time, he was the chairman of the Senate Appropriations Committee. That might have had something to do with it.

Much later, after the climb succeeded, we went to Washington, D.C. and visited Ted Stevens' office. Norman said, "Ted, we were in big trouble. I know I should have asked you first, but what did you do? It was immediate." Senator Stevens said, "Oh, it was easy. I just told them one of my constituents was having a hard time. He's well-loved by my whole state, and, oh by the way, when was the last time we audited you?" And that's how the problem got fixed. Permission, permission, permission with a little bit of political finesse. On Thanksgiving, we were so happy we had tears in our eyes.

We were just getting ready for the eight-hour trip to Antarctica the next morning at about 4 a.m., when we got a phone call. We had three flights, and the first one carried the dogs and the radio equipment. I decided to let Norman sleep in for a couple of hours, and then I knocked on his door. I said, "Sir." He said, "What's up?" I told him our plane had crashed. He did not go wild or anything. He got into survival mode. First, he asked who was hurt, and then if any of the dogs were hurt.

The dogs were on the first flight because they had been sitting around in sixty-degree weather for too long, and we wanted them to get back to where it was cold and more comfortable. At that time, all flights went into Patriot Hills. There was poor visibility. There was definitely bad weather, and the Adventure Network International people on the ground warned Bruce, our pilot. But he thought they were just trying to scare him off because it was his first flight there as a competitor. But no, it really was bad weather. They called it right and he didn't believe them. He had window fogging problems. He couldn't see real well because of a ground blizzard.

More than likely, the altimeter was off because it was Antarctica. I call it the Polar Premium. There is lower pressure at the poles than there is at the equator, so the altimeter doesn't function properly. The co-pilot told me they thought they had one hundred feet of clearance, but they did not.

Bruce was six miles out, and he had just pulled the nose up for final approach and a few miles from the runway, the wheels hit the snow at 120 miles per hour and the plane slid on its belly. The propellers were wing-mounted and they hit the snow. They were spinning at like five billion revolutions a second, and when they hit the snow on the right side, they went cart-wheeling out across Antarctica. The props on the left side tumbled into the DC-6.

Jerry, the vet, was sleeping in line with the props with his head against the left fuselage. Later, I went to examine the wreck. You could see where there were multiple whacks, three or four, bop, bop, bop, bop, and the first whack was right about where Jerry's head was. The second one was a bit further down where his arm was. The third was where his leg was. The fourth whack from the propeller cut through the plane and ripped his seat loose. He pitched forward and that kept him from getting killed by the propeller, but he was thrown into the fuel drums and was a mess.

He was strapped into his seat, asleep, when 2,000 pounds of force hit. Jerry was hit so hard, the suture joint in his head opened and shattered his temple bones. A whole section of his forehead swelled out about four inches. But that saved his life, because it relieved pressure. An ANI medic, who coincidentally was from Girdwood, Alaska, right outside Anchorage, was there and treated Jerry with morphine and brain-shrinking drugs to keep Jerry from being crushed by his own brain swelling.

In Punta Arenas, we arranged for a rescue flight and sent in Zafren, the doctor, and Brian, the medic. They picked up Jerry. Bruce came back with the plane. Larry, the dog handler, cracked some ribs, but by acting quickly was able to hop out the back of the plane and get the dogs removed before it caught on fire with the help of George, the radio operator. The dogs were not really hurt in the crash.

The fuel tanks were in the center of the plane, and the fuel was much more volatile than the kind of gas you put in your car. Larry feared the fuel was going to create a fireball. Some of the dog cages were crushed, and some dogs were loose and fighting. He began taking them out one by one and trying to tie them down. The problem was that in Antarctica there is only snow and ice, nothing to tie them to like a tree. So he tied some of them to pieces of the wreckage.

ANI knew the plane was supposed to land, but then it disappeared. They sent out snowmobiles for a rescue. What they realized was that if a fire broke out, everything down wind behind the plane would burn, including the staked-out dogs. They cut the traces and while you might think the dogs would just scatter, they did not. They got into a big brawl. They went crazy in the midst of the fuel, the blood, the flames, and the chunks of airplane.

They went berserk and the handler was in the middle of it all, smacking them in the head, trying anything to keep them from fighting. He tried to find places to tie them again, with their cut traces, and they were chewing on each other and anyone who got too close. Finally, Larry and the ANI helpers got most of them corralled and transported Jerry temporarily to a hut at Patriot Hills. There were about thirty dogs, and they were still wild. That's a handful for a few guys, some of whom had just barely escaped the crash with their lives.

About four of the dogs were seriously injured in the big dog fight and wandered off. We suspect they went off to lick their wounds and disappeared. They were probably covered by drifting snow. People searched for several days, but they were never found. We think they probably died like that. Food was even left out for them, but they never came back.

It was just horrible, but our main concern was Jerry, who was in a coma from his head injury. He also had a broken arm. His leg was broken in twenty-two pieces. I saw the X-ray. His lower leg looked like a jigsaw puzzle.

When you suffer that much damage, things compartmentalize. So much blood coagulates that the swelling is massive, and you can't get the circulation going. Doctors had to cut his leg open just to relieve the pressure. He was in a coma for two weeks. We visited him every day in the hospital, and when he finally opened his eyes, just about the first thing he said was a joke! We all said, "Jerry's back."

It was a relief to know his sense of humor was intact, because that is a subtle thing and, with a head injury, you just can't tell what is going to happen. He looked like a human being again. As soon as he was conscious, he was medevacked out, and we got the dogs out. Most of the dogs had been loaned to Norman for the trip, and he was very broken up for a long time about the four that were lost. I know human life is more valuable, but it messed him up.

We had put together a great team of great people, most handpicked by me, a mostly Alaskan team, and the whole trip ended in a complete fiasco. You couldn't write failure in bigger letters.

But guess what? It wasn't over. We didn't give up. After Jerry was sent home and the dogs were taken care of—there were sixteen others— Norman made a little speech. He said everything had been terrible and devastating, but he still had his dream. "So what do you guys want to do about it? I still want to do this." I said I was still in. Dolly said she would come back to Antarctica. The other guys had families and businesses and pretty much had to go. Norman said, "Let's take a break for Christmas and come back in January. We'll try again."

We had reduced personnel, but some of us were still there. None of us, not me, Dolly, or Norman, had any money. Norman had sponsors, and he even raised money from school children who donated. It was an uphill battle to get all the funding in place, but it finally happened, and we returned to the ice. We were on the ice at Patriot Hills and got socked in by a storm, one storm, for seventeen days. We had budgeted twenty-two days for the whole trip.

Our plan when we returned in January of 1994 was to go without dogs. We were going to ride snowmobiles with nobody backing us up. In a way, the delay represented the storm of good fortune because we all could have died if we carried out that snowmobile plan. In retrospect, I praise the Lord for sending the storm.

Rob Hall, the famous guide who died on Mount Everest a few years later, was working there for ANI, and he broke the news to us we couldn't go. It was too late in January. They were going to break down the camp soon, and we did not have enough time to complete the trip. He said, "I need to tell you, it's not in the cards. You have a very small window, and it is still raging outside."

The southern winter was coming. Just to provide some context, Robert Falcon Scott and his group died in February. Rob said it, but we all knew it. We just weren't voicing our concerns out loud. We had just kept our fingers crossed hoping the storm would stop and we could start. When Rob delivered the official news, we kind of all cracked simultaneously. We all cried.

There was another guy waiting who had been trying to make a trip to the South Pole. Instead he was trapped with us. His name was Charles Givens. He wrote a book called "Wealth Without Risk." It was about flipping houses and he made a lot of money doing it. He said, "You guys have a great story and it is a great dream. I'm the kind of guy who believes in that kind of stuff. I think you guys could have done it if things had been different. You shouldn't give up on it." Then he wrote out a check for $100,000, saying, "Would this help you get started for next year?" Norman was not a guy inclined to give up anyway. I passed the check to Norman, and it put a smile on our faces.

There had actually been a National Geographic camera crew around us, waiting for fruition on this crazy trip. They went back to their offices in D.C. and said, "No story, but a hell of a lot of drama." The editors went, "This is priceless. You can't script this."

We never saw the pilot again. He kept the money and went off and died with it. In my mind, he was the skunk of the world. He should have gotten insurance money, but instead he kept our money. I kept telling Norman, "He's got our money!" I figured he owed us $500,000 back. I was learning about life the hard way. How I looked at it was he screwed this old man out of half a million dollars. Norman kept telling me to settle down.

The story of our colossal failure starting getting told and people started saying, "He almost died. He didn't make it." But people liked the appeal of what we were doing and that we weren't quitting. Funding started coming out of the woodwork. Norman went on tour around the country talking to businesses and pledging to make motivational speeches to their employees.

He said, "I'll do motivational speeches for you guys. I'll do a half-dozen." And he did do talks for several years afterwards. And the funding came through. I don't know where it all came from, but a well opened up. It was such a dramatic story, and Norman is unique because of his age. Everybody dug deeper and corporate America got on the bandwagon. Big companies in Alaska came through.

Norman Vaughan smiles while standing in front of the mountain named after him, Mount Vaughan in Antarctica

So we were able to go back and try again. No dogs, though. That year, in January, sled-dog use was permanently banned in Antarctica for fear they would transmit diseases to the seal population. We left at the very beginning of December, and Norman and I wanted him to be on the summit for his eighty-ninth birthday on December 19. The crew was not exactly the same, and some people told their wives they would be home for Christmas. National Geographic told the camera people to keep it short. They had already spent like a million bucks, and they were running out of money.

Some of the donors, who were covering the cost of the plane, wanted to come. They were hooking on to Norman's dream. I was thinking, "This is his trip." Norman likes to placate people and keep everything going smoothly. Those guys definitely wanted to be home for Christmas. The idea of hanging out at base camp in a frozen wasteland was not their idea of a holiday celebration.

I was thinking, "Damn, it's only a couple of days more till his birthday. Norman was accommodating. He seemed to want to please them more than himself. There was good weather, and ultimately we went up to the summit before his birthday.

Mount Vaughan is in the Queen Maud Mountains. There is a long ridge to the top. Base camp was at 6,000 or 7,000 feet. We planned to put in two camps on the ridge, and then a high camp at 9,000 feet. We planned to go to the top at 10,302 feet, from there.

I climbed with Norman. I wanted to make sure he was steady on his feet. He wore a heart monitor so we could keep track of his health and make sure he did not get his heart rate up too high. That was doctor's advice before we left. I was making good steps, and I was tied to Norman on a short rope. We had someone behind him as a stabilizing factor in case he fell over. We could catch him. We just kept working our way up, step by step. Norman was slow, but he was rhythmic. It was steady. Norman's mood was terrific. His cheeks were rosy, and his smile widened

He was sweating, but the higher we got, you could see relief. For him it was, "Here I am. A sixty-year dream becoming reality." And I thought five years waiting to climb Denali was a long time until a payoff.

Norman carried a stuffed dog with him to the top as a tribute to the sled dogs that had meant so much to him in his life. Admiral Byrd had named this mountain for him six decades earlier. The cameras were panning him and the scenery all around. Carolyn was right there with him, and on the summit, Norman and Carolyn made me kneel down and kissed me right on top of my bald head. It was December 16, three days before Norman's birthday.

Mount Vaughan has a nice, rounded top. There was a slight breeze, and it was minus-twenty. It is Antarctica. We're all laughing and celebrating and making a big hullabaloo about getting there. Norman was hot and sweaty. You don't notice it when you are moving around, but when you stop and you're an old man and you don't have a lot of fat reserves, you chill down quickly.

Before I knew it, Carolyn yelled, "Norman is going down." I go, "Holy shit." Remembering the lesson of Lynne Salerno, I had brought a tent, stove, and sleeping bag with me just in case. I knew Norman wasn't going to sprint up the mountain.

All of a sudden, on the summit, Norman got hypothermic. I hurriedly put up the tent, slammed him in the sleeping bag, and got the stove going. Norman spent the night resting on the top of his mountain. Not everybody knows that part of the story. We came down the next day and were back at base camp for his eighty-ninth birthday.

The other guys who tagged along—granted they helped finance things—didn't seem to be worried enough about Norman, and I was pissed off by that. There were supposed to be two planes flying out in tandem for safety, and they were all saying Norman should just descend the mountain and sleep on his plane on the way back.

Norman said, "I'm exhausted. I need to sleep." They wanted to throw Norman on a plane, and I said, "Norman is not going anywhere." They go, "What the hell are you talking about? We're getting out of here." I made a stand on Norman's behalf that he needed to rest and, as far as I was concerned, he was going to get that rest. I damned well was not going to lose Norman Vaughan because they were in a hurry.

Norman was an old man, turning eighty-nine, and they wanted him to sleep sitting up in a plane after climbing the mountain? This is his trip. He is exhausted. My god. So I had pilots in my face, guides in my face and the National Geographic film crew shouting. This man is tired. All the others want to kill me. I am his safety officer and I go, "He is not going anywhere. He needs to be sleeping. And the longer you guys yell, the less sleep he's gonna get and the longer we're gonna be here."

It's not like we were delayed long, not even a full day. Norman just wanted eight hours of sleep. Finally, they backed down. The sponsors took off, but by his birthday, Norman was down at base camp. He was still on his mountain, and I wanted that for him. I thought they were a little bit selfish.

As it turned out, after they left us, their plane was ordered down. It was the safety plane, and we were supposed to go in tandem, so they had to land in the middle of Antarctica and wait for us. They had to camp out under the wings of their plane in the middle of nowhere in Antarctica. Everyone was upset with me, but it was all pretty clear to me. Who was calling the shots? The film crew? No. The sponsors? No. It was Norman. I wasn't calling the shots. I was just his advocate, and it was up to me to make sure he was safe.

Norman Vaughan and Mount Vaughan

You know, he almost died of hypothermia the day before. It isn't any surprise that he was exhausted and wanted to sleep. I thought the tail was trying to wag the dog. I said, "You guys want to fly? You can do whatever you want." I also wanted to see a little respect. National Geographic was going to make a ton of money off the video of him. The guides were getting paid. The sponsors were theoretically there to support him. I was the only volunteer there besides Carolyn. I wasn't getting anything out of it besides being able to help my hero. Norman got his sleep, and then we descended and flew back to Patriot Hills.

After the others left the continent, Norman, Carolyn, and I stayed at Patriot Hills with the Adventure Network International staff for Christmas. Norman loved it. Norman was in Antarctica because he loved the place. Those other guys didn't even ask how Norman felt about rushing to leave. They just climbed over each other to get out fast.

When we were leaving, he said, "You're coming to Washington, D.C. with me." I said, "I'd love to." I wanted to get back to Alaska, but I was happy to go wherever he wanted me to go.

Norman became Alaska's hero with a big reception in Washington, D.C. National Geographic set up a press conference and all of the networks were there. The Bosnian War was going strong, and I think Norman's achievement got glossed over a little bit, knocked off the front pages.

But Norman definitely had his moment in the sun. We ate with Ted Stevens in the Congressional dining hall. There were five-piece settings. One piece of silverware looked like a rake. I felt a bit awkward, but Norman dragged me around with him everywhere and I was happy to be in the background of his limelight.

Norman wanted me to help him get back to Mount Vaughan for his 100th birthday. I said sure, and we planned it. Norman's scheme was to sign up a French champagne company for a sponsor. On the summit, he would take a drink and say, "I waited a hundred years for this." Although Norman worked on that idea for years, it really wasn't meant to be. I telephoned Norman in the hospital on his 100th birthday from Antarctica.

I asked, "How are you?" He said, "I'm not feeling so well, but hey, you know what? I drank some champagne." I asked, "How was it?" He said, "It tastes awful." After all that… "tastes awful." I think if the champagne sponsor had come through for the climb and he did it, Norman would have sweetened up that comment a bit.

Norman died a few days later. A few years after that, I was back in Anchorage and I visited Carolyn. She was living in a nice four-plex. "How did you guys score this lovely place?" I asked.

She told me the insurance money came through from the first trip. The insurance company paid Norman. That was my understanding. I don't know exactly how it all played out, but it does sound like justice was done.

How great a story is all of that for Norman? Dream Big and Dare to Fail was Norman's motto. He worked hard, dreamed big, got spanked, got back on the horse, rode it, and got a four-plex out of the deal, too. Norman Vaughan is truly one of my heroes.

SOUTH POLE-NORTH POLE

As the known world shrunk with sailors exploring the oceans blue and mapping uncharted territory, one of the last remaining areas where man had not landed was the South Pole. Famous adventurers and scientists set out to plant flags at the Pole and earn glory as the discoverers and first humans to stand on that spot on earth.

Robert Falcon Scott, who later died on an Antarctic journey, led an expedition between 1901 and 1904 that sought to push its way to the Pole. One of his compatriots on that trip was famed explorer Ernest Shackleton.

They got only so far in 1902, and later Shackleton returned to try again. He made progress in 1909, but did not get to the Pole. Later, on another Antarctic voyage, he saw the trip turn into one of the most incredible, forbidding, and magnificent survival adventures of all time.

In-between, in 1911, Norwegian Roald Amundsen had claimed the Pole, just beating Scott to the location.

The South Pole is the southernmost point on earth, the polar opposite of the North Pole. The South Pole is at the center of the Southern Hemisphere and is referred to as the Geographic South Pole. There is also a magnetic South Pole, but that position changes.

There is a Ceremonial South Pole, located 590 feet from the South Pole Station, which is used for scientific research. Flags mark the spot. It would seem inconceivable to such explorers as Scott, Shackleton, and Amundsen that tourists regularly visit and snap photographs at the South Pole. They do not endure life-threatening journeys of hundreds of miles, but are flown in, and in some cases merely ski the final miles to the Pole. Other adventure companies offer more daunting 730-mile, two-month-long ski treks to the South Pole.

There is no mountain to climb at the North Pole, no Seven Summits tie-in, only one of the most unusual and memorable places on earth.

The North Pole differs from the South Pole in significant ways besides that. The Geographic North Pole is not on land. It is on the Arctic Ocean. In recent years, the ice over the Arctic Ocean began melting for longer and longer periods each year, leaving open water. That warming trend is expected to continue, making it more difficult for people to approach the Pole on foot and easier for ships to reach the Pole by sea.

Because the North Pole is not on land, there is no scientific station at the North Pole as there is at the South Pole, and the location of the Pole seems to move. This is because the ice of the Arctic Ocean is constantly moving due to the wind and currents. A flow of two-to-three miles an hour is common. However, the Russians have been establishing temporary, annual sea-ice based stations nearby for several years. Remarkably, the water depth at the North Pole has been measured at only 13,980 feet.

Explorers first began trying to reach the North Pole in 1827. Although American Richard Peary, with Matthew Henson and four Canadian Inuit, was credited with being the first to reach the North Pole in 1909, years after their deaths, studies indicated they perhaps had not reached their final destination.

All early claims of firsts have been questioned. But in 1926, Roald Amundsen, who was the first to the South Pole in 1911, and his patron, pilot Lincoln Ellsworth, reached the North Pole via airship designed by Umberto Nobile, whom Amundsen insisted be the pilot. It is likely the matter of the true first arrivals will never be conclusively settled.

Unlike the on-the-premises partnership in Antarctica for scientific cooperation, claimed possession of the North Pole is murkier. Five countries, Russia, the United States, Norway, Canada, and Denmark share territorial claims. However, following international law, their right of possession only extends 200 miles into the ocean from their land boundaries.

As the Arctic Ocean melts more frequently for longer periods, nations are vying for North Pole area supremacy via the sea. In the meantime, civilian adventurers seek to visit the Pole one way or another, sometimes merely flying over it.

Given his many mountaineering trips to Mount Vinson, it was natural that Vern Tejas would cast his eyes on a visit to the South Pole. He was already most of the way there. Tejas has been on several ski treks and wheeled expeditions aiming for the Pole and has reached it six times. And he has also managed to guide skiers to the North Pole, making him the only one to have guided the Explorers Grand Slam: both Poles and the Seven Summits.

The South Pole is a neat place given all of the exploration history surrounding it. Not very many people have completed the Seven Summits and gone to the South and the North Pole, which I have done as a polar guide. It is somewhat remarkable to think that those who gained the earliest fame trying to reach the South Pole in some cases gave their lives to the quest. Robert Falcon Scott and his men died trying to get home from the Pole. Shackleton shipwrecked, but miraculously got his men home alive.

My first visit to the South Pole was under the direction of the National Science Foundation. I was working as a mountaineer for the U.S. Antarctic Program, which put four of us in the field trying to scout an overland route to the South Pole. There was one particularly promising route down the Leverett, a glacier that we needed to analyze from the air to scout a good path through the crevasses.

We hitched a ride on a South Pole C-130 fuel resupply plane and, after off-loading our fuel at the Pole, returned to McMurdo Station via the Leverett Glacier. So we got a good look. The captain of the plane took the craft in low and dropped the tail ramp down. Harnessed to a safety line we sat on the tailgate, legs dangling out of the rear of the plane. Thus positioned, we were able to take photos and video for a lengthy time as we flew 100 feet off the ice all the way down to the glacier.

A few days later we returned to our pre-scouted route with snowmobiles and two weeks' worth of supplies for a more intensive examination of the route. Our efforts paid off. That glacier was key to connecting the Ross Ice Shelf to the Polar Plateau. Now most South Pole fuel travels overland via the path we scouted that day. That has limited the need for resupply flights and saved the U.S. taxpayers hundreds of millions of dollars.

The first time I skied to the South Pole was in 2006. There were three people on my commercially guided trip. This trip involved skiing to the Pole from sixty nautical miles away, also known as "the last degree." We skied and did quite well without any hassles. Trips like this cost $63,000, most of which goes to transportation. In this remote location, fuel is drop for drop more expensive than fine brandy. And while that seems very expensive, some adventurers will somehow find the means to take the trip.

There was a Chinese group there at the same time. These skiers were quite well-funded, but their guide wasn't an experienced polar navigator. We were going straight each day, and after a while they noticed they were kind of zig-zagging. They were doing many more miles than we were, but we ended up camping near each other each night. After a while they figured it out. Around day three or four they began following us. I really did the navigating for both groups until we got close to the South Pole.

The Chinese leader seemed to be self-aggrandizing. He was one of the most famous climbers in China, though nobody knows his name unless they are Chinese. He wanted his group to be first to the Pole. After following us for several days, they bolted for the pole on the last day.

We had been making about ten miles a day, a steady ski pace. Now that they could see where they were going, they wanted to race. We did not take the bait, but skied at our normal, steady pace and came in about thirty minutes behind them.

When they got close, they saw the flags and the Ceremonial Pole, a stationary pole used for photos, and went there. I told our people, "Come on over here guys to the real Pole," and led them to the geographic South Pole, which is 100 yards further. The Chinese looked confused so I hollered to them, "This is the real South Pole."

We had taken all of our photos there when they came running over. They were like kids. They went, "Ahhh, we want to get that photograph." So they scrambled to the true South Pole after us. As the Chinese group swarmed around the true South Pole, we went over to the flags and got our pictures of the Ceremonial Pole without them in the way.

Tejas gets a picture of the Southernmost spot on Earth

Due to ice movement, the North Pole seems to be constantly moving over the Arctic Ocean. Also, due to flowing ice, the South Pole seems to move about ten feet per year. It's not too hard of a target to hit. The North Pole, the spot is there for a second and it's gone. The South Pole is on a glacier. The snow gets higher every year. People remeasure the geographic South Pole every year on New Year's Day. The Ceremonial Pole is a drifting barbershop pole, and that's where the flags are. It's more photogenic that way, but it's not exactly at the South Pole.

At the permanent station, you can go in and buy souvenirs. Visitors can use the restroom and you can get a drink of water there. There is a post office on the premises, too. You can't mail anything, but you can get your passport stamped. After doing it once, I haven't repeated. It just burns up another page in my passport.

The station is all about science, and they don't want to detract from the science by having visitors. But who is paying for the science? The taxpayers. So it is tricky to deny access to people who are actually your employers.

Many of the people who come to the Pole are movers and shakers. Since it costs so much, they are generally well off. It's not riff-raff off the street. There are people who know U.S. Senators. Some of them are U.S. Senators and governors. They wouldn't take too kindly to being told they can't use the bathroom.

Will Steger made the first dog-sled traverse of Antarctica in 1988 and 1989, covering 3,471 miles in the International Trans-Antarctic Expedition. When he got there, they wouldn't let him in the station. He was told the employees would love to have him, but they were just following orders from people higher up the ladder. This was an internationally famous guy doing something that had never been done before.

I have actually been to the South Pole several times, just haven't always skied a long distance every time to get there. I have been there a half dozen times. In 2010, I was part of an overland driving trip to the South Pole in specially made large vans.

In 2012, I became a North Pole guide for a company named Polar Explorers. I was not going to Everest that year. I wanted to attend my son Cayman's graduation. He was summa cum laude in physics. (Did I mention he took after his mom?)

So I called up my friend Rick Sweitzer and asked if he needed a guide. He said he had a lot of clients for the North Pole. The trip was for April, right in the middle of the Everest season. I had always wanted to go to the North Pole, but for the previous ten years, I had been guiding Everest. There were three guides and I think eight clients. North Pole trips cost almost as much as South Pole trips, between $40,000 and $50,000. Obviously, not everyone can afford to go, yet there is still constant demand.

Since we were not going to swim or take a kayak, we had to arrive when the Arctic Ocean was still frozen. There is a base-camp ice station run by the Russians on the frozen part, and you fly by helicopter to one degree of latitude shy of the Pole. The last degree is a circle, so you can be put down anywhere to ski the last sixty nautical miles.

The pole is stationary, but the ice is moving, so it is not good to be put down on the lee side of the ice pack. If so, you have an upstream battle. You lose distance while you're sleeping. The season is very short, pretty much the month of April, and they try to put out several expeditions a day at the height of the season.

There is nothing there but ice and polar bears. The helicopter is not dropping you off at a landmark or a place, just one degree, or sixty nautical miles from the Pole. Hopefully, on the upwind side. There are no guarantees. The wind shifts and currents change. All of a sudden you might face a crosswind. If you are downwind, that can be really tough. Once, a guy got really antsy about the flight and just decided to go for it from the downwind side. He spent two weeks out there skiing really hard every day, and at night he lost five miles because the ice was just being blown backwards, away from the Pole. Wise people know you must be patient and work with nature to be successful.

We were shooting for a ten-day trip max, though with good conditions, a week is ideal. The organizers want to turn the groups over. They put out a lot of people on the same day that hopefully finish on the same day because of the basic rate of travel. The fewer people strung out on the ice, the less hassle they have. The ice can crack, and all of a sudden there will be an opening, splitting the teams. Things can happen.

As soon as the helicopter drops you off, you strap on the skis, hook up the sleds hauling supplies, and you start going. The guides pull out a GPS and say, "It's that way." You start skiing and pretty soon you kind of clue in to which way the wind is blowing, where the ice leads are broken and you can almost navigate without really having to look at the GPS.

The ice is your scenery. While skiing to the North Pole, you never notice the movement unless you're right at a lead. At an open lead, you might be able to see that the ice is breaking apart or coming together. The weather is basically somewhat dismal. There are low clouds and wind. The wind is usually consistent from one direction. If you are fortunate, it is at your back.

In April, the temperature is most likely going to be around minus-twenty. A month earlier, it would be minus-forty. Now, almost year-round, there is some open water. The South Pole is actually colder than the North Pole. By May there is too much open water to ski to the North Pole. There is a huge swing in a short amount from March to April and April to May. That's why April is the time to go.

By April there is also considerable daylight. The sun feels like it is up all of the time. You navigate a little by the sun depending on what time it is. I like to travel with my shadow falling in front of me because you don't want to be going into the sun. You get glare all of the time. You're squinting even with glacier glasses on, and your face gets sunburned. Skiing into the sun is bad for your eyes and worse for navigation.

You want to travel with the sun at your back. That's what I found with polar travel. You also want to be able to navigate by the wind if it is consistent, so you don't have to check your compass all of the time. Some people hang a little string or a piece of yarn at the end of their ski pole. If the string is blowing at the same angle all the time, they are probably going pretty straight.

This was a good group. I had one of the guys as a climber before in Antarctica, an older gentleman, jolly, fun, not a great skier, so he ended up walking a good chunk of it. There was snow on the ice, but in some places it was blown clean and you could walk right on it. It was sea ice and had some grip to it. It had salt in it and it was rough, not completely smooth and slippery.

Every couple of hundred feet there were pressure ridges where the ice was stacked up or opened up. It was discombobulated. There were places where you balanced on one slab of ice and jumped to another with your skis on. There was some risk of falling into the Arctic Ocean.

Besides the weather, there is objective danger from the water. If you go through the ice you can be in a bad situation really quickly. It did not happen on this trip, but I have heard stories of things going wrong and people getting wet from time to time. You are not roped up on this travel. If you fall in you grab your ski poles by the baskets and use the tips to help you haul out.

Sometimes you have to pick crossing points over open leads. The leads can be melting and the current can be strong underneath. This is freezing cold water. The leads can be opening or closing. You have to worry about falling into the water, but you also have to worry about what the ice is doing. It can be shearing and breaking into little pieces.

During the night, you might have started with a nice, flat place to camp twenty feet from the water, but overnight your spot could end up in the water. If you hear grinding noises, you have to get up and figure out what is going on. If you get a big cross-current where the water is going one way and the wind is blowing the other way, the ice can stack up twenty feet tall. Or you can get this shearing motion where the ice is grinding itself away. That's scary, too. You can end up in the drink.

On this trip things went pretty smoothly. We saw polar bear tracks at one point and decided to head in the opposite direction. The destination is north and the bear tracks were on our west side, so we went east for a couple of miles before turning north again.

Polar bears can range 100 miles. If they want you for dinner, you're going to have to do something. You have to carry a shotgun through there. But we never saw the bear. Another night we reached a place where there was open water. It looked as if the lead went for miles each way. It is so flat that you really can't see too far in the distance. The most you can see is probably two miles to the horizon. We couldn't see closure in the ice in either direction, so we camped. By the next morning, the open water had closed.

What had been ice sections 100 feet apart were ten feet apart and had frozen over in the lead right in front of us. I crawled across the freshly frozen lead, trying to keep my weight distributed, and found the ice would hold me without carrying a pack. I then skied across it a couple of times and returned to our skiers and said, "Hey, guys, we've got a road in front of us." So we packed up and everyone got across without any problems.

Things like that happen. The reverse could have been true. We could have made camp and found out the lead opened overnight. If you can't cross a big lead, just have patience. That's the best thing you can do. I had wanted to get to the North Pole for some time and it was a cool trip. I liked it for the sheer rawness of living with the primal forces of nature.

Unlike the South Pole, with the research station and the Ceremonial Pole as landmarks, finding the North Pole combines using your GPS and pretty much guessing. We knew on the morning of our last day we were about five miles away, so we were closing in. You should be able to ski five miles by the afternoon.

When we reached a place where we should have been about a half mile from the Pole and realized how fast we were going, we went, "Holy smokes! It's moving towards us right now." It got within about a hundred feet, tick, tick, tick; it was coming closer. It looked like the Pole was coming to us.

We were sliding across the ice and two or three guys got out a GPS. We were going, "Here it comes. It's right over there." That's what I mean about the North Pole being a moving target. Everybody ran to that spot and looked for something significant like a stack of ice to plant a flag on. You don't need to be precisely on the Pole to say you were on it. After all, it's only going to be in one place for a second or two. You can only pinpoint it for a brief moment and then it moves away.

A couple of British guys brought their country flag, stripped down and posed for a picture with their naked legs sticking out the bottom and their naked torsos above it while holding it. Stripping down? They were as nutty as me. They whipped out cigars and brandy. I wish I had taken out my guitar to celebrate, but playing at those temperatures in the wind is painful. There is nothing at the North Pole except for ice. In fact, ten feet from where we decided the Pole was on the GPS, there was open water. The North Pole was breaking up.

Climate change is definitely happening and that's why there is more water. I met a fellow who believes he made the last, complete over-ice approach to the North Pole. Some adventurers are bringing portable boats now because there are so many openings. They stop, take off their skis, paddle for a bit, stop and put the skis back on. Some guides are practically getting people to the Pole by kayak. You can use kayaks that double as a sled. So the equipment is a sled on the ice and a boat in the water. If you've got two of them you can turn them into a catamaran, lashed together, and put up a sail. People have done that.

The change is happening much faster than most people believe. In the future there will be more boating and less skiing. On the last-degree ski trips some people are actually carrying dry suits so they can swim across leads. They might find a polar bear in there swimming with them one day, too. They will be hungry, and polar bears can swim like crazy. You might be able to out-paddle a bear—they go about four miles per hour—but probably not out-swim one.

For the adventurer, saying you got to the South Pole and the North Pole is an attraction. Some people call Mount Everest the third pole, but to me it is the first pole. The other two are much easier, the challenge of skiing that last one degree. If you go overland to the South Pole, that's a whole different story. You can still take an epic trip across the Arctic Ocean, but eventually it's going to be a lot more paddling than skiing.

As the water stays open longer, we're about to see the beginning of an age of shipping freight around the North Pole. Then there will be tourism boats. There are debates about who owns the Arctic, but they should keep it like Antarctica with all nations sharing. Right now we have that 200-mile, offshore territorial claim for each country. The ships will have to cross between each other's territories. Twelve different countries claim chunks of Antarctica. All of the claims look like pieces of a pie.

Everyone will also need a share of the North Pole.

ERNEST SHACKLETON AND MOUNT VINSON

Sir Ernest Shackleton is one of the most famous names of Antarctic exploration. He is probably best known for the brilliant way he salvaged what could have become the worst disaster on the continent.

There is always risk in exploring the unknown and the unexpected does interfere. Through a series of events relying on his good judgment and the cooperation of the elements and God, a journey that could have killed all of his men was instead transformed into a triumph of the human spirit.

Shackleton was born in 1874 and led three British explorations to Antarctica. The aim of his 1914–1917 trip was to cross from sea to sea via the South Pole. Serious problems began when his ship, the Endurance, was frozen into the ice-pack and was gradually crushed. From then on, the journey was not of exploration, but one of survival.

For months, the crew endured on an ice floe. Then, relying solely on lifeboats, Shackleton and crew managed to reach Elephant Island. While taking them off the water, the island did not offer prospects of long-term survival or, because of its remoteness, great odds of rescue. The majority of the men hunkered down in bleak circumstances as Shackleton, gathering a small group of men, set out in a small boat to cover 720 miles to South Georgia Island to try and save them all. There, he knew whaling crews inhabited the land.

Shackleton promised to return and rescue the men on Elephant Island, but the odds of him ever being seen again were astronomical. Shackleton reached South Georgia, anchored offshore in hurricane winds, and then he and his men were at last able to set foot on land. However, they were on the wrong side of the island to reach the whalers. Shackleton's crew was forced to trek thirty-two miles across the island, over snow-covered hills, wearing the remnants of their clothing and only normal boots.

They managed it in thirty-six hours. Previously given up for dead, his home country was astonished to hear the men were still alive. True to his word, although it took three attempts, ships guided by Shackleton sailed to Elephant Island to rescue all the others.

Historians and outdoorsmen always wondered what Shackleton and his men confronted when they landed on South Georgia Island and just how remarkable their journey was to reach the whaling station.

One hundred years later, Vern Tejas was part of a group that retraced the steps of those hardy men who were on a life and death mission.

Ernest Shackleton was probably one of the greatest exploratory heroes of the last century. After he lost his ship, he was able to bring back all his men alive after two years in Antarctica. It was a pretty amazing trip. The very last part of it was the trek across semi-charted land. Nobody knew where the mountains and glaciers were in the interior of South Georgia. In the course of their crossing the island, they explored a new place. They didn't have anything much in the way of supplies as they did so, either.

They just basically fought their way through the snowy mountains to the whaling station as fast as they could. The island was only fifty miles across, and they were in danger of missing it altogether.

The stakes were incredibly high. So many people's lives depended on him getting it right, from his own and those of the men in the boat, to those of the men left behind camping on Elephant Island.

Their overland trek was chosen because they did not want to risk going back onto the water to circle the island. The winds were powerful, they feared being blown out to sea and never being able to get back. This was the only place where they knew other humans who could possibly help them.

So Shackleton crash-landed the boat on the shore and the men made their way overland. Modern-day adventurers have replicated his desperate boat crossing from Elephant Island to South Georgia Island. Doing what they did, seeing how hard it was, and seeing how quickly it can be done in the modern age has appeal for some people. Naturally, they don't want to spend a couple of years duplicating what happened to Shackleton, but the overland part has always produced curiosity.

Twice I have been asked to guide the overland route. That traverse is fun, challenging and historical, certainly more fun for citizen adventurers than for those men whose lives were threatened. Polar Explorers contacted me and asked if I would like to join them and lead the trip, and I said sure. The first time was a little over three years ago. It was coming up on the 100th anniversary of Shackleton's trek. You had to take a ship for a week even to get there and another week going back.

Let's say it was easier for us. We had skis, tents, and food. In Shackleton's crew's urgency, they spent only thirty-six hours reaching the whaling station. We took three-and-a-half days while carrying all of our stuff. We were not starving and did not have others waiting at the other end to save our lives. There were eight of us and our pace was definitely more leisurely.

We started on the west side of the island, up a fjord onto a glacier, climbed up high and got above the animal line. There was so much wildlife there you had to part your way through penguins, seals, and birds to get across the beach.

Crevasses can form or close quickly
and pose a significant danger to climbers

Shutterstock / Gusakov Andry

Shackleton's men were starving on the boat, but when they reached the island, they could choose from foods they had forcibly become familiar with. They were out of western food, so they ate all they could

147

kill. Those marine animals have high fat content and fresh meat gives you vitamins, but when it comes to survival, oil is very important. It is one of the most concentrated forms of food energy on earth. Eskimo natives in Alaska survive on it.

The traverse is pretty much a straight line from west to east. You follow the compass and the wind. In the process, though, the route goes over the spine of the island and one of those vertebrae is the Trident Peaks. This is where Shackleton and his buddies scouted around to look for a safe way down and they couldn't find one. So they coiled a rope they carried from the boat, jumped on it and, while holding on, tobogganed down to the bottom of a very serious slope.

It took us several hours of looking around before we found a safe enough place to go down. The right place was on an avalanche slope about 1,500 feet high with crevasses and snow berms hanging over it. As a mountaineer, it was not a place I would call comfortable. Once again, I had to use the Tejas Snow Wheel as a protective technique. I had the rest of the team make a double-wide tire of snow to roll down.

As the wheel went downhill, it opened a couple of ankle-biter crevasses for us to avoid, which was nice. But it also seemed to indicate the slope was stable enough for us to descend. Instead of skiing down, we walked, pulling our rough-locked equipment sleds behind. Rough-locking is a dog-sled technique wrapping copious amounts of rope around the sled to provide lots of friction. We kept on walking once we reached bottom in case an avalanche followed us. We didn't stop for another quarter of a mile or so just to be safe. Never hang out below a potential avalanche slope.

It was a great group, an international team of Americans, Europeans, and Kiwis. Good people. There were very strong winds going against us. I remember getting blown down a dozen times. I don't blow down easy, but everyone was getting knocked over. The Southern Ocean is known for high winds. All of Patagonia is raked with winds, and Antarctica is the windiest continent on Earth. We continued our trip despite the wind, as Shackleton would have.

Shackleton returned to Antarctica for a third time and died on that trip in 1922. He was back in the South Georgia Islands at the time and is buried, by his wife's request, at Grytviken. The Grytviken whaling station is on Stromness Bay. We visited the grave site and poured a little brandy on it. That kind of wrapped up our adventure. It was a challenging traverse, but it was one of the best historical trips I've ever taken. I did it again in 2015 and would go back in a heartbeat.

The wildlife is fantastic. You see whales on the ocean and marine birds. There are all kinds of penguins by the thousands. I saw rookeries of albatross, maybe 30,000 nesting birds. King penguins, fur seals, elephant seals, skuas: it's like the Serengeti of Antarctica. South Georgia Island is right by the convergence of the South Atlantic Ocean and the Antarctic Ocean. There is an upwelling of huge quantities of nutrients which plankton live on. The krill live on that, and everything else lives on the krill, from the birds to the fish to the marine mammals. The biggest animals in the world, whales, live on the krill.

Overall, it's a beautiful trip. But there are massive storms. We used a better ship than Shackleton did, but even with a 300-foot boat that holds between 50 and 100 people, there are days you get tossed around so much you don't want to get out of bed. If you do get up, you spend your time sitting in the galley watching the water submerge the windows. There are times the boat lists so dramatically that you are looking at blue water out the window, looking through blue water. You would be in for some stomach distress, for sure. When you get around the islands, it's calmer, especially if you are on the lee side.

I loved the trip. How often do I get to do something these days I had never done before? It seemed fresh and exciting and different. Several well-known mountaineers had done it for a TV special; Reinhold Messner, Dave Hahn, and Alex Lowe. They were working their way through all these crevasses. We didn't do that with our climbers. Those guys went over stuff. We went around stuff. We can't know exactly what the snow conditions were like for Shackleton and his men; they made their traverse later in the summer when there was probably less snow. We go when there is more snow and take skis.

Shackleton was there out of necessity; we were taking people on an adventure vacation. What was once for survival, 100 years later is for an active vacation.

I really have been on great trips to the Antarctic region, from guiding Norman Vaughan to the top of his mountain, to following in the footsteps of Shackleton, and, of course, my regular trips to climb Mount Vinson. When I first climbed Vinson in 1988, I would have been amazed if anyone told me I was going to do it an additional thirty-five-plus times.

KOSCIUSZKO

Mount Kosciuszko is the tallest mountain in Australia. For Americans, according to their geography lessons, that means it is the highest mountain on the Australian Continent. That also means that when Dick Bass set out to climb the Seven Summits, he included Kosciuszko.

Kosciuszko is not a very challenging mountain. It involves some hiking, but no technical climbing. Its elevation is 7,310 feet, which does not place it in the category of one of the world's tallest peaks. Kosciuszko is by far the easiest of the Seven Summits to climb, and a mountain which has gained fame around the world solely because it is one of the Seven Summits. From base camp at the lodge to the summit represents an elevation gain of only 1,273 feet.

Yet there are those who choose not to recognize Australia as one of the seven continents, mostly non-Americans. Basically, that means they learned their geography in another country. This is the only messy part of the Seven Summits. Those other mountaineers know the seventh continent as something called Austral-Asia or Oceania. That opens up additional mountainous territory not specifically located in the Australian islands which have taller mountains.

Patrick Morrow, a Canadian climber, who also sought to climb the Seven Summits early on, decided his seventh summit was not going to be Kosciuszko, but Carstensz Pyramid in New Guinea. That is a much more formidable mountain, pretty much in the middle of nowhere. It is hard to reach and much harder to climb than Kosciuszko. The elevation is 16,204 feet above sea level.

When Bass climbed the Seven Summits and wrote his book, he introduced a new challenge to the world of mountaineering and defined it as climbing to the top of the tallest mountain on each of seven continents. Nobody pretended that Kosciuszko was in the category of Everest or Denali. But it was the geographical feature that fit the description.

Morrow muddied things with his version of the Seven Summits. All of these years later, the point remains debated as to how the seventh continent is defined and therefore which mountain is the right mountain to climb to complete the Seven Summits. For the citizen adventurer, the choice has leaned towards Kosciuszko. It is easier, more accessible, and is easy to knock off. Nobody is going to fail to complete the Seven Summits because of vicious weather on Kosciuszko.

Many top-notch mountaineers chose to polish off Kosciuszko, but also take on Carstensz Pyramid. They did not want to wake up one day and hear someone say they didn't climb the real Seven Summits because they left out Carstensz Pyramid. Those climbers typically climb eight peaks to make seven.

To them, it was possible that some day in the future, the concept would be redrawn to exclude Australia. For sports fans who don't believe such a thing could happen, they never imagined Major League Baseball would re-define no-hitters and remove dozens of games from that honored list which had been pitched decades earlier. So climbing Carstensz as insurance was not such a bad idea.

More recently, some even have sought to define the continent as including New Zealand, but not New Guinea, which would make New Zealand's Mount Cook, at 12,218 feet, the tallest mountain there. New Zealand was once part of Australia, but long ago broke away.

Kosciuszko is situated in Kosciuszko National Park in the Snowy Mountains. Located nearby is Mount Townsend, which stands 7,247 feet high. That ranks as the second tallest mountain in Australia. In a peculiar twist of geographic naming, it was originally believed Townsend was taller and it was given the name Kosciuszko. When it was the discovered to be the other way around in 1892, the New South Wales Land Department swapped the names.

Originally, the name Kosciuszko was attached to a mountain in the region by Polish explorer Paul Strzelecki in 1840. He named it after General Tadeusz Kosciuszko, a national Polish hero from the Polish-Russian War of 1792.

There is a bridge in New York City called Kosciuszko that is named for the same guy. He was a Polish freedom fighter who worked as a general for George Washington. He was a big enough name that explorers chose to name the mountain after Kosciuszko. He went all over the world helping people in their battles against the establishment. He was a worthy man.

Kosciuszko is so accessible and easy to climb that it is estimated about 100,000 people visit it each year during the Southern Hemisphere's summer. Since 2004, an ultra-marathon foot race of 150 miles ascends to the summit of the peak.

Many skiers visit Kosciuszko. The mountain is pretty much in-between Sydney and Adelaide. Sometimes I have hitchhiked there several times.

I have hitchhiked around the perimeter of Australia and it's a funny place. I met a lot of characters. If I am asked what the culture is like, I say Deep South fifty years ago. I grew up in Texas. People I met in Australia were really into their prejudice against local natives. There was lots of beer drinking, a lot of rough-cut characters. It definitely reminded me of the Texas of my youth.

Sydney, of course, is different. There were your doctors and lawyers, but things got real rustic, real quick in the Outback. I worked my way around. I got picked up and someone would say, "Hey, do you want to work?" They needed help putting up what they called burly barbed wire fencing. The guy said it was fencing of steel poles because water buffalo would walk right through a wooden pole fence. I did that for a couple of weeks at a time, got a little pocket money, and moved on.

The fastest approach to the mountain is from Sydney, because it has a good freeway that goes to Canberra, and you just sidetrack from there. The freeway is so good that I have received speeding tickets for going a bit too fast.

Kosciuszko is by far the least challenging of the Seven Summits. It is only 7,000 feet high. That said, people do die up there if the weather turns bad and they are not prepared for it. Same old story. They get lulled into carelessness because it is not a big mountain.

It can get windy and wet. The clouds roll in, the wind comes up, and that can lead to hypothermia. The National Park has a nice environment. Low on the mountain there are ferns and trees: things that koala bears like to eat. Marsupials like kangaroos, wallabies, and wombats hang around and thrive there. Near the bottom of the mountain, you can see kangaroos and a variety of birds. The higher you climb, the plants start shrinking in size, and then the last 1,000 feet to the top is tundra.

Thredbo is a ski resort that has been around since 1957, and most climbers access the mountain by going through that community.

You have the choice of hiking over a nature trail—that's where I saw the wombats. Or, if you wish, you can take the ski lift. The lift goes pretty high up on the mountain. It leaves you off on tundra, and with so many people walking over it, a steel mesh grate was installed for protection of the fragile tundra.

That steel grate goes up for kilometers, bringing you to within about 300 vertical feet of the summit. In older days, there used to be a bus that drove tourists to the top. They did away with bus rides years ago because of the environmental damage. But the bus trail still exists. The parks people are trying to grow it over and return it to a more natural looking state, but it hasn't happened yet.

Some people in decent shape just run up to the top. There is no super steep angle. Near the top it becomes rocky and the rocks often lead into snow.

Kosciuszko is no more challenging than many of the mountains in the front range of the Chugach Mountains overlooking Anchorage. The highest those mountains reach are 5,100 feet or so, so Kosciuszko is taller, but no more difficult. The rocky stretch takes over high on the slope because the snow that falls prevents the tundra from growing there.

Shutterstock / Greg Brave

Kosciuszko, Australia's tallest mountain, is not a challenge but can be fun to hike at 7,310 feet high

You may invest a couple of months in climbing Everest, and it may take you three weeks to climb Denali, but you can reach the top of Kosciuszko in three hours from the parking lot to the summit. I have done it twice in a row in one day. On another occasion, when I was doubling the Seven Summits, I climbed it one day, returned to the base, slept in the car, and climbed it again the next day. Then I drove back to Sydney and flew out. I was only in Australia for thirty-six hours that time.

I was trying to make more Seven Summits swings at the time, and it is expensive going to Australia. It was even $1,000 from Indonesia. So, if I completed my fourth series of Seven Summits and spent the night and climbed Kosciuszko again, I was starting my fifth series right then without having to leave and come back into the country. I rang the bell three times in one visit.

Many local people like to climb it as part of a visit to the National Park. A couple of times, I have gone up with locals who were just on an outing. One guy said he wanted to follow in Norman Vaughan's footsteps. He was an older gentlemen and he was bewitched by Antarctica. He was mentally meshing the reality of an Antarctic expedition with his physical conditioning. We were just talking, and I just said, "Hey, come join me. Let's go up this thing." So he did, and we went up Kosciuszko together. It was fun training for us.

Locals do go to Kosciuszko. I don't know if I have ever gone up on a Saturday when there weren't maybe a half-dozen people on the summit when I got there. There's always someone there. That's in the summer. But I have climbed it in the winter. Winter weeds out a lot of trekkers. No matter where you go, in the winter the numbers go down.

My way of thinking is to climb when you can, because if the mountain is in a distant foreign country like Kosciuszko, you don't know when you will get back. You could even run into a storm day on another trip. If you are there, do it. You have it in your pocket that you climbed it in winter.

The first time I climbed Kosciuszko was actually with my friend Mike Gordon from Anchorage. I said I would guide it and the cost was basically transportation. It was great to go with a friend, and his wife Shelli came, too, but I also wanted to fly off the top. At that time I was trying to do the Seven Plummets. Meaning I was trying to paraglide off the top of each of the continental mountains. I still haven't completed that. I did not paraglide off of Carstensz Pyramid. The summit ridge is very narrow, and there is no place to set up your glider.

So I flew off Kosciuszko, but the wind was so strong, so malignant, I actually flew backwards through these large boulders, crashed myself into the rocks at the top and hyper-extended my leg. That shows you how things can go wrong even on the easiest of the Seven Summits. Climbing wasn't hard, but flying off was dangerous and almost got me killed.

I laid out my wing. I had seen some birds soaring and that is usually a good sign. I got what we call "ridge lift." The wind hits the mountain and the current is deflected upwards. Just as I stepped off the ridge I got lift, but right about that time I noticed all of the birds descending. They must have sensed a big, bad gust coming. They didn't want to get blown backwards so they all landed. I popped up and was blown backwards.

It probably carried me at ten to fifteen miles per hour through the boulder field in a matter of seconds. The boulders were the size of a kitchen table and it hurt. I cracked a knee pretty badly. There was a lady up there and she saw me go down. She came running over and said, "Are you OK? I'm a physical therapist." I told her I was pretty sure I tweaked my knee. She unfolded it very carefully.

We got to talking and she sounded American. We did the whereabouts thing, and she was from Anchorage, Alaska, too. There we all were on the summit of Kosciuszko, four Alaskans at the same time. I got her card and went in for some therapy when I returned to Alaska.

Actually, very few people can say they get paid to guide Kosciuszko because people don't need a guide. I wanted to be able to say I guided all of the Seven Summits. Mike gave me $50 and covered the food, hotel, and transportation. I think most people would be pushing credibility to say they guided it, but I did.

The paragliding did not work out so well, but I did fly off the peak. I've still got a couple of serious ones I haven't done yet. I have flown off Aconcagua from 21,850 feet, but not from the summit. That was a scary flight. It is also illegal to paraglide off the summit of Mount Kilimanjaro. There is only one occasion I heard of officials opening it up for that, and it was for a TV show. That law may soon be repealed, and when it is, I will fly.

I usually don't paraglide if I am guiding. Kosciuszko that time was different. That was part of my guide-to-glide program. Usually spectators, people standing around, like it and think it's exciting. Of course, people also say, "That's crazy." I think I have the first known flight by paraglider from the highest mountain in Europe, Mount Elbrus; the highest mountain in Antarctica, Mount Vinson; Denali in Alaska; and Kosciuszko. Not a lot of people try it. In fact, few people are crazy enough to even consider it.

In the early 1980s, I broke my ankle when I popped off a rock climb in Yosemite. In a simple twist of fate while paragliding at Hatcher Pass, about fifty miles north of Anchorage, I re-broke it. Always check your lines!

Kosciuszko

For all of the grief Kosciuszko takes because it is not a difficult climb as a member of the Seven Summits, the view from the top can be beautiful. It's just the highest of hills, so you're not looking miles and miles away like on some of the really tall mountains, but you can see the Tasman Sea and coast-line from there.

It can be plenty cold if you go in the winter. While there another time, I also climbed Mount Townsend, the second highest mountain in Australia. I have done it more than once. So I have climbed the second highest mountain on that continent. If I ever go after the Second Seven Summits for each continent, I will already have that one checked off.

CARSTENSZ PYRAMID

Another name for Carstensz Pyramid is Puncak Jaya, though westerners do not generally use it. If not for Canadian Pat Morrow's own quest for a slightly different Seven Summits, probably five total mountaineers in the entire world would have heard of Carstensz Pyramid.

No one thought of Oceania, or Austral-Asia, as a continent. Until Dick Bass's success on his Seven Summits journey, no mountaineers cared about Mount Kosciuszko either. It was too insignificant a bump on the terrain to bother with. Then it gained full-fledged notoriety as one of the Seven Summits, stoking international interest.

Carstensz Pyramid is a whole different animal. It rises 16,024 feet above sea level, compared to Kosciuszko's 7,310. It is in a remote location, and much more challenging to climb. Carstensz is situated on the island of New Guinea in the West Papua region of Indonesia. It is the tallest peak between the Himalayas in Asia and the Andes in South America.

A nearby neighbor is an industrial giant, the Grasberg Mine, the largest gold mine in the world, as well as the third largest copper mine. Grasberg is less than three miles away from the mountain and is a gigantic operation employing about 19,500 people. This sometimes can create complications for mountaineers who are focused on the outdoors and the environment and the mine owners who jealously guard their wealth-producing site.

Carstensz Pyramid was named for a Dutch explorer named Jan Carstenszoon. Carstenszoon first identified the peak in 1623. When he returned to Europe and reported the findings of his journey and told people he saw snow near the equator, nobody believed him. There are actually three summits close together near the top of the mountain.

The three peaks are East Pyramid, Ngga Pulu, and Carstensz. However, in an unusual twist, when a Dutch team sought to climb the highest point in 1936, it was Ngga Pulu. Later glacier melt diminished its size, leaving Carstensz as the highest point.

Partially slowed by bad weather, the Dutch expedition climbed the other two high points, but not Carstensz. It was not until 1962 that Carstensz was first climbed. One member of that group was Heinrich Harrer, the mountaineer who was the focus of the movie *Seven Years in Tibet*, who made several impressive first ascents during his career. Harrer also wrote a book about Carstensz Pyramid.

A year after that inaugural ascent, the Indonesian government changed the name to Sukarno Peak to honor the national leader. Still later the name was altered again, this time to Puncak Jaya, translated as Victory Peak. However, that switch never caught on in the mountaineering world.

An individual cannot simply show up to climb Carstensz. The government controls permits, and awards them to adventure travel companies for a fee. Between 1995 and 2005, the government shut down the mountain to climbing.

Initially, Vern Tejas was not attracted to climbing the Carstensz Pyramid. He completed his Seven Summits with Kosciuszko and was satisfied with that. Later, however, he decided he should climb Carstensz to make sure he covered all of his bases for eight summits, just in case the issue was ever called into question about the true Seven Summits.

Tejas has since reached the summit of Carstensz Pyramid three times.

To begin climbing Carstensz Pyramid, you fly to what used to be called New Guinea, but which some call West Papua now. The only reason why Indonesia wanted to annex New Guinea is because of the gold and copper deposits they are mining right next to the mountain.

The mine area is huge. It has eaten up other mountains. If Carstensz did not have the designation as being the tallest, they probably would have blasted all of the way through it to get the mineral deposits beneath it. Carstensz has been spared that. The mining industry is hard-rock mining from the inside out. Carstensz is the national symbol, the highest thing in the country, so they really can't destroy it. Other former mountains, next-door neighbors, are now lakes.

One way or another, that area certainly produces income, whether it is from mining or tourism. The mine is the biggest taxpayer in the entire country, and the government protects the miners. Government officials do not want environmentalist climbers going in there and taking photographs of the environmental travesty going on. They don't want bad press. The mine is linked up to the highest officials and the military. The top people in government are very protective of the mine.

The mountaineers are supposed to just slide by the operations and maintain the peace. The last time I was there, we accidentally ruffled the miners' feathers pretty good, though.

For a while, there was a six-day trek into Carstensz Pyramid, but then a rebellion got underway and native rebels with guns that resented the Indonesian takeover were trying to fight back against the people that took over their country. To keep the tourism dollars flowing and the mountaineers coming, a helicopter landing pad was built. That way you skip some of the jungle hiking and hassling with all of the rules around the mine. You can just zip in and zip out after the climb. I heard of one guy not long ago who took a helicopter in, and, establishing a speed record, climbed the mountain in four hours and took a helicopter ride out.

Carstensz Pyramid got ramped up on competitive people's lists who didn't think climbing Kosciuszko was sufficient. It's a hard climb. You need some rock climbing skills, and you need to be comfortable with fixed ropes. It is more technical than the other seven mountains. Still, some people are doing one Seven Summit, and some people are doing the other. It's like 7A and 7B. I've done all eight of the Seven Summits. There are not any bones to pick, but you could hear someone saying later you didn't do the real thing.

The main route up Carstensz is actually the most technical of the Seven Summits. It involves quite a bit of technique. I heard that there has been a three-strand cable bridge installed where the Tyrolean traverse used to be. The mountain is only 16,024 feet high and the climb begins at 14,000 feet. You're only going 2,000 vertical feet to get to the summit. It is technical, but the elevation gain is not difficult.

The route is a zig-zag, so you can ascend pretty quickly. It's not straight up. A typical climb takes a day. Of course, you have to be acclimated so you don't get turned back by the altitude right away. The guys who are doing the Seven Summits can face a problem unless they are acclimated. You should be pre-acclimated. That's an advantage. The climb is just in and out, but still, you can have problems up high– lightning, hypothermia and rock fall, to name a few.

When climbers reach the actual summit point of Carstensz Pyramid they can be in for a surprise. It is pretty small. Mount Vinson's summit spot is very small, as well. It's kind of got a ramp, but the top is rocky. You can fit maybe four people on the summit of Carstensz at once. Most people never step on it. They step all around it, but not on it because it is just a point. I have put my foot on it.

Being a point and dropping off sharply at seventy degrees, you don't want to stretch too much. About three feet away, you can stand with your body higher. People can touch the point if they want to, but their head can be higher, so I count that. To actually try to stand on top of the point would be scary, if not suicidal. If you slip, you die. You don't want to be screwing around. There is more room on the summits of Denali, Everest, Aconcagua, and Kilimanjaro. But on Everest people certainly don't stand on the north end of the summit because it sticks out in space. You can sit where the top of your head is higher than the actual top. Most people don't want to stand at the precise spot anyway because there are prayer flags there.

Carstensz Pyramid, Oceania's tallest mountain, is difficult to reach and even more difficult to climb at 16,024 feet high

Doing Carstensz the long way, with the trek, means you absorb more culture, although the culture may not always be friendly. I don't think I want to get an arrow in my butt. The local Mani and Dani Tribes often block the way, extorting you for money. I can do without going through the jungle when it is wet, slippery, infested with bugs, and falling down, coping with landslides and near-hypothermia. Really, I can. It's good to do it that way once, for sure. Now that I have done it three times, I look forward to going to the mountain by helicopter.

Of course, I am not sure I wish to return there after my 2013 trip if anybody is going to remember me. The mine personnel, for instance, could remember me because I exited from the mountain through the mine.

I went through the mine after a climb, on my way out of the country. One of our porters died on the way in, so the other porters basically dropped their loads to take care of his body and get it out of the jungle. The way the tribe sees it, if a man is working for you, he is doing your bidding, and if he dies, he is your responsibility.

He was an ill-clad older man, and the weather turned. The porters don't dress warmly because it is much warmer where they live twenty-five miles away. He was wearing shorts and a T-shirt and we were high up in elevation and the rain turned to blowing sleet and it got icy. It was a miserable day. The porters live at about 7,000 feet, but we were up to 14,000 feet. It turned to mixed snow and rain. It was colder than the area where the porters lived. They hunt at high elevation, but they don't go out in weather like that. They only go if the weather is good, so he did not have experience in the cold. He got hypothermia, which he had no knowledge of, so he did not know that he was dying or why he was dying.

We hadn't even hired him directly. He bought his way onto the trip for the work. He bought someone else's employment to have extra money. We had twenty porters on the trip carrying equipment.

So the man died in my employ, making me responsible for him. In that region over there it is an eye for an eye, a tooth for a tooth, a life for a life. As soon as the man died I called our office in Seattle and said, "We've got an issue." I told them, "Please figure this one out. We're going to finish the climb, but as soon as we finish we want to know what we're supposed to do." I called back and my orders were to cut through the mine. I said, "It's illegal." They said, "Go through the mine. We don't want you going through the jungle with the natives. You might not make it to the other side."

There were five of us and we tried to exit through the mining territory. They had their reasons why they didn't want westerners passing through the mine. I was the western guide and we had a local guide and assistant. The local guide and assistant got off the hook for going through the mine. The rest of us, me and my climbers, were detained and told, "No, you can't cross through the mine." So we sat at the edge of the operation for four days.

In the meantime, Todd Burleson, the Alpine Ascents boss in Seattle, was trying to reach Alaska Senator Lisa Murkowski. The Department of State got involved. The Department of Transportation got involved. They were working the phones and trying to resolve the impasse.

Alpine Ascents got the climbers' wives involved, too, calling their representatives. They called and told the officials, "We've got an international incident going down."

Ultimately, the mine's higher officials realized something was brewing. They understood porters and the family were pissed off because one of theirs had died. They had had trouble with the local natives before and walked a fine line with keeping the peace. All of a sudden we were thrown into the middle of this situation. We are camping near the mine right on the edge of their lucrative backyard. They did not want anybody killed and they did not want the scrutiny if anything happened. Eventually, they hustled us out of there.

They seemed to have a policy that if anyone was trying to flaunt the rule against crossing through the mine, they kept them waiting for a week. They just didn't want people crossing their land. They did not want trespassing. Trekking out through the jungle only took four days, so they figured most people would give up and exit through the jungle. In this case, we were warned not to go through the jungle, so we were going to sit it out. We held out hope that they would eventually give us crossing permission. They did so in about three-and-a-half days.

Finally, the security guys for the mine came over and got us. They were carrying machine guns and said, "Get in the car. You are going to talk to the head of security." That guy was from Louisiana, and I was able to build a little rapport because I grew up in Texas. We chatted. "Hey, how are you doing?" "I've got a brother in New Orleans." I told the guy I owned 1,000 shares in the company because I had been following their prospects. I said, "I like the company." I am not sure what kind of credential that was, but it was better than nothing. He knew I was basically a small fish. I was kind of casually suggesting he not get too hard-ass on me. But sometimes shareholders showed up, so it didn't carry that much weight. Fortunately, he didn't come down too hard on us. They made us put on flak jackets and helmets to drive out just in case there was an incident on the way.

The security people took us to the community of Timika, but did not just abandon us there. They warned us to check into a hotel and stay inside. "You are getting on the plane tomorrow," we were informed. They didn't want us seen on the streets because they felt we might be a target of revenge on behalf of the porter. That was the last time I went to Carstensz Pyramid. I will go back, but I will have to go by chopper.

When I was younger and made the solo winter ascent of Denali, I wore a thick beard. I shaved it off a long time ago. But maybe if I was going to go back to Carstensz I would grow my beard back as a disguise. When I last went, you flew into a small air strip that

Christian missionaries built fifteen or so years ago. That's where the walking began.

Carstensz seems a lot more interesting to me now because it's like I have a price on my head. Also, with those helicopters you can fly over the jungle and the mine. I wouldn't have to deal with the locals. It would be so much cleaner avoiding all of the hassle. No imbroglio.

Overall, the trip was getting to be a zoo there. Bribery is rampant. The rebels wanted a cut. Local chiefs wanted a cut. And everybody along the trail through the jungle wanted their cut. A guy comes up to us with a machete standing at one end of a vine bridge going across a river. He says, "My brother built this bridge. You can't cross it. He told me to make sure nobody crosses it unless they pay." He's saying it's not really him, but it's his brother who is the asshole, right?

We stood there and negotiated for two hours. I didn't have any money for a bribe. So the local guide eventually opens up his backpack and hands the guy enough money to buy five cartons of cigarettes so we could cross. This was happening over and over again for the first few days of the trek.

It wasn't that surprising. When my climbers landed in Bali, I met them and provided a briefing. I told them the trip would be fun, but they had to be really tolerant and smile a lot. Don't give anybody any money. Don't get riled up with anybody. At one point, we were on motorcycles and a tree was down in the road. We figured we could just move the tree out of the way. But no, there was a guy there with a bow and arrow who didn't want us to move the tree until we paid him. You're moving a tree so you're sitting ducks.

When we got to a village, we paid people for staying in a room. They could have called it a toll, but this was an exchange, making it a little bit more civil. They were not extorting money from us. They were renting us a place to stay.

The rate of payouts slowed down when the number of people diminished along the route. But it was heavy duty baksheesh the first day-and-a-half. Baksheesh is a tip or a bribe or the cost of doing business. Once, I stepped over a little pig fence. Everyone there was raising pigs. I looked up and there was this little lady with a paring knife in my face going, "That's going to cost you."

I try the negotiation thing. The lady wants to cut my eyeballs out with a knife. In some ways, it was hard not to laugh. These guys were wearing nothing but a penis gourd and carrying a bow and arrow. There were kids with slingshots. I tried to make it clear I was not the one to talk to. She needed to talk to the local guide who had the backpack full of money and cigarettes.

In the beginning, you are crossing through a jungle and that's where you see the people. Maybe next time I should bring some pigs for bribes. They're very valuable. As you go higher you cut through a rain forest and get wet. There were no wild animal threats to us. The people had pretty much killed everything for food. We were above the crocodile line. Crocodiles were down low. We were above the mosquito line, so we didn't get bitten and catch malaria. We were above the leech line, too.

It's a real adventure. There were some people with bones through their noses. The only other place I saw such things was in *National Geographic* magazine. One guy was a classic. He had a bird through his nose. The beak was over here and the tail on the other side. It was a show-stopper. The girls turned their heads. "Oh, he has a bird in his nose. Wow!" You go, "OK, that's wild." I see a lot of body piercings on the streets of New York City, so I am used to it, but I have yet to see anyone else with a bird piercing.

These people are like a half a generation removed from cannibalism. Some may be wearing that penis gourd. Others are walking around wearing New York Yankees T-shirts. Probably the missionaries provided them. People ship boatloads of clothes over there. Otherwise they would be basically naked, and I guess the missionaries don't like to look at naked bodies.

The people are supposed to all be happy. I heard they have sex any time they want. The women wear grass skirts. Maybe they used to always go topless, but they switched to baseball team T-shirts. In one generation, they have gone from eating one another to only occasionally killing one another without eating them. That's progress. They eat a lot of pigs. That's why they are so valuable. The pigs are what they've got because they hunted out all of the other wild game.

I would like to go back and climb the second highest mountain there. Who knows what day that will be?

At this point, I have probably visited fifty countries to climb mountains. When I get my passport stamped, I just hope the marks don't take up too much of a page. I have run out of passport space before and obtained extra pages while abroad. I also try to get passports renewed overseas. It's cheaper than it is to get it done in the United States. The last time I renewed, I did it in Greece.

I look forward to returning to Carstensz Pyramid to climb again. I know I definitely won't end up with nearly as many ascents of the eighth summit as I have of places like Aconcagua, Vinson, and Denali. However, a few more summits will suit me fine.

MOUNT KILIMANJARO

Known as "The Roof of Africa," Mount Kilimanjaro was often identified from a distance by a cone of snow on the summit. The 19,341-foot peak is the tallest mountain on the African continent, but its snow and glaciers are disappearing, changes blamed on global warming.

A dormant volcano, Kilimanjaro is located in Tanzania. While impressive in height and scope, Kilimanjaro can be one of the easiest of the Seven Summits to ascend. That is because the weather is generally benign and there are no crevasses or avalanche dangers. The altitude represents the significant challenge.

The origin of the name Kilimanjaro is murky. Those who studied the matter well over a century ago attribute the label to words in native languages such as Swahili, essentially translated as "great mountain," "white mountain," or "mountain of caravans."

Kilimanjaro is one of the best-known mountains in the world and it is visually arresting from a distance. It stands high, and, if not quite alone, stands out individually against the skyline.

Recorded history does not explain when Kilimanjaro first became known to Africans, but by 1860, explorers had identified it. The first ascent of the mountain recorded by Europeans took place in 1889. German geographer Hans Meyer and Austrian mountaineer Ludwig Purtscheller were credited with this pioneering climb. Purtscheller was a renowned climber for his era who took his greatest pleasure from route finding in the hills.

There had been numerous attempts to climb Kilimanjaro during the intervening thirty-year period between its recognition in the West and the Meyer-Purtscheller ascent. Some of those attempts were repelled by snow and some by altitude. The actual climbing route up Kilimanjaro that has been popularized is not terribly demanding. The challenges in no way resemble the difficulties presented by Mount Everest or Denali. The trail can generally be covered in a few days and it rates as no more than a strenuous hike. The main caveat for the climber, as is the case on many mountains that stand more than 10,000 feet high, is acclimating before pushing up too high.

The success rate is around sixty-five percent, but reports of altitude sickness are quite common amongst those who did not sufficiently train or rushed their climbs. The majority of people who die trying to climb the mountain suffer from some kind of altitude illness, although some have perished from pneumonia.

In August of 2014, a Swiss-Ecuadorian man named Karl Egloff actually ran up to the summit of Kilimanjaro and back to base camp in six hours and forty-two minutes to set a speed record. The oldest person to the summit was eighty-six years old. A man pushing a wheelchair has also reached the top. A Nepali friend of Vern Tejas' climbed it going backwards a few years ago.

Tanzania, which borders Kenya, is at the heart of some of the world's most fantastic wildlife viewing. Those two nations feature several game preserves and the opportunity to sign up for the additional excitement of taking wildlife photo safaris in conjunction with Kilimanjaro climbs. For the most part, hikers and climbers do not cross paths with the big game animals of Africa while on Kilimanjaro.

However, nearby opportunities abound to see elephants, lions, Cape buffalo, zebras, rhinos, warthogs, wildebeest, impala, leopard, Greater Kudu and others.

Kilimanjaro has also been featured in popular culture. The book, *The Snow of Kilimanjaro*, written by Nobel Prize-winning author Ernest Hemingway, is famous worldwide. The mountain can be seen on film in *The Lion King*.

Vern Tejas has made the journey to Africa a dozen times and has climbed to Kilimanjaro's summit seventeen times.

The first time I went to Africa, I flew to Nairobi, the capital of the Kenya, on my own and took a bus to Moshi, the closest community to Kilimanjaro. This was not for a guided trip; I was doing Kilimanjaro on my own.

You have to cross the border between the countries and sometimes that can be tense and other times it is easy. Basically, the best thing to do is keep your head down and keep shuffling. Do not get into debates with the guards. They can turn you away if they feel like it, and they're carrying guns.

There is a lot of weird action at the border. Some residents make their living by hanging out there trying to hustle wealthy foreigners. They try to sell beads, beads, and more beads, and anything else that they think you might like.

Mount Kilimanjaro

I made my way to the YMCA in Moshi and asked around to see if anyone was doing a climb of Kilimanjaro. There are local guides. In fact, you have to hire local guides. That's part of the local economy.

My motivation at the time was to climb Kilimanjaro as the sixth of my Seven Summits. I was on my way to Everest that spring to complete the Seven Summits, and I wanted to get Kilimanjaro done beforehand. I was looking for the cheapest trip I could attach myself to, and I think it only cost me a couple of hundred dollars to join up with a bunch of backpackers. I was pretty acclimated, but I wanted to do the climb quickly, not spread it out over many days with camping in the designated huts. By then, the early 1990s, I was doing this sort of thing for a living so I was pretty much always acclimated from going from one mountain to another. Still, if I was going to climb it fast, I knew it was going to hurt. I had my pressure breathing techniques and a rest-step pace.

I also wanted to fly off the summit with my paraglider. I was crazy, because it is illegal to paraglide off Kilimanjaro. If you get caught, you get punished. You can get put in prison and fined. Part of the fine goes to the person who caught you so there is incentive for them to turn you in. Despite the appeal of the flight itself, it was not the best idea I ever had.

Climbing Kilimanjaro does not demand the time investment of an Everest or a Denali. Guided trips only take a few days. There are obvious designated camps for cooking and spending a couple of nights. There is a welcoming hut system where groups sleep. The climbers tote their sleeping bags up and spread them out on bunk beds. They are good resting places, but they are not heated. They are stopovers. The group turnover is pretty swift. Your group might hang for five hours, but there is always someone coming behind you that needs some rest, too.

Roughly 30,000 people a year try to reach the summit of Kilimanjaro. About two-thirds of them make it. The hut system is an aid. There are half a dozen available routes to choose from, some taking a little longer, some steeper. One popular trail is the Marangu Route. Typically, the climbers reach the Kibo Huts at about 15,500 feet, eat dinner, go to sleep, and wake up to depart at about 1:30 a.m. If they are lucky as they climb the route, the sky will feature a full moon and stars, and they might not have to keep a head lamp lit. The goal is to reach the top by sunrise, early in the morning, and gaze out at the spectacular scenery from the roof of the continent.

There are various well-known spots on Kilimanjaro: landmarks, much like on Denali, which have had prominent spots named. One place near the true summit is Stella Point. There are signs there informing climbers that the mountain is a World Heritage Site. There is also Kibo Point, Gilman's Point, and Uhuru Peak. Uhuru is the highest summit on the Kibo volcano crater rim.

Uhuru is Swahili for freedom. When Kenyans and Tanzanians sought to remove themselves from European influence, "Uhuru" was the rebels' battle cry. It was the most powerful and symbolic word in their struggles for independence through the 1950s and into the early 1960s.

My game plan to paraglide kind of ran up against the standing bounty for the locals to turn you in. People were wondering why I was carrying a conspicuously bigger backpack. Everybody else was carrying little daypacks. My pack was much bigger. My story was that, since I was training to climb Mount Everest, my pack was full of rocks. I needed the extra weight for the workout. I actually reached the point on the climb where I could carry the pack balanced on my head the way that the porters carried the supplies. I got to the point where I could hold the balance for forty-five minutes to an hour without even touching the pack with my hands. Looking back on it, it was definitely goofy.

Carrying the pack on my head was just an idle activity, giving me something to think about as I hiked up the trail. I didn't have any responsibility to clients on this trip. There were a couple of Europeans on the trek, but they were feeling the altitude much more than I was. By the time we got to the Kibo hut, one of them was puking. He did not respond to the call to get up and go to the summit. The others did. We reached Gilman's Point and then Stella Point. When we got that high, some of the guides started asking me why I was carrying such a big pack on summit day. I kept telling them it was rocks for my training, but they started going, "Yeah, right."

The local guides got after me. They didn't believe me. The porters do not speak much English, and they weren't really paying much attention. The local guides are the ones who will get fined if you do anything wrong. They definitely didn't trust me and I didn't know what was going to happen. When we hit Stella Point I excused myself to go to the bathroom. I ran behind a ridge and I stashed the paraglider there and did put rocks in the pack. I had a feeling I might be searched.

I rejoined the group, put the pack on my head and went to the summit with everybody. Everyone congratulated everyone. We had hugs and kisses and the guides asked, "What's in the pack?" I said, "Rocks." They still didn't believe me and said, "Show us." I dumped out the rocks from the pack and they all said I was crazy. I just went "Yeah, yeah." I also put the rocks back in the pack, because I knew when we got back to Stella

Point I was going to have to do something to pick up the paraglider. But if I said I needed to go to the bathroom again, the guides would be really suspicious.

One thing about Kilimanjaro, once you reach the summit, they hustle you down as quickly as possible. They were in no mood for stops for anything. We just kept descending past certain points, including Stella. We zoomed past Kibo, which is already below Stella, and zipped down to the next hut. Most guides stop at one point to give people a rest because summit day is a long day. You get up in the middle of the night, climb up, and then descend. Normally, they pause at a hut to let people take a nap. But these guys were just pushing us. I'm thinking, "What am I going to do? I left my glider up there." That thing was expensive. It was worth a couple of thousand bucks, and I was a poor mountain guide.

Finally, when we stopped and were tucked into bed for a rest in a hut, I opened the window, jumped out, and ran all of the way back to Stella Point in the dark. I grabbed the paraglider and was going to fly off then and there, but there were too many clouds. The most dangerous thing about paragliding is any lack of self-control. You want to fly whenever you can, but if you allow yourself to fly in the wrong conditions, it can be very dangerous. It takes a certain amount of self-control.

It was the middle of the night, I was away from my local guides, and I had my paraglider back, but I realized it just wasn't safe enough. I had tears in my eyes when I put the glider back in my pack. It was 2 a.m. and I was heading down.

But guess what? Here came another group climbing up to make their morning sunset summit. I couldn't let them see me because there was no explanation for me being there alone. They could hear me coming down in the scree. I'm hustling along. They were in a ravine and my choice was to either go down past them, or go off trail and try a different direction I hoped would let me reunite with the trail below them. I could hear them coming up. They were investigating because of the noise I made on the gravel scree. I could see the lights of their head lamps bouncing up toward me in the dark.

They were going up, so it was harder for them. I had gravity on my side. I had the ability to move quicker, even though they were hardened Kilimanjaro guides. Because I was going downhill, I was faster. Probably about fifty feet before they were going to intercept me, I bailed out to the left. I chose the left because they were coming up from the ravine from the right. They had clients, so they couldn't really run off in any direction. They couldn't abandon them and roam too far. Even if they want whatever reward money is being offered, they can't leave the group behind.

They come running up the hill, and I could hear them yelling at me to stop. That was about as far as they could go because they couldn't skip out on the clients. I head left for freedom and dash all of the way back down. Going back up to Stella Point meant I had pretty much climbed Kilimanjaro twice in one day. I got back to the hut and climbed in the window about thirty minutes before dawn. Before you know it, the guides are knocking on the door and shouting "Breakfast is ready!"

I put on an act, giving a big yawn and stretching like I've slept real well. But I was exhausted. We went all of the way down to the base and out the gate of Kilimanjaro National Park. I definitely put out a lot of energy and made things tough on myself. I didn't get to fly, but I didn't get caught. I did climb the mountain for my first time.

Many times since, I have returned to Kilimanjaro and climbed it again and again, but I have still never flown off with a paraglider. It is still illegal. Actually, it is illegal because of me. In 1988, when I climbed Denali in winter, I took a kite with me. I was planning to fly. The weather was a whiteout, very poor flying conditions, and windy. So to fly was a death wish. I left my glider on Denali. Later that year during the guiding season I climbed it three more times. Each time I took the paraglider to the top with me and every time the weather was bad. I brought it farther down the mountain and parked it, hid it, again. I left it cached on the mountain. That wasn't legal either, but nobody was looking for it.

In 1989, I was invited on a University of Alaska trip to re-measure the mountain. A professor of engineering there, who taught a surveying course, organized the group. They asked me to join, and I said I would be part of it if I could fly off. The National Park Service thought I was getting paid to guide, but I wasn't. The only thing the group was paying for was the food and transportation, but they were doing that for everyone who was part of the team. My tradeoff instead of being paid as a mountain guide was to be able to paraglide off the summit to the Football Field at 19,000 feet as a test. Back to the guide-to-glide program.

I didn't know how the air would react with the foil. The air density was half as much as it was at sea level, so everything can happen twice as fast. It means you take off twice as fast, land twice as fast, and have to think twice as fast with the half the amount of oxygen you usually have. That's not a great situation, but I did it. I did maybe a 700-foot vertical flight and learned it was possible. I had a good flight. After I stowed the paraglider back in my pack, I ran back to the summit to make the big jump. But the professor was showing signs of altitude sickness and I could not let him descend on his own. I roped up to him, slung the paraglider on my back, and, with a sad heart, left with him. So I did not fly from the summit, not taking the big leap I had always envisioned. I took only a small flight.

We dropped down to high camp above 18,200 feet, where the professor recovered. We stayed there because the plan was to run two state-of-the-art GPS receivers on batteries for four hours until they died and then return the next day with fresh batteries to do it all again.

The others asked me if I flew, and I said I had. It was not the biggest flight in the world, but I had achieved my goal of flying off the top. They said they missed it and asked if I could do another flight. I told them if they carried my gear down to the 14,200-foot camp, I would do another flight from 17,200 to 14,200. They were totally on board.

All kinds of people saw my second flight. They saw me launch from 17,200 and land at the 14,200 in a special spot. The spot was marked by wands, and it seemed like a safe place. Boom! I landed right in the middle of this landing zone. As I was folding up the paraglider I saw a sign reading, "Water Supply of National Park Service. Do Not Disturb." Right where I had just landed. They had a regulation that said you can't land in the Park. They meant airplanes. It did not say anything about landing a paraglider. However, the next year the regulation was amended to include paragliders.

Unbeknownst to a lot of people, national parks all over the world talk to each other. At Kilimanjaro, when they found it was illegal in the United States, the park service there decided to do the same thing. They followed the Americans' lead from Denali, which was all because of me. So I played a big part in making it illegal on Kilimanjaro without realizing it. This all came out when I was speaking with the superintendent of Tanzania's national parks seeking direct permission to fly off Kilimanjaro.

He said, "No. Sorry. Can't make exceptions." That said, they did make an exception a few years ago. They did grant permission, although the paragliders faced such bad weather that they did not pull it off.

I figured the story would continue indefinitely, but surprisingly park officials may have changed their minds now to allow paragliding on Kilimanjaro. If so, Africa, here I come!

Kilimanjaro, nicknamed the Roof of Africa, stands 19,341 feet high

Kilimanjaro is an annual stop for me, anyway. I have climbed with guided groups, by myself, and even completed a speed ascent. The one trip that sticks in my mind the most was when one of my former Everest climbers wanted to take his whole family to climb Kilimanjaro in 2007. When I say whole family, we had sixteen- and seventeen-year-olds and extended family. There were probably about a dozen people climbing.

We were having a great time until we got to high camp. The day we moved up high, a huge storm rolled in. It raged all night and put climbers' summit tries on hold. That meant high camp was overloaded with people who had not gone up the day before as scheduled. The whole system works on people cycling through. Instead, we got all clogged up. Even worse, we began hearing stories. One porter died of hypothermia because of the ice storm and another porter slipped on the ice, hit his head on a rock, and died from a concussion. All of a sudden, this was not as much fun.

So many people congregated at this hut that we had to move to an even higher camp known as Kosovo where the porters had stopped. When we got there, all of the porters who were supposed to be putting up the tents were just sitting there, huddled together, and there was no shelter ready. I said, "Get me a tent. You, you, you, give me a hand." It was very windy. We started setting up the tents as fast as we could and throwing cold, wet, miserable family members into them as well as the porters, who were freezing. They were hypothermic. We had to get them out of the elements, as well as hold down the tents. Everybody's body warmth helped each other.

It was postman weather: sleet, hail, rain, and snow. And it was going postal on us. Meanwhile, my friend's wife got really cold and was shivering uncontrollably. He thought he was going to lose her, so in the morning, when everything had settled down, we did not go to the summit. We could have spent another day there resting and recuperating and gone the following night, but he said, "Let's get the hell out of here." I had wanted them to have an enjoyable trip, but he was worried about losing family members. I said, "Man, you're right. Let's go." That was one of my more memorable trips on Kilimanjaro, but not for the best of reasons. We had to turn back on what normally is one of the most straightforward of mountains. I had never done a family outing before.

Remarkably, a couple of years later, the same friend came back with me to climb Aconcagua with two of the sons who had been with him on Kilimanjaro, and we got blasted by the weather there, too. Same scenario. We ran, just got the hell out of there. After that he gave up on the family trips, I think. He is in his sixties now and is finding other things to do that did not put his family at as much risk.

Usually, Kilimanjaro is a great introductory mountain in terms of getting up high in a famous place without too much hassle and with no technical climbing. It has also become easier to reach with flights over the years. You can fly direct from New York to Amsterdam and then to Kilimanjaro International Airport, as they call it. It leaves you between Moshi and Arusha, two nearby cities.

One of the spectacular bonus parts of going to Kilimanjaro is being able to take a wildlife safari. Alaska is great that way, too, of course. When I first saw a moose in Alaska, I saw it from behind, just its hindquarters sticking out of a bush, and I said, "I didn't know they had wild horses in Alaska." Then his head came up.

The Serengeti in Africa is one of the most remarkable places on earth. There's nothing that compares to it in terms of seeing a wide variety and volume of animals.

Just hundreds, thousands, hundreds of thousands of wildebeest. Animals from the smallest to the largest on earth, from little shrews and other itsy bitsy things to giraffes, zebras, and elephants, to all of the predators in between. Despite all of my time spent in Alaska, Africa is the wildest place I've ever been. There's nothing that compares to it. It's you that it's in the cage with wheels on it driving around to see them.

The animals are just out there running around doing their thing, and it's pretty impressive to watch. One time, we drove up on a very big male lion mating just five feet away. That was pretty up close and personal, and it is still an amazing memory. Just the rawness of it was impressive. When they finished mating, she turned around, growled, and tried to hit him with her massive paw. Wow. OK. That is what life is all about.

Elephants are so mega. They are so big you think they shouldn't even exist on earth. I've been in the Serengeti, the Masai Mara National Game Preserve, and seen hundreds of thousands of animals, and this incredibly cool experience was part of my job. I have managed to pull off about a half dozen safaris as a byproduct of Kilimanjaro climbs. If I go, I don't even have to interpret, because the driver-guides speak perfect English. I merely rebroadcast what the driver-guides say to my clients. I learn a lot this way.

Such amazing things have been spotted on those drives, from mating lions to fighting giraffes. You would not believe how nasty those guys can get. You know those little prongs on their heads? Those are battering rams. They swing them. They swing their whole heads and collide with their opponents' chests. It all seems in slow motion because there is like seventeen feet of extension. The other guy is going, "Oh, damn, here it comes." Their necks alone must weigh 300 or 400 pounds. When they smack into the other guy you can hear a thump. It has got to bruise the other animal. Then the other guy does it. They are jousting for mates. It's one of the most bizarre acts of fighting I've ever seen.

When I say it's like slow motion, it may take ten seconds to unfold. Sometimes the recipient will raise his leg in anticipation and try to step down over the other giraffe's head and pin him. Once the first guy gets going, he can't stop. The other guy wins if he pins the first giraffe's head. It's like, "OK, I'm smarter. I'm stronger. I'm faster." It's something to be experienced. When giraffes run, it may seem like slow motion, but they are hoofing it. They're traveling ten yards in a step, moving at thirty miles per hour.

Hippos and Cape buffalo are very dangerous to people. So are crocodiles. Crocs take like 1,000 people a year. Most of them are in small communities, so not everybody hears about it. Crocodiles know other animals have to obtain water. They've been on the job for sixty million years doing the same thing. They go, "I'll just stay here by the waterhole and look like a log. Something will come down to drink. I will eat it."

The hippos are very territorial and surprisingly nimble. Once they open their mouth, you're not long for this world. They don't eat you, they just crush you, which is small consolation. They've got these massive, sixteen-inch saber teeth, and they make a deep impression when they clamp down, to say the least. They're bad news, and very aggressive. I suspect that is from coping with crocodiles for eons. They do not want you nearby. Even crocs avoid them.

Hippopotami are dangerous animals if they don't want you around. But if they don't really know you are there, no big deal. Different story if they see you in the water. They flip canoes over. They'll crunch a swimmer. I wouldn't want to go swimming anywhere in Africa, to tell you the truth. If it's not the big things that kill you, the little things will. No thanks. Pass. I have swum in Africa, but only in a hotel pool. That's it. The pool was safe from hippos.

Leopards are hard to see. I saw one in a tree lounging around. It wasn't going anywhere. It must have just eaten. Leopards will ambush a hunter. Sometimes you see profiles of one, but it was pretty cool to see this one hanging out in a tree. Baboons hate them. They eat baboons. But if there is a troupe of baboons around, they can actually kill the leopard. Get ten of them together biting—and they have good-sized teeth—the leopard is going down.

Cape buffalo look leathery and tough, and they are. It has been said they always look mad, as if you owe them money. They are, and you do! Buffalo have terrible eyesight, which makes them real edgy. They attack first and ask questions later. Anything that moves is a target. Good to know when one confronts you at close range. Don't move, even if your mind is screaming "Run!" They definitely seem left over from a prior age.

Mostly, I have not faced threats from animals, but I was charged by an elephant once while riding in a Land Rover. Unfortunately, we were trying to out-run him in reverse. We were very surprised by how quickly the elephant could move. The same bull flipped a vehicle the day before. Our driver-guide's quick reflexes allowed us to get away.

I know of people who reached up while rock climbing and grabbed hold of a snake. Some of the smaller animals, rodents or birds, can be camp robbers stealing your food. Once, all we were left with was Brussels sprouts. But most of the mountaineering for Kilimanjaro takes place above tree line, and therefore above most animals.

Most of the time when you're on Kilimanjaro, the weather does not interfere. The extreme weather that my friend and his family ran into is not common. But it is a reminder when you are on a mountain, above 18,000 feet, or even at 15,000, anything can happen. People should never underestimate mountains. Hypothermia has probably killed more people than anything else in the mountains, and you don't need a blizzard with fifty miles per hour winds to have that problem. Falls occur, but that can happen at sea level. You get above tree line, and you're in weather. There is no place to hide then, even on 7,000-foot Kosciuszko, it can ruin your day. At 19,000 feet, near the summit of Kilimanjaro, if it starts to sleet, it can be serious stuff. When the wet sticks to you and freezes on you, that can bring down the strongest of porters or the hardiest of mountaineers. You've got be prepared with warm, water-resistant, wind-resistant clothing.

On Kilimanjaro, you pass through different climate zones. Near the bottom, on the beginning of the hike, you pass from jungle to rain forest, to cloud forest, as they call it, so you actually work yourself up to where it's raining much of the time. There is moss growing on every tree and the ferns are fifteen feet tall. Then, when you get above the clouds, things start drying out. You get giant heather and smaller, bushier plants. Then you're in a sub-Alpine zone. It's more like tundra with short shrubs and small grasses. Above that it is so dry it's a desert. They say on Kilimanjaro you can see all of earth's major environmental zones. You see jungle, forest, bushland, tundra, desert, and near the top it's Arctic, with snow and ice.

I enjoy the contrast. I like the changes. There can be a lot of mud on the trail. Welcome to Africa. It can be slippery and quite nasty down low. I try to book it through the rain forest section quite quickly. You can go through in one day. Conditions improve the higher you get.

With the culture and the wildlife, as well as the height of the mountain, Kilimanjaro is one of the most exotic trips you can take. You get a hiking challenge, but not the mountaineering challenge, because the porters carry the supplies. Clients only carry fifteen-pound packs. You cannot climb Kilimanjaro without a local guide, and the local guide will not take you without the porters. It is about a five-to-one ratio, one climber, and five staff. It creates a lot of jobs. It is good for the economy, but it can also create the false impression that mountaineering is just a walk in the park. It is there, but if the same climber goes to Denali and expects the same thing, with all of that hauling help, they are going to be surprised.

Mount Kilimanjaro

If they got spoiled on Kilimanjaro, they had to learn quickly that other mountains were going to be harder, and they were going to be expected to work harder on the climbs. They may come away from Kilimanjaro thinking, "This is great! This is easy! I love it!" And as a guide on Elbrus you go, "OK. Let's see if you're ready for the next phase." That means you carry a little more stuff. There's a little more risk involved. There's more commitment to the mountain. On Denali you are fully responsible for the movement of your gear and the safety is on you. In the process of climbing the Seven Summits, a transformation takes places as the effort required to reach the top gets progressively harder. I watch some of the people trying to climb the Seven Summits advance from beginners who just like a hike in the park to people intrigued with the experience who are willing to work very hard to take on more difficult challenges. Everest may be a much tougher climb, but your stuff is pretty much being carried by Sherpas like Kilimanjaro. Of course, Everest is like ten times more difficult than Kilimanjaro. To me, the main obstacle on Everest is the lack of oxygen. You also have much more snow and ice than Kilimanjaro, too.

You get lots of people on Kilimanjaro. Going to 19,000 feet is a big deal, but there is a major difference in going to 29,000 feet. They get 25,000 people a year climbing Kilimanjaro. Due to the two rainy seasons, the majority of folks climb during the two dry seasons. You end up with hundreds of people on the mountain at the same time during the height of the season. That is way too many really. It's never going to be a solitary experience that I enjoy. Why wouldn't you want to be on the summit at sunrise with 300 of your closest friends?

On one trip to Africa, after I had climbed Kilimanjaro and was acclimated, me being a self-competitive type guy, I wanted to challenge myself. I decided I wanted to climb the second highest mountain in Africa. This was about ten years ago. It is a day's worth of driving to Mount Kenya, where the summit is 17,057 feet above sea level.

I hired a local guide who knew the route. We got up in the dark, put on a climbing harness and ropes and headed for the rock. It involved twenty-one pitches of very reasonable rock climbing. The climb is delightful, just 5.7 or 5.8 in rating, easy scrambling. It was pitch after pitch. We reached the top and tagged the summit and took a photo and then retreated, racing the dark. It was a very long day, dark to dark.

Being acclimated made the whole thing better for me. My guide and I were well-matched, so we could keep moving. I was pleased to top out on that peak in grand weather, with good company, in good conditions.

It made for a very nice experience. We did not see anyone else during the climb. Mount Kenya is barely climbed compared to Kilimanjaro. It is like Mount Foraker in the Alaska Range compared to Denali. About 1,500 people a year might try Denali, and ten will go to Foraker.

Other things the authorities do not appreciate on Kilimanjaro are people who want to do solos or who want to speed climb. I returned from Kenya to Kilimanjaro to visit with their park service. There is no unguided climbing on Kilimanjaro. I had to hire a guide who said he wanted to do it in one day like me, but also had to pay the cost of a week's worth of garbage removal and a week's worth of porter services even though neither was involved.

So I paid for a week's services even though I knew I was going to climb it round-trip in less than a day. The entrance gate is at around 6,000 feet and you're going to 19,300 feet. At 3 a.m. I put on a head lamp and told the guide, whom I had climbed with before, how we were going to go fast. He said, "I can do this in a day." I said, "Great, because we're going to be moving. Please keep up." He said, "Yeah, right." As the day wore on, he kept falling behind. Twice I left him for twenty minutes at a time. After I taught him the pressure breathing, we were able to stay together. That was important because we had to pass a ranger station and I wasn't supposed to be alone.

I made one mistake before we started. I ate Indian food that night for dinner hours before we started and the first thing I did when I put on the boots at 3 a.m. was run to the outhouse. I got sick. The choice of food was not such a good one for me. I blew my brains out in the outhouse before we started. That haunted me for the rest of the day. If I got ahead of the guide, I ran into the bushes. Not feeling so great after my bout with the bad Indian food made it harder to snack. Things were going out as fast as they were going in.

We reached the summit in between eight and nine hours and came right down. I got really tired on the way down. Overall, I was out around fifteen hours and forty minutes for the whole thing. You are going up 13,000 feet and coming down 13,000 feet. That's 26,000 feet round trip. You might not think about it at first, but that's pretty hard on your knees.

On the route we took, it would probably ordinarily be five days to the summit. Most people do not take the Umbwe route. It's very direct, but not as gentle an ascent. We reached the summit about noon and returned to the road just after nightfall. It was a very busy day. We came down a different route that I had been on several times, so I knew where I was at when it was getting dark. At that point, the guide fell far behind me, met some friends, and I think smoked a doobie. He fell far behind me, but I was close to the exit gate.

I was past the last checkpoint and I knew if I checked out without him they would understand. The climb was pretty much over. My girlfriend at the time was able to convince the park people to let her meet me on the road, so she came up a little ways. Even then, I still felt sick and had to stop at outhouse on the way out.

It was not a record time, and I was not even thinking about a record time. Since then, the fastest time up and down Kilimanjaro has been lowered to below six hours. One of my rules is that I do not run, and people who are setting those kinds of records are running for at least part of the climb.

One reason I wouldn't run is that I suffered a broken ankle on a rock climb years earlier and I wasn't really able to run. I figure that if you're striding out without damage, you will last longer. I feel like I can move reasonably fast without the jarring of running. Now I am just blown away by how fast some people can go in the mountains.

The first time I ever thought about going up a mountain as fast as I could was on my solo of Mount Vinson in Antarctica in 1988. It's a fairly benign mountain by the standard way. I had just done the route, so I knew where there were crevasses. From my perspective, there was nothing major to be concerned about. I also had climbers I had to get back to rather swiftly. I have done all of the Seven Summits each in less than a day except for Mount Everest. Guiding on Mount Everest, I can't do that. I have clients to watch over. I would like to try to do it in a day. It has been done. I know several people who have done it in less than twenty-four hours. I think I could, too.

Opportunity, good conditions, being in position, being fit, and being acclimated all are critical components. You can't even think of a speed climb up any of these mountains without those elements in your favor. When I tried Kilimanjaro for speed, I had recently climbed it, and gone over and climbed Mount Kenya, which is also quite high. I was prepared by the first two climbs.

You can try those things without being as acclimated, but it's a different game with far more risk. You're going to hurt yourself trying to go fast while not acclimated. I've learned a few things from all of my experience on the Seven Summits. Oxygen is really good and more is better. Technique, pressure breathing, taking Diamox, using rest steps, all of it helps. If you're smart you use all of those things. When I'm guiding I am all about pace for the group and maintaining a margin of safety. When I am on vacation, not guiding, I can do anything I want. That's when I pick up the pace. I move quickly, efficiently and that is the freedom of the hills to me. I am trying to make fluid movements through a challenging place to the best of my abilities and within my limits. One of the most pleasant experiences in life is to move efficiently and at a fast pace through a harsh environment.

MOUNT ELBRUS

Mount Elbrus is a tricky member of the Seven Summits. It is the highest mountain in Europe, yet if not for its prominence as one of the Seven Summits, few would highlight it as a climbing destination, or even be aware of its status.

There are a couple of reasons for that. If asked, the average non-mountaineering person would likely say the more famous Mont Blanc in France is the highest peak on the European continent. And to boot, although Elbrus is in Russia, it is not close to being the tallest mountain in that country.

That unusual delineation is due to the fact that Russia spans both Europe and Asia. All of its tallest mountains are in the Asian portion of the country, yet they are all much shorter than the tallest peaks in Asia. That group includes Mount Everest and the Himalayas.

Mount Elbrus stands 18,510 above sea level. It is situated in the Caucasus Mountains in the southern portion of the country, not far from Georgia. Lenin Peak, in the Pamirs, is the best-known and most eagerly sought summit in the region. The top is at 23,406 feet, substantially higher than Elbrus, and, for its height, it is one of the easiest mountains in the world to ascend. It is estimated hundreds of people reach the summit each year. However, despite the quirk of being in the same country as Elbrus, Elbrus gets more of the attention for being one of the Seven Summits.

Similarly, Mont Blanc is the tallest mountain in the Alps at 15,774 feet, and has had a long climbing history. The first ascent of Mont Blanc is dated 1786, and in an average year these days some 20,000 people reach the summit. The mountain is widely known and admired, but those who believe it to be the tallest peak in Europe are incorrect. That title belongs to Elbrus.

Elbrus is a dormant volcano with its last known eruption in 50 AD. Photographed from afar, its lower bulk can be viewed as green with the upper slopes covered in snow and ice. Elbrus actually features two distinct summit points, East and West, with only a matter of about seventy feet of height separating them. The lower east summit was first climbed in 1829. The slightly higher west summit was climbed in 1874.

What is called the normal climbing route on Elbrus, the easiest way to the top, starts with a cable car ride partway up the mountain. This is an approach from the South. The cable car deposits people at 12,000-plus feet, and from there it's about 6,000 feet to the top. People cover the lower part of the mountain via snow cat. The descent can be accomplished in only a handful of hours. The main issue for climbers, as it is on any high mountain, is to be acclimated.

Weather can also play a part in halting climbs. Typically, on the normal route, there have been few crevasses on Elbrus, but that seems to be changing with global warming. Extremely cold temperatures in the minus-thirties, significant snowfall, and high winds can hamper climbing progress and contribute to climber deaths. In 2004 alone, there were forty-eight mountaineering deaths, and in an average year between fifteen and thirty people perish on climbs there.

Vern Tejas has climbed Elbrus thirty-eight times, and it is one of the regular stops on his annual world tour of the continental high peaks.

The start time for the climb to the summit of Mount Elbrus is about 3 a.m. The adrenaline is going. You are climbing the highest mountain in Europe and people are nervous. Still, Elbrus is very civilized with the cable car and the snow cats helping you out.

The summit day is a very big day of work. The camp is at 12,000 feet and you are going to 18,000 feet. That is 6,000 feet of gain, which is really a big gulp. To make that more reasonable, I typically employ

Elbrus's dual peaks reflect the sunset during clear weather

Shutterstock / Alexander Zharnikov

a snow cat to shuttle us back up to our previous high points at 15,000 feet. Starting there is still more than you would gain in altitude during a single day on Everest. We drop down to 12,500 feet afterwards.

Not long ago, I had brunch with a lady who had been on an Elbrus climb with me the year before. She said when the climbers were riding the snow cats, they were all nervous. Then I broke out my harmonica to start playing music. The tension went away. The woman said, "When you pulled your harmonica out it just broke the ice."

However, it was cold and windy, and I sensed some diminished confidence. People were wondering if they had it in them to reach the summit on a day with weather like that. I kept playing the harmonica, hoping to wake them up and get their adrenaline going. One thing I played was "Suwannee River" by Stephen Foster and "Old Joe Clark," an old, traditional song. "Suwannee River" has a nice marching beat to it and that's what we were going to be doing for the next five hours or so of our lives. We were going to be marching up this hill in the dark and cold. Most people don't know what to expect or what they can do. For them it was like the pre-race jitters. Music helps calm the soul.

One thing about a harmonica, compared to carrying a guitar or a fiddle, is that it can go anywhere just tucked in your pocket. It's easy to get at. Sometimes when I am waiting around in line for the cable car, I'll pull it out. It may be only for two minutes. The locals, the Russians, love music. You can have an impromptu jam while you're waiting. They're clapping and goofing. It's fun. The woman I had brunch with was in New York organizing a Dixie Chicks concert. She deals with musicians all of the time and she remembers my harmonica as a magic moment on the climb. It being a highlight for her made it rewarding for me. I also brought a guitar on the trip, but I left that at the hut. The guitar has gone all over the world with me, too.

The music all goes back to what Jim Hale told me when I first started out on Denali. "The mountains are hard enough, so make sure you have fun." Sometimes people are just gritting their teeth and pushing their bodies. I am hoping to get them to relax a little, especially during a storm. Look for some enjoyment in just being there.

One thing about planning to play music on anything bigger than a harmonica when you are high on mountains is the size of the instrument. I have a regular guitar, but I usually carry a baby guitar. It is down-sized to be lighter and smaller and can fit in a pack. It's called a lapstick. You also have to prepare to carry extra weight, but it's always worth the extra effort. That is easier to do on some mountains than others.

The lapstick is made for practicing really. It's been beat up on my climbs, but it is durable. It's electric and you can plug it in to earphones on planes and trains. You've got to go out of your way to find something like this or make it for the purpose. I found the baby guitar on the internet. It was my Christmas present about nine years ago. It has been to all Seven Summits. There is another little accomplishment for my resume. I am sure I am the only person ever to play a guitar on the top of each continent.

I guess if someone played a piano on each summit they would beat me out. Of course it would not be a real piano, but maybe a keyboard. A friend once brought a keyboard to Everest base camp. Playing the mini-guitar on the summit is esoteric, but it is still cool.

In the beginning of my climbing career, I carried a fiddle, but it was too awkward, too hard, too finicky in the cold, too everything. At least I wasn't trying to carry a bass fiddle. You've got to choose your instrument correctly. The baby guitar was really durable and could go anywhere. I had a guy on a recent Elbrus trip who was a repeat climber and he said, "I remember when you played that thing in South America."

We were on our way to Mendoza after a speed climb of Aconcagua, and I was hitching a ride with some guys. One had a little electronic cable for a Walkman and I was able to plug right into it with the guitar. I played it through the stereo system in the car and we rocked for three hours into town. I did it long enough to get tired, but we had a great time. Although everything about it has to be lightweight and small, I can still plug the guitar into a big amplifier. Then I get a big sound out of that little guitar.

Although I am used to carrying more weight in the mountains than the climbers who sign up for the trips, I still have to be careful, as well. On most of the Seven Summits trips, the packs climbers carry are not that heavy. Porters are required on Kilimanjaro. There are supporters on Aconcagua. Most of the camp gear is carried by Sherpas on Everest. Kosciuszko is a day hike. Denali you have to carry the heaviest packs, sixty pounds or so. On Elbrus and some of the other mountains, the climbers are basically not carrying more weight than they would be if they were carrying a suitcase.

The weight of the pack might seem heavy to them because they are carrying it at altitude, which increases the work your body has to do. They are aware of it, for sure. Numbers get thrown around pretty loosely at times about weight, forty, fifty, sixty, seventy pounds. There is some weight, but not that much most places. Carrying weight can be a big factor at altitude, but the climbers for the most part are not forced to carry those heavier weights. However, the workload on Denali can crush people if they are not ready for it. They have trained to build endurance, but they may not have trained to carry so many pounds. A lady who climbed in 2016 started calling her pack "the little monster." You can imagine how she felt carrying that pack. Her pack included an outer jacket, a sleeping bag, and some other things. It probably weighed thirty pounds. To her, that felt like a lot.

Anything sixty pounds or more is a worst-case load. That's at the beginning of a climb when we are moving everything up to establish camps. That kind of load can be sixty pounds on your back, but you will also be pulling a sled with sixty pounds of supplies on it. The supply carry might be for three or four hours. It's a lot for people to do, but is normal for Denali.

Russia is one place on the Seven Summits circuit where I really enjoy the company of the local people—the peasants, if you will—in the remote areas. They have suffered a lot through the decades under Communism, Joseph Stalin, World War II, Stalin again, and more Communist upheaval. They drink a lot and it seems as if every eighth Russian you come across sings the blues. The Russian blues have a lot of misery behind them. It seems as if every family you come across, you hear somebody in the clan has been lost, whether it was during the war, being sent to gulags or pogroms. All of those wounds seem fresh to them.

It has been estimated, in his dictatorship reign, that Stalin's actions caused the death of something like fifty million people through imprisonment, torture, executions, or starvation. That's a lot of people. He may have disappeared more people than Adolf Hitler.

The Russians I meet these days have heart. They've got soul. I like the Russians. It is a grimmer culture in many ways, but they do know how to party. They do love vodka and drinking. I think vodka prevents more people from killing themselves. I have helped take people to the hospital from overdrinking at a celebration.

The first time I went to Elbrus in the late 1980s was with my friends from Hong Kong who were trying to complete the Seven Summits. They had climbed with me on Denali. Two of us went on to climb Everest together and finish the Seven Summits.

The country was the old Soviet Union, not Russia, and driving through Moscow was bleak. It was very cold, very dark, very dreary, and we rode in a military van at a high rate of speed with no seat belts. The whole city was very drab.

During the Soviet era, there weren't any bright signs. Everything was gray. When we got to our only lodging option, the Intourist Hotel, the national basketball team came in. They ducked through the doorways and had hands that went down to their knees. They looked like greyhounds of the human species. They were giants.

All foreigners had to stay in Intourist hotels, which made for easy monitoring of our movements, and the local Soviets were supposed to stay away. Authorities did not want any unofficial mingling. You could get in trouble. This was the government's way of keeping all of these foreign troublemakers in one place. The hotels were huge buildings that held thousands of visitors. I know they had surveillance on us. We made jokes about how they were spying on us. About ten seconds after we walked into the room, the phone rang and someone using rough English asked, "Do you want a woman for tonight?" I said, "No woman for the night, thank you."

Another thing was trying to drink safe water. You could get Pepsi in Russia. China had the Coca-Cola concession. It was just like the powers of the world dividing up the continents. So did the soda powers. Bad water is one reason why people drank so much vodka. At least they knew it was safe. Even the Pepsi tasted like it had zinc in it, but it beat boiling the water to sterilize it. From there, we flew to the Caucasus Mountains and caught a military van to the ski resort where they had the tram, or cable car.

My god, everything was archaic. Everything was in disrepair. The tram was scary. We could even see a fallen car crushed 200 feet below that they didn't even clean up. Above that was a chair lift, but it was broken and the guys there to fix it were drunk. This experience made me wonder how the Soviets were going to bury us with their military might when they couldn't even handle the most basic machinery. They were a nuclear and military power, but were so backwards at home. How was this possible? It was all a show. Everything they did was a show for the West. They did nothing to improve the life of the average Russian, not one iota.

Americans benefited from scientific development in the space race, but it seemed as if the Soviets' work impoverished the people. They didn't have bread on the shelves. They didn't have good service. You could walk into a store and the lady would be smoking a cigarette. If you wanted help, she would just scowl. I said I wanted to buy a loaf of bread and she said to come back when she finished smoking the butt. In western society, money talks, so I employed that philosophy. I said I wasn't coming back, gave her $10 worth of rubles, and that bought me service.

Service is supposed to be linked to accountability and accountability and service should be rewarded. I'm still trying to show local guides that if they are good to the climbers they will receive good tips. Many don't get the connection. We are still working our way through the medieval effects of Communism in Russia.

On the first Elbrus trip, we reached what they called the highest hotel in the world on the mountain at 13,000 feet. It was not. There are higher inns in Nepal, at 14,000 feet. There was nobody there. We came late in the season, October, and there was no one around to unlock the door. We forced the door and checked in. We had some supplies with us and were trying to heat up some water on our stove in a hallway.

The only other person on the mountain was an American woman named Peggy Luce. Peggy was on her Seven Summits quest and that year, 1988, she became the second American woman to climb Everest. The next day, we had a Russian guide come along, and we started up. When we got near the top he said, "You go here. It is very good. It is the highest point in Europe." Actually, it was not. He was steering us to the East peak instead of the West peak because he didn't want to work hard. I had a map with me so I knew. I said, "Isn't that the East peak." He said, "Yes, East peak, highest point." I said, "Well, actually, we would like to go to the little bit higher West peak over there." He goes, "Oh, no, this is the highest peak." It was not going to go over well with the people I was guiding if we went to the wrong peak. I told the guide, "This is the right peak for us."

I refrained from getting in a really big argument. I just told the guide we were going to the West peak. I thought the map was smarter than he was. The difference is 18,510 feet to 18,442 feet. But it is a difference. We went to the West peak. Then I unloaded my paraglider from my pack and said, "This is why I'm here guys." I flew off the top saying, "See you back at the hut." By the time they came down with the local guide, I had dinner on. I didn't believe anybody else had flown off the West peak. The guide confirmed I was the only one to fly off the highest point in Europe.

One of guys took a good picture of me in flight. From the summit, the whole Caucasus Range was spread out 100 miles south of us, all of the way to Mount Ararat. You're looking down into Georgia, Azerbaijan, and on and on with the sun in the background. The picture was so dramatic it was published and seen all over the world and that was before the advent of the internet.

Going to climb Elbrus you get some great sightseeing in, too. When we are on our way in for the climb we enter the country through St. Petersburg, which used to be called Leningrad. When we leave we go through Moscow. We have one day for sightseeing in St. Petersburg and there is a lot to see. We make sure to visit the Hermitage museum and we tend to visit the most famous churches and galleries. I have seen the Fortress of Peter and Paul and where the remains of Czar Nicholas and his family were returned to St. Petersburg after they were dug up in Siberia. We do a day of art, cathedrals and monuments.

One of the main reasons sightseeing is tacked on, in addition to the basic opportunity to sample Russian culture, is to ensure that all of our baggage has caught up to us. There seems to always be one bag that goes AWOL, and by staying around the city another twenty-four hours, the lost bag is usually recovered.

On the way out, we stop in Moscow to see the capital. We do a city tour, see Moscow State University, and drive by the 1980 Summer Olympic setting. We see a bunch of churches and the Kremlin and maybe go inside the Cathedral of Christ the Savior that was rebuilt. That church took forty years to build and it was consecrated in 1883. In 1931, Stalin demolished it because under Communism atheism was the state's equivalent of religion.

Stalin planned to build a huge palace of government in its place. Although construction started, the new seat of government was never finished, waylaid by World War II. The new version of the cathedral was built between 1995 and 2000 at the behest of the Russian Orthodox Church. It is a magnificent church.

We always go to Red Square, too. Usually we eat dinner first and see it at night because it is so impressive under the lights. We go back the next day and visit the big government store and shopping center. In 1988, the first time I ever visited the store, G.U.M. it was dismal. There was no food on the shelves. At the time, Mikhail Gorbachev was in charge and was introducing the first policies of perestroika and glasnost, restructuring and openness. It was early. Now that area is all Gucci. The G.U.M. store has been modernized. It used to be that young people wanted to buy jeans right off your body, or your watch off your wrist. Now the goods and services are in one of the nicest malls in Europe.

If you read the in-flight magazines and Duty Free publications, all of the stuff advertised in those pages is going to be in those stores. They have high-end brands, all the big product names. I don't keep up with that stuff, so I am not familiar with a lot of them. There was definitely a time when it would be difficult to imagine speaking the words G.U.M. and Gucci in the same sentence. Before, Moscow was not exactly a shopping mecca.

Years ago, you were not excited to go out to eat in Moscow. Now we have lunch in Red Square in a nice Soviet-style cafeteria: a workers café, they call it. It's actually become a cliché. The waiters tell you, "Comrade, clear your plate." It is very Soviet, like nostalgia. The workers from the G.U.M. store used to eat there, but now it has become a tourist attraction. It is a good value, but so many people know about it that there's a line. I hate to spend an hour for my lunch, so maybe in the future we will try other places.

The food used to be terrible, but it is good now, excellent. It's still Russian food, if that's your taste, but the quality is there. There is a whole mall complex on the east side of the Kremlin, and a park strip. There are three stories of underground shops. G.U.M. carries expensive Gucci, and the girls who work there go to the more trendy underground shops.

Russia is very different than what it was in the 1980s, transformed in many ways, but Elbrus is still the same mountain. It is neither the easiest, nor the hardest of the Seven Summits to climb, but it is a challenge at a respectable altitude, and a trip to climb it gives you access to all kinds of cultural and historical experiences in St. Petersburg and Moscow.

And maybe more vodka than you ever planned on drinking in one sitting.

GUIDE LIFE

The task of being a mountain guide is a challenging one. It involves acquiring experience and in depth knowledge of selected mountains, developing wisdom and applying techniques. A guide must have people skills, a sense of responsibility towards others and put others' well-being ahead of his own goals.

For all of the freedom of the hills that comes with the job and even being acknowledged as one of the best in the world at what you do there is also not a tremendous amount of money to be made. Guides do not work 365 days a year, or fifty weeks of the year with two weeks of paid vacation. For the most part, theirs is seasonal work, so the odds of becoming wealthy are lower than in almost any other profession. It is a true labor of love.

In many cases, being a mountain guide can be a short-term career, much like that of a professional team sports athlete. Even then, only a small percentage of guides develop a wide reputation where new climbers seek them out.

Compared to all but a few people worldwide, Vern Tejas has kept his guiding career going much longer, by many more years, than other mountain guides. He has also been able to perpetuate his reputation, particularly on Denali, and on many of the Seven Summits peaks so that citizen adventurers seek him out.

During his decades of guiding, Tejas has also added a storehouse of knowledge to draw upon, so he lends expertise to the routes being climbed on several of the world's most important mountains. When it comes to the Seven Summits, he knows his stuff and the climbers know he knows his stuff. In a high-risk profession, which can be a short-lived career, Tejas has maintained his health and stamina.

When it comes to the climbers and citizen adventurers who sign up for trips, I have learned it is human nature to think you are in better shape than you are. I've seen it over and over again. The bane of guiding is to have climbers who believe they are ready to go, but they are not. It's what we do as humans.

We make mistakes, and many of those mistakes could be avoided by doing our homework and training. They can be avoided if the people really work hard to prepare. But they have family responsibilities, a boss that demands they work late. So they skip the gym. They skip it a few times, and then they are off their training regimen. But they have paid in advance for the trip, so they are going to go anyway.

They underestimate the mountain and overestimate their preparedness. It is classic. It happens so often. We want people to be as fit as they can be. Sometimes they are not. The percentage of people who are not that fit almost exactly reflects what our success rate to the summit is. The seventy-five percent who come fully prepared represent the summit success stories and typically succeed; the twenty-five percent who don't recognize the trip is going to be harder because of that training failure are the others.

This is where good guiding comes in. How much weight am I going to carry of theirs? A lot of guides don't carry weight. In Europe, especially, the guides have the attitude, "If you're not fit, don't come." In America, where we value the dollar, I'm going to try to give you the best I can give you. I can't fix everything. I can't make you healthy if you get sick. I can't make you strong and fit, but I can help you with your load.

Carrying someone else's pack weight is a generous move by a guide. Usually, it is appreciated, and I see that in a return in tips. I helped the weakest guy on a recent trip, and he knew I helped him the most and gave me a good tip. Mountain guides do not make much money, so tips are welcome. I will carry excess weight. I make sure somebody gets a meal closer to their preference than somebody who is on another team. I go out of my way to customize a trip the best I can, but personal fitness is an important element that can make or break a trip.

Things do not work as well if the person who is not in shape affects the group and makes the whole team suffer. You find out fast if somebody did not do what was necessary to get ready. You do a reality check. I have said to someone, "Before I ever take you on another mountain, you've got to lose twenty pounds." They come back and I look at them and say, "You didn't lose twenty pounds, did you?" They go, "Well, I lost ten, but gained back two." Reality catches up to them on the mountain. Either I turn them back, or I work extra hard carrying a bunch of their weight. That's my training. This seems to happen with a higher percentage of climbers on Aconcagua than it does on any other mountain. Climbers might say they have done Denali, which is a high mountain, but Aconcagua is almost 3,000 feet higher. The way you feel on the top can be very different.

As the group leader, I spend a lot of energy ensuring the safety of my team. An example of this was when we changed the route on Mount Vinson in Antarctica. When we climbed the older way, we worried. There were always hanging glaciers on both sides of the old route. I called this place the Valley of Death. If you were in the valley at the wrong time, you were dead. That was in the 1990s. We guides frequently talked about the hazards of the route.

We changed our course in 2000. A year earlier, there was an avalanche that spewed ice all over the place. There was a huge wind blast, and debris was sent everywhere. Friend and fellow guide Dave Hahn of New Mexico suggested a creative solution by installing a fixed line up a nearby ridge. We all got on board and his idea made the route safer. In fact, it also made it a little bit quicker.

A big aspect of guiding is anticipating problems and mitigating them before someone gets hurt. As a guide, I always start out with a plan when we begin climbing a mountain. I try to put the building blocks together for success. Sometimes we have to adjust. Sometimes things happen or the weather is bad. That said, I have a ninety-nine percent success rate on Vinson. Not so on less predictable mountains like Denali, Aconcagua, or Everest.

You can get the worst weather. You are freezing your butt off, plastered by the wind. You have every inch of skin covered, so that you won't get bitten by the wind. I have been in minus-forty with high winds on a climb, and we have received four feet of snow. You don't move. There is no reason to go for a summit on a severely windy day when it's cold. If you have wind, snow, or whiteout conditions, it is going to impact your chances of reaching the top. If you have two of those going on, the chances are reduced to about fifty-fifty. If you have all three, you don't even think of going. The wind gets in people's faces and blocks the vision from their goggles. You get wind burned, snow blinded, hypothermic, and frostbit.

On Vinson, you regularly have temperatures at minus-thirty or minus-forty, but the weather has been warming up the last five years. Some climbers get frost nip and walk around with these little white patches on their faces. I tell them it makes us both look bad. The wind can rip your face off. People can get frostbite and lose skin. The fact that I have never been turned back on Vinson is amazing to me. Everything has to go right, and for that to occur, you have to be patient.

Sometimes people turn back before we have really started because they are caught off guard and can't take the cold. A few years ago, an

Australian guy took off his gloves while we were setting up the tents. A few minutes later, he was in the warming tent complaining about the loss of feeling in his hands. Game over. He just blew it. He froze his hands right away and couldn't go on. Frostbite doesn't get better. It gets worse. It was a failure on my part to not watch him like a hawk. It was a failure on his part not to watch himself. These days, that's a $40,000 mistake. That's a lot of money for a few minutes of cold exposure. You can't really watch everybody that closely. It is cold out there. Welcome to Antarctica. He had never been in weather like that before, never had that threat before. He lives in a place where it doesn't freeze, so he doesn't know what to expect or really how to prepare. Though I had warned the team to protect against the cold, it wasn't enough. I failed to anticipate his needs early in the climb. I do stress self-care with my team. It is crucial for each climber to be responsible for taking care of himself. I teach the importance of consciously being aware of having enough oxygen, hydration, calories, and the right clothes.

This is a process that requires hourly input. If they cannot do all of those things, they will soon be a liability. Be selfish and take care of yourself first and then you can contribute to the team. The classic rookie mistake is pulling into a new camp site with everybody being in a rush to put up tents. If they put on some warmer clothes and eat and drink first, they will be able to complete the task comfortably. If they forget to take those self-care steps, they set themselves up for hypothermia. It happens way too often, and what starts out as a minor problem can quickly mushroom into a life-threatening situation. So the best thing for the team is for everyone to take care of the basics—oxygen, water, food, and clothing.

I do give pep talks at the start of climbs. It's a little John Wayne-like. "Listen up! This is the first day of the rest of your life. It's your choice to make it a good one or a bad one. How would you like to begin the rest of your life?"

They're all saying, "Let's go climb a mountain."

"Yes," I say, "but let's do it safely."

When we get to base camp, sometimes before that, I am a joker. I have already gone over the gear list with them. We have already gone out to dinner. I want to make things fun at that point. I tell them to make it a good day, to make good choices. That gets the group thinking about things. There is humor involved. I learned from Jim Hale way back that humor helps people relax.

I go over my game plan for pressure breathing, my particular method for getting more oxygen. Pressure breathing is when you exhale forcefully, and it's very disturbing to anyone around you because it sounds as if you are ready to blow up. I think it is one of the most basic things to learn about altitude climbing. It doesn't matter in rock climbing. It doesn't matter on low mountains. But when you get up on the big boys, on the continental high points, you had better have some techniques to help yourself through. You literally blow your cheeks out as you are expelling air. For me and many others, this works. I tell the climbers that if they are with this particular guide—me—to humor him. Pressure breathe and laugh at his jokes.

With repeat climbers, they know the punch lines of my jokes before I get to them. That's one thing, but the pressure breathing a technique they can count on. I tell them they don't have to embrace it, but if they're gasping up high, I'm going to teach it again so they might as well learn it right away. I tell them that if they know of a better breathing technique that they should teach me, but no one has tried that recently. I've had many people come up to me after they climbed the mountain and say, "That was the best thing." I don't know exactly how it works, but it does. People tell me they used it on other mountains after learning it from me and it worked. That's the kind of feedback I like.

Team building is important for safety and enjoyment also. I start off easy with talking about how we are all reliant on one another and how it is in the best interests of all of us to look out for each other. That requires good, open, two-way communication. Before we go anywhere, we need to know how everyone is doing. Typically, I will ask each member how they slept and how they feel. I also encourage the climbers to ask each other. If someone is having a bad day we need to know. We can help out by going slower on the trail or carrying some of their pack weight. We are a family and we move together and help each other.

One of the most delicate of balancing acts is to get strangers of different abilities to work together as a cohesive unit. The melding of individuals into a team is the guide's masterpiece if done right. The ideal situation is that everyone completes the climb as friends after having a great experience together.

I have had a sixty-five-year-old man and a sixty-five-year-old woman both make it to the top of Everest on different trips. That's not bad. How did they do it? They employed good pacing and plenty of oxygen. They did not have the kind of extensive mountaineering background I did. I tell them what I have learned. I tell people that if they come away from the mountain knowing how to pressure breathe, I have done my job because every mountain you climb from now on, it can help you out.

Believe me, with a thousand samples or more to choose from, I know slower can be better. I may be slower ascending than some other guides, but I have a better success rate as a team leader. There is a better outcome, with less frostbite and fewer headaches, fewer people wadded up in a ball in pain, broken from the climb. I have watched faster trips on Denali where the guides took people up and the climbers did not feel as well as my climbers. Slow is beautiful. Everything improves from the oxygen intake, to digestion, to staying warm and avoiding hypothermia. The basics don't change.

It is very important for the guide to take care of himself, too. If I am not healthy, I can't help other people. I have traveled in the mountains for a long time. I have lost too many friends to accidents. I have been very fortunate to avoid accidents, stay ambulatory and still be able to climb in high places when I am in my sixties. I know one guy who guided Everest at seventy, and, although I don't think I will be doing that, I can say that I am still strong. Call sixty-four the new forty-four.

However, many years ago, in 1982, I did have an accident that hampered me for a long time. I was rock climbing in Yosemite and I had a crash landing that injured my ankle. It hurt for weeks, but when I got it examined, all they could do was put it in a cast. About five or six years later, I was paragliding in Hatcher Pass, north of Anchorage, and I landed hard against the hill. I was trying for a flat spot, but slammed into a hill with my right ankle.

I killed cartilage in my subtalar joint. It was an issue for years. Finally, in 2010 I had surgery. The doctors put bolts in the top and bottom of the joint, pulled it apart, and injected stem cells into the cavity where the cartilage used to live. They became cartilage, and now I can run again. It was a first for those doctors. They had done knees before, but not that joint.

They seemed pretty surprised I had been climbing mountains on it for all of those years. In the past, they just would have fused it. I couldn't deal with that. Screw that. I had to be mobile. Sometimes it bothered me. I could complain or whine, but it would not do me any good. I might be out walking with friends in New York City, and they would notice. "You're limping again." That's when I decided I needed to do something about it. Probably walking on all of that concrete in New York was the worst thing I could do for it. Dancing all night was pretty tough, too

I knew I was really in trouble on Denali when I got to the place high up that they call the Autobahn. It is a severe slope from high camp to Denali Pass. You have to crank your ankle. You have to align your foot with the angle of the slope. It really tweaks your ankle. The injured spot had atrophied over time. When I crashed and the cartilage disintegrated, it became bone on bone. That's why I limped. I had no padding. There was no lubrication between the two bones. It also threw my hips off when I walked. Norman Vaughan had fused his ankle, and it threw his knee off, and ultimately he needed hip replacement surgery. I did not want to fuse my ankle. I needed mobility. I needed to be able to flex my foot in all directions. If I had it fused, I would have had to retire from guiding. I just tolerated the pain it until I heard about an alternative surgery seven years ago and had the operation. The surgeon cut into my right ankle and drove in bolts in the spot.

For a couple of months after the operation, I wasn't very happy. I was on crutches and I had bolts going through my foot. You really have to keep the bolt holes clean so you don't get an infection and have the bone start rotting. It was a real drag to have the operation, and it kept me out of commission for a couple of months. My first expedition back guiding was to Antarctica, and it did not stress the ankle at all. When I did the South Pole traverse in vans, I arrived there with a cane. I spent hundreds of miles flexing the right foot on the gas pedal. It was good therapy.

Tejas's "guide to glide" program gave him the opportunity to paraglide off of many mountains

From what I understand, this procedure was a Russian medical invention, not by a doctor, but a veterinarian, who applied it to sheep with broken legs. The trick was to slowly jack the break apart while it heals in the correct position. In my case, it was my subtalar joint, but the principle was the same as that applied to the sheep. It grew and grew until cartilage took hold. It's really kind of a miracle that they can do it. They can re-integrate instead of disintegrate. My life got better from this operation. And since then, I have had crippled ballerinas and basketball players call me up to ask how my surgery worked out.

RETURNS TO EVEREST

At 29,029 feet, Mount Everest is the tallest mountain on earth. And because it is the tallest, it is always going to have an allure for mountaineers. To say you stood atop Mount Everest is a rare boast, an accomplishment without parallel that every layman can understand and respect.

Not everyone may comprehend just what such a climb entails, but people do know it is a grand physical achievement. Although Everest was sighted in 1852, for many years the only known way to approach it was through Tibet, and that country was a closed society. The British organized the first attempts to try to climb Everest. The famous George Mallory and Andrew Irvine expedition took place in 1924. They did not reach the summit and died trying, but Mallory spoke eloquently of mountaineering, saying, "Have we vanquished an enemy? None but ourselves. Have we gained success? That word means nothing here. Have we won a kingdom? No...and yes. We have achieved an ultimate satisfaction."

For various reasons, including World War II, Everest was not first ascended until 1953, by Sir Edmund Hillary of New Zealand and Sherpa Tenzing Norgay. That was the true milestone, the British people's ultimate satisfaction.

A quarter of a century later, Reinhold Messner and Peter Habeler became the first humans to climb Everest without the use of supplemental oxygen. In 1980, Messner returned to the mountain and made the first solo climb, again without additional oxygen.

Dick Bass's completion of the Seven Summits triggered an entirely new way of looking at climbing Everest. For the most part, over the decades, most of the major expeditions to the Himalayan peak were groups representing nations. After Bass threw out the Seven Summits challenge, privately guided trips were organized by adventure travel companies.

More than 5,000 people have now reached the summit of Everest, and more than 260 have died trying. Some terrible events have unfolded on the mountain's slopes, including the deaths of guides and clients in a vicious storm in 1996, the story of which turned into the best-selling book *Into Thin Air*, by Jon Krakaue. Also, in 2014, an avalanche caught people unawares and caused the death of sixteen Sherpas in the Khumbu Icefall as the climbing season began. In 2015, an earthquake caused many more people to die in base camp.

It took Vern Tejas three times to make his first successful climb of Everest, but he has reached the summit ten times. Only nineteen people, most of them Sherpa climbers, have climbed Everest as often or more frequently than Tejas.

The Seven Summits created a demand from people who wanted to climb Mount Everest. Usually, they have climbed the other continental peaks before trying Everest. They know it is going to be expensive, around $65,000, and time-consuming, requiring the investment of a few months on the mountain, and at least six months training. Some people figure if they can't complete the other mountains then there is no point in going to Everest. Everest is the Big One in several ways. By itself, it provides bragging rights. Tying it in with the completion of the Seven Summits provides an even more powerful tug.

Being paid to guide on Everest also provided me with the opportunity to get to the top of the world and get there more than once. When I completed the Seven Summits the first time, I did so by climbing Everest last. I looked at it as the crown jewel.

There are never any givens on Everest. Bad weather is always possible. High winds can come up at an inconvenient time and keep you from the summit. There are crevasses. There is danger from falling ice blocks in the Khumbu Icefall. It is not uncommon for climbers to push themselves too hard and run out of gas. People may suffer from altitude sickness. There are only fourteen mountains in the world taller than 8,000 meters, or 26,000-plus feet. The area above 26,000 feet has been labeled the death zone because of the thin air: the lack of oxygen.

I have never had a climber die on a trip with me there, but there are deaths on Everest every year—many of them. They occur with chilling regularity.

The main reason it takes months to complete an Everest adventure is the time spent acclimating to the high altitude. Generally, groups fly into Nepal, to the capital city of Kathmandu to meet. The trip begins with a two-week trek to Everest base camp. The trek starting area has changed over the years, but most recently, we have hiked from Lukla, which is at 9,383 feet.

The Everest base camp trek is one of the world's grandest hikes. You used to cover about 100 miles, but from Lukla you spend about ten days to cover forty miles instead. As you trek, you are surrounded by porters and yaks carrying all of the equipment. That is similar to the old British expedition method of doing things. Everest base camp is above 17,000 feet of elevation. The trek is a trip in itself, and I have guided many of those for non-climbers. It is a tremendously beautiful area, and you see all of the great peaks of the area up close.

While hiking, the terrain goes up and down, but basically you are always gaining in altitude. For an Everest climb over the 100-mile approach, there are probably 300 porters carrying tents, bags, stoves, food: everything needed on the mountain. When I first did it, it was the most marvelous aspect of the whole journey. I loved the history and traveling old-style.

The trips have been shortened somewhat now and much of the gear is flown in. That has changed the role of the Sherpas. In the past, support from the locals involved carrying all of the supplies. A large number of the carriers were dismissed at base camp. The remaining Sherpas were climbing Sherpas, who not only transported heavy loads on the mountain, they climbed it, in many cases all the way to the top.

Recently, people began flying supplies above the Icefall to diminish the number of times Sherpas had to cut through and risk their lives. Still, the Sherpas took over the role of placing the fixed ropes for the climbers.

On the approach march in older days, tents were used more regularly. Now we stop at tea houses more often. Every little village has several tea houses. They are about a day's distance worth of hiking. At each village, you sleep, and the trek resumes the next day. The porters don't usually stay in the teahouses because they do not want to spend the money. They camp out and get up at dawn to pack their loads, put them on their heads, and hike until 10 a.m. before taking a break. When the sun rises, everyone warms up and cooks.

Each supply box is the same because they are predicated on airline travel and the airlines have fifty-pound limits for checked baggage. Some porters are strong enough to carry two at a time and collect double wages. The boxes are actually waxed in case of rain. Large numbers of men traveling through the wilderness carrying supplies like that very much resembles scenes in old movies. Sometimes fewer porters are used and the group relies on yaks as pack animals to help. One yak can carry two loads.

The guides arrive at Everest base camp ahead of the climbers. Until then, there is no food or shelter for the group. Mountain guides get there with the first porters, days ahead of the climbers, to set up. We go faster. They go slower to acclimate. The guides have to be in better shape than the climbers. The Sirdar keeps track of all the porters, counting them to make sure they all arrive. Once we are all gathered at base camp, we have a puja blessing ceremony, a Buddhist tradition where we ask the mountain to grant us permission to climb it and safe passage.

A monk is on the scene, and an altar is built. You lay some of your foodstuffs, or your equipment, on it for the blessing. It might be an ice axe or a climbing harness. We pray for a safe return and burn juniper. The smoke wafts around us. A prayer pole is raised with prayer flags on it. Flags are all over the camp so that everyone receives the blessing. Each flag represents a prayer, and each flutter of the flag in the wind is another prayer being said. You are blessing the entire area many times over. Everybody wants to be standing under the prayer flags. You look for an auspicious sign, perhaps a raven, or yellow-billed chough. If one of the birds lands on a prayer flag, it is a good omen. They may be attracted to the food or just checking out this scene, but meaning is read into it. The birds alight on the highest point in the vicinity, and that's auspicious because birds represent the spirit of climbers. Donations are made to the monk.

After the delivery of supplies, the herd of porters clears out. Their job is done, and remaining are perhaps twenty-five to forty-five Sherpas who will be with us the rest of the way: carrying loads, assisting climbers, and climbing with us.

The first thing on the agenda as the group begins moving up from base camp is making sure everyone is acclimated. People know climbing Everest is going to be hard work, but I always stress the idea of having fun in this beautiful place. The late mountaineer Alex Lowe said "The best mountaineer in the world is the one having the most fun."

Team members have just had two weeks walking, but they probably need forty-five days at high elevation before they can go to the summit. Additional acclimation is gained is by climbing up and down the mountain between camps ferrying supplies. Base camp is about 17,600 feet. Camp I is a temporary camp, an interim stop where you acclimatize. Camp II is at 21,000 feet. Camp III is between 23,000 and 24,000 feet. There are several groups climbing the mountain at the same time, and not everyone can be at Camp III at the same time. The teams spread out. You start to get multiple uses out of the same shelter with not everyone in your team at the camp at once.

Camp IV is at 26,000 feet. By then you are higher than you would be on almost every other mountain on earth. Sir Edmund Hillary had a Camp V, closer to the summit. With that additional camp, you need more Sherpas up high, more equipment, more everything. High camp does give you a good shot. We do not go up to 26,000 feet until we are acclimated. Time is spent at Camp I and then Camp II. We spend a couple of days there and go back down. We'll rest and recuperate and then we'll do it again. Only we'll spend three or four nights at Camp II that time. When we move up to Camp III we spend a night. That's the equivalent of camping on top of Aconcagua. By then, the climb is probably three weeks in. It can be hard to spend the night at 24,000 feet without oxygen, but we do not encourage people to use oxygen there.

Prayer flags similar to these at Everest Base Camp
pay respect to the mountain and bless the climbers

Shutterstock / Daniel Prudek

What we're trying to do is make the body work really hard and go into overdrive to manufacture more red blood cells to adapt to the elevation. We want the system to freak out, to stress. Then we drop back to Camp II where there is more oxygen. A day later, you drop back to base camp. We go down as far as we can, retreating from the mountain to a village at maybe 11,000 feet. Some climbers will even fly back to Kathmandu, but they risk their summit if weather keeps them from returning to base camp.

One year, in the early 1990s, we went up high, and I came down with a sick climber just before going up to Camp III. I got very tired during the evacuation and re-ascent. After spending the night at 23,000 feet, I went down to base camp to consult a doctor. She said, "You have pneumonia." She said I must go down to a village and recover before I climbed high again. I took the advice seriously and ingested all of the antibiotics she gave me.

I descended to a small village called Deboche and laid out for two weeks. Through creative visualization, rest, recuperation, and good medication, I got healed enough to climb back up. While I was recovering, a whole Russian team came down from the mountain and I asked what they were doing there. They said they always retreated for a rest at lower elevation for a little bit to breathe thicker air before making their summit push. They ate and drank while they were there, too, but they were mainly sucking in more oxygen before they went for the summit. The idea is to go as low as you can, but also stay close to the mountain.

I was not in the best mood. I was pretty somber. I was being paid to guide and be up high with the climbers. Many people develop a severe cough, called the Khumbu cough, which can be a precursor to pulmonary edema or pneumonia. Either one drops your overall resistance and can ruin your climb. I didn't need that, especially when trying to recover already.

The Khumbu cough can easily slide into serious issues. Fluid accumulates in your lungs. You get very weak. Your ability to climb is compromised. As a guess, I would say about sixty percent of the people on a climb get such a cough. They go hard, and they get the infection, and it may lead to edema or pneumonia.

When I lay there recuperating, I tried to build strength in my mind. I did a lot of visualizing of taking the final steps to the summit. To complete the circle, I also visualized me celebrating at base camp after I got down. I pictured those final steps to the summit, feeling how cold the air was, pressure breathing. I visualized all of the components of what it would be like to summit. That gave my psyche something to grab hold of while I was sick. I wanted to fulfill that dream. I was antsy as hell being stuck there.

By the time I regained my strength and departed Deboche, the team had acclimated. The climbers were moving out the day I caught up. I knew the schedule. Camp I was closed. We were on to Camp II and then Camp III. Boom, boom, boom, we were on the move to reach the summit in five or six days.

This was the culmination of the big adventure. It might even be the last big adventure for many team members if they were trying to top out for the Seven Summits. There can be a lot of anxiety amongst the climbers. Everybody is a little bit on edge. There is also the relief that here you are, making the move up. You are no longer training. You are not resting. You are acclimated. You have heard the weather report, and it is positive for the next several days. This is it. It feels right. You throw the dice hoping the weather holds, knowing it can change suddenly.

There are other groups climbing, too. Some are going faster, some slower. Occasionally, there can be bottlenecks where more than one group is trying to travel through an area and has to adjust its pace because of another group. At Camp IV, 26,000 feet, you are in position. This is the last stop before the top. Sometimes, members of the group will assess their physical situation and take themselves out of the running here. They will realize they will risk their lives if they try to push higher. They will admit, "I don't think I can do this."

My first couple of times climbing Everest, the trips were from the North. In 1992 and since, it has been from the South. Not Tibet, Nepal. Coming out of high camp it is fairly flat and open, but you are crossing rocks. You are wearing a big mask for oxygen intake. The bottle is on your back. You're wearing crampons, but the steps are uneven because of the rocky surface. In some ways, you are a little bit like a space man, and that gets to people at times.

You ascend to a dome and then you are on a fixed line. Next on the route is a triangular face, and that is a steep part of the mountain. There are fixed ropes, so people are basically climbing safely. But your pace can be disrupted if you get behind someone else going slower. There is nowhere else to go. You are stuck behind them.

The South Summit is 300 feet below the North Summit, and a half a mile away. You cross what I call the Death Traverse where people can fall off. Sometimes the terrain can be as benign as a sidewalk. But to the right, there is a cornice. If it breaks, the fall is two miles into Tibet. If you go a little bit to the left you're overlooking the Southwest face of Everest, and it is a couple of miles down. Stay on the straight and narrow. The narrow is very narrow.

The Hillary Step is a bottleneck. You can't pass people up there and they can't pass you. The step is too complex. Basically, if you are behind other climbers, you stay there. If someone is attempting to reach the summit in front of you, you are going to have to go at his pace. On the '92 climb, we got stopped and sat around sucking oxygen for an hour-and-a-half. You don't want to be wasting an hour-and-a-half. You want to finish the climb and start the descent before people run out of energy or the weather changes.

The air is so thin, I wrote down what I was supposed to do at the summit on the back of a mitten as a reminder. I still have that mitten. The first instruction was to breathe. Then check the oxygen supply. Then take summit pictures. I wanted to remember to give a congratulatory hug to my climbing partners. The last one said to check the oxygen again and get the hell out of there.

Your self-confidence goes up when you accomplish something like climbing Mount Everest or when you succeed at something like climbing the Seven Summits. That is true for everybody. As a mountain guide, it is even more significant. There really are not that many mountaineering guides who have guided all of the Seven Summits. Doing that gave me a type of confidence that went beyond climbing. It provided me with the confidence to walk into a room and talk to a crowd of people. For a long time, I had low self-esteem. After succeeding at those climbs, I don't feel sub-standard on any level. It still bolsters my self-image. I want to stay in this career for a long time. I know I have something to offer. People want my guidance. They want my experience, my expertise, and my stories. If people want to climb a mountain, they know they can ask my advice, and I can provide good answers because of my background. There are very few people in the world who are real experts on this topic.

Just about everyone in the world knows Mount Everest, even people on the street who have never seen a mountain. I travel all of the time, and after people ask what I do, and I tell them I am a mountain guide, the first thing they ask is, "Did you ever climb Mount Everest?" I reply, "Yeah, ten times." That's when they drop their jaw. Some of them don't even believe me, but it is documented. I can feel the conversation change, and I earn some respect.

The number one thing the average person knows about Mount Everest is that it is the highest mountain. They also think of it as dangerous and wonder how many people get killed on it. When I guide people on Denali, I tell the climbers that going for the summit is probably going to be the hardest thing they do in their lives. Everest is harder. That's why so many people die up there. Thank God I have never lost a client on Everest. Not everybody makes the summit, but no one climbing with us—thank God—has died trying.

If someone comes to me who has never climbed, but is athletic and fit, and asks me what to do to start climbing, I tell them to contact their local climbing club. It might cost $20 in dues a year. Even the flatter parts of the country, like Kansas, has a mountain club. For one thing, it means you will meet people with similar interests. I happened to start climbing in Alaska, so the first thing I did was get involved with the Mountaineering Club of Alaska.

When you get connected to people who have experience, you can learn technique and safe methods. Even if there are local politics in the group, there are kernels and nuggets of knowledge to take away. Older climbers especially are glad to share. They have a wealth of information. As a guide, I get paid to share information all of the time. But I also get emails asking me about the quality of boots and if certain clothing will be warm enough on cold-weather climbs. I'm an advocate for going with the warmest boots you can get.

Also, I tell people if they want to take guided trips, start low with an easier mountain. Mount Rainier, outside of Seattle, is more than 14,000 feet high, you need crampon and rope training, and you cross crevasses. It also doesn't cost nearly as much as an overseas trip. See if you still like doing it after a climb like that. After you have been spanked by the weather a few times or fallen into a crevasse, see where your head is at. If you don't like mountaineering anymore, you haven't spent much money, and you haven't wasted a lot of time. Chances are you haven't risked your life. If you want to take on more, sign up for a bigger trip. Kilimanjaro is easier to do than Denali or Everest.

On Rainier, you can get so many nasty conditions. It is a very good training ground. Many Pacific Northwest guides go on to do Everest. But it is still only 14,000 feet high. You're probably not going to get altitude sickness or die from it. Don't jump into things by saying, "I'm going to Aconcagua next week." You can get hurt. You don't know enough. I love to see people who want to climb take a shot at medium height mountains. They're getting experience.

Anyone who starts out by planning to climb the Seven Summits all in one year, well, they can kiss their job goodbye, kiss their family goodbye. They must stay acclimated for the entire year. They can't stray from training at all. They have to climb other mountains in-between the continental high ones. But chances are they are not going to succeed in one year. I think completion of my first set of the Seven Summits took me more than ten years.

Climbing the Seven Summits makes the most sense if you climb them sequentially, easiest to hardest. Work your way up. Kilimanjaro is a good place to start. Then go to Elbrus. If you go to Vinson, hop over to Aconcagua since you are in the Southern Hemisphere. Then go to Kosciuszko and Carstensz while you are in that neck of the woods. That's when you get really committed to the tough ones: Denali and Everest.

There are other big mountains in the Himalayas that are not as high as Everest and don't cost as much to try. You find out if you can really deal with altitude. You also find out if your boss or your wife can handle you taking off for forty-five days. She might say, "Forty-five days, what the hell?" And Everest is more like a two-month commitment, even longer when training is accounted for.

If you are going to try to climb Mount Everest, you want to be in the best shape of your life. It can be life-threatening, so you must give it your best. You reap what you sow. The absolute worst things can happen to the best-prepared people. Everest doesn't discriminate.

The best-known tragedy on Everest occurred in 1996 when the weather blew in and battered climbing groups that stayed up high or on the summit longer than planned. Eight people died, including famous guides Rob Hall of New Zealand and Scott Fischer of the United States.

The main climbing season on Everest is in the spring, around the same time as the main climbing season on Denali. That year, I was guiding on Denali and was with my good friend Marty Raney when we heard what was happening on Everest. A fellow known as Makalu Gau, who was with Scott Fischer when he died—and nearly died himself— came to Alaska for frostbite treatment. The news was going worldwide in newspapers and television broadcasts, and as friends of Scott, we wanted to know how he died. Marty and I visited Makalu in the hospital, and he told us what happened. He lay there in his hospital bed with a spoon taped to one hand and a fork taped to the other, feeding himself that way because of the frostbite.

Makalu seemed a bit removed from reality. He made the summit of Everest, watched his buddy die, suffered severe frostbite, but pledged he was going back to the Himalayas to climb all of the other 8,000-meter peaks. He was not facing the frightening consequences of how the frostbite might screw him up for life.

Actually, Makalu couldn't really give us the complete picture. We picked his brain, but there were a lot of rumors swirling that did not all match up. Many books have been written about that tragedy. Movies were made. Some of the best guides in the world were there and they died. If you are a guide you call that all bad publicity. But as the old saw goes, even bad publicity is publicity and amazingly, after the dust settled, more people wanted to climb Everest. That caught me off-guard. Alpine Ascents called me and said, "The phone is ringing off the hook." They told me climbers were calling left and right wanting to do Everest. I didn't expect that at all; I had expected a lull. I was seasonally guiding on Denali, working on the North Slope on the communications towers and trying to raise a kid. The word got out that (duh) Everest was dangerous, but you could hire a guide to help you climb it. It was a great opportunity to follow my passion. I stopped climbing towers and started climbing mountains full-time.

These climbers were mostly well-off people. They were doctors, businessmen, software writers, people who made the grade in society and now they wanted the challenge of making the grade in the wilderness. They had the time, money and drive to go and try it. Our climbers were for the most part very successful people. They knew the value of preparation and persistence. They knew how to set goals, train hard, and learn new skills, and were willing to work. I learned as much from them as they did from me. This has been one big reason I have kept guiding for so long: I really dig the people I'm sharing time with in the mountains.

As perverse as it may seem, the tragedy of 1996 did not deter climbers, it motivated them to become high altitude mountaineers. The result was that it ended up being the Golden Age of westerners guiding in the Himalayas. However, now we seem to be in a transitional phase. The Sherpas will take over Everest guiding slowly. They're stronger on the mountain than we are, and they're going to be working near home. They will also work for a lot less than a western guide will. As their climbing and language skills develop, so will their capability to control their own destinies.

I am fortunate to have climbed Everest ten times. That would not have been possible without the help of my Sherpa friends. Some of them have made the summit twenty times, an amazing accomplishment. A few years ago, I decided ten times was enough for me. That was plenty. Plus, it was a nice round number. I figured so much time in the Death Zone was bound to be killing off brain cells, and Lord knows I need all of the ones I have. That's when I began guiding other Himalayan peaks.

In 2014, I was in the Himalayas, had just led a trekking group to Everest base camp and departed to return to Kathmandu when an ice avalanche struck, killing sixteen Sherpas who were on the mountain carrying the first loads of the season. Three of the bodies were never recovered. A year later, an earthquake of 7.8 magnitude killed more than 9,000 people in Nepal and nineteen more people at base camp while injuring sixty-one.

I had just left the area in 2014 when the Sherpa guides were killed in the Khumbu Icefall at about 19,000 feet. I knew Sherpas who died, one was a very dear friend named Ang Tsering who worked with me on Everest for eighteen years. Four Sherpas were from the Alpine Ascents team. Our trekking group said good luck and a few days later, four of those people were dead.

Due to whatever reason—God sneezing, or global warming—a big chunk of ice dropped. It does that from time to time. We don't like going through that area for that reason. When I pass through there, I am looking up. I have another friend, still living, who was climbing there once and was blown into a crevasse by an avalanche. They only found the boots of a Sherpa who was with him. They don't even know where his body ended up. That friend was lucky. He took cover. I know he still climbs, but I haven't seen him in Nepal since. That kind of thing changes your life. We know ice collapses every year. Hopefully, it doesn't happen when we are there. Unfortunately, this time people were there, and there was a big traffic jam underneath the dangerous slope.

The following year, when the earthquake roared through base camp, I had just met one of the base camp managers before heading back to Lukla. A beautiful woman, a medical officer, and four days later she was crushed. Things are transient in life, but being in the mountains ups the ante a bit. You are much closer to the edge. You would never think of people being killed at base camp and yet, bam, they were dead. The earthquake triggered things and took down an unusually large serac that turned into a huge avalanche and tore through base camp with the force of a bomb. I had another friend there that was thrown 150 feet. She doesn't even know how she survived it. She was a doctor, and she got right back up and began treating people.

Avalanches are probably the number one killers of my friends in the mountains, from Alex Lowe, a well-known climber who died on Shishapangma, a 26,335-foot mountain in China, to a girl I used to dance with who was taking an avalanche course when she was buried. At lunch, she went out to ski a few turns with some of the other students. She and all of the rescuers had avalanche training, but she got buried, and by the time people got her out, she was dead. You have to make a note of it. You have to learn from that. I learned to stay away from skiing steep, deep stuff. Climbing and avalanches go hand-in-hand. A couple of years ago, a guide I knew and his son were in the Himalayas. They just disappeared. Nobody really knows what happened to them. They just didn't come back from the trip. More than likely, they died in an avalanche. Another couple I knew got hit on K-2. She made it, he didn't.

He was right behind her and an avalanche took him out. They were in the wrong place at the wrong time, but sometimes you have to go through the wrong place to get to the right place.

Going back to Ray Genet on Everest in 1979, he died of exposure at around 28,000 feet. He was used to spending the night out high on Denali, but Denali is much shorter. He was guiding a woman, and they stopped to spend the night and spent the rest of their lives.

You hate to lose people. These are friends, not just names. Boom, there goes another really good climber. You are emotionally affected, but when I hear of something happening to somebody, I try to learn from the accident. You have a loss, but you'd better have a gain. People take unnecessary chances. I have fun in the mountains, but I don't have to try to have fun right over the edge. Sometimes people want things they can't have. Gravity never sleeps. Snow cornices come down eventually. Sure, you can avoid avalanches altogether by going to the beach, but I love mountains. I try to take educated guesses and make educated decisions. I like ridges better than gullies for a reason.

People close to me never try to talk me out of returning to the mountains, but I have had close calls on Everest several times. I have had pneumonia three times, and I was in an avalanche on the north side that half-buried me. That was close. You do pause to think about the situations that might have killed you, and begin thinking differently about Everest: "Let it be."

When I was younger, I didn't think I'd live to be thirty because of my lifestyle. But I did make it to thirty, forty, fifty, and beyond sixty. I've doubled my life expectancy. I'm getting more conservative; I'm not going as close to that edge. I have more of a wait-and-see outlook. Still, statistically, the longer you're a mountain guide and going to these high and potentially risky places, the greater the chance of something happening. Whether I'm mellowing out or wising up, something is making me more conservative in my middle age. Perhaps it is just reduced testosterone production, but I'd rather think it is accumulated wisdom.

Maybe, going way back to what Brad Washburn told me, "Do something really difficult when you're young and then live a long time." That's what I'm doing. That's how you get the laurels. If you do a lot of risky things, maybe you have to dial it back a bit. The great mountaineer Mark Twight, who undertook many extreme climbs, talked of prioritizing which risks were most rewarding and curtailing the extraneous ones.

Maybe I'm just luckier than my friends. When you lose a dozen friends to avalanches and another dozen to bad judgment, miscalculations, falls, and pulmonary edema, I think you get a bit more philosophical. You also gain a bit more knowledge and think, "OK, reel it back in."

I don't process emotions well, and it affected me deeply in 1996 when Rob Hall and Scott Fischer died. Scott was a friend, as was Rob. I worked with them and had great respect for them. These were big, strong climbers on Everest, and they died. There was a message there. You don't necessarily want to be going to the edge too often. Don't get complacent, smug, or let your ego make decisions for you. Anything can go wrong. They were guiding on a house of cards that crumbled in one storm.

The last time I climbed Everest was 2013. It was a very successful trip. The following year, the Sherpas died in the Icefall. Then the earthquake rumbled through base camp and a lot more people died. I had already decided not to guide Everest anymore and led base camp treks both of those years. And I still just barely missed being caught up in the tragedies on the mountain.

So I have been very fortunate to climb Mount Everest ten times and to be able to walk away with my health and love for the Himalayas intact.

DENALI

For most of its time in the spotlight, from early sightings through early climbing, until well into the 2000s, the tallest mountain in North America was called Mount McKinley. Although for decades Alaskans preferred the name Denali, the native description of the 20,310-foot peak, the English name of McKinley stuck.

Mount McKinley was named after President William McKinley by a back-country prospector in 1896, and was formally adopted as the name in 1917 when Mount McKinley National Park was created by the National Park Service. It was an honorific since McKinley never went near Alaska and certainly had no history with the mountain. Over the century following his death, the Congressmen who represented his Ohio district zealously guarded this portion of his legacy. Periodically, there would be stronger movements to rename the peak Denali. Ebbing and flowing over time, they never carried the necessary weight to lead to a change.

In Alaska, one was just as likely to hear usage of Denali as McKinley, even though the designation was unofficial. The meaning of Denali appealed to all: "The Great One" or "The High One."

During the summer of 2015, President Barack Obama wielded the executive authority of the White House to change the official name of the admired mountain to Denali. For most, it was surprise news, and in Alaska, it was definitely welcome news. The announcement came on the eve of the president's visit to Alaska.

In recent years, about 1,200 people annually attempt to climb Denali with a success rate of about fifty percent. An estimated 32,000 climbers have tried to reach the top and about 100 have died trying.

Vern Tejas owns the distinction of being the first person to make a successful solo climb of Denali in winter. He also has the most ascents with fifty-seven.

After first viewing Denali (as he has always called it) before his twentieth birthday and being awed by the peak, the mountain became a huge part of his life and only rarely has a May-to-July climbing season passed without his making a visit to the summit.

When I first climbed and began guiding on Denali, I had no idea it was going to be my career. The solo winter ascent opened up opportunities, and then the climbing world became fascinated by the Seven Summits. To climb the Seven Summits, you must climb Denali. So I became a guide in demand. I knew the mountain, and I got to know it better and better from repeat ascents.

The weather can be anything on Denali. You can run into minus-forty temperatures, high winds, and terrific storms, but I also believe climate change is altering the picture. If you are up there often enough, you are still going to get whacked some of the time. The main climbing season up the West Buttress route, the one where we guide our climbers, is primarily May to July, with some starts in April. I wonder if we will be climbing in March if it keeps warming up.

The West Buttress route was established by Brad Washburn in 1951. He was a brilliant aerial photographer, and he knew it was actually the best and easiest route to the top even though when he went to climb it that year, everyone said it was impossible and he was going to die trying.

It actually should be called the Washburn Route. He defied the impossible and gave us a great route. If he had not, a lot fewer people would have made the summit, and a lot more people would have gotten hurt trying.

The last couple of years, I have not always worn my warmest clothing to go to the summit. I haven't worn a down suit on top for several years. I still have it with me. I wear it sitting around camps. I just wear finger gloves, not my warmest mittens. I wear two shirts and a jacket, but not the down suit to climb in because it is too warm. Minus-forty is head-scratching cold, and I remember a Summer Solstice Day, June 21, some thirty years ago when it was that cold. But that has not happened recently.

Such change is noticeable in all of these places where I climb. The snow is melting more, exposing rocks, and in some cases taking down big hanging glaciers. It is like that on Denali, in the Himalayas, on the Matterhorn. Things are falling apart. Places that are only held together by ice are melting and freeing rocks. They can fall on you. People are getting killed by these circumstances. The glaciers on top of Kilimanjaro melting away might have only twenty years before they are gone. It still snows near the top, but it goes away in a day. It's not permanent. In South America, it's the same thing. Where there used to be ice fields, there are pocket glaciers here and there.

Denali

In Indonesia, where climbers go for Carstensz Pyramid, the snow melt is so extreme that it's changing the heights of the triple-summit peak. The snow is melting so fast on top that people are no longer sure which one is the second-highest peak and which one is the third.

The world is warming up. I don't care if it's manmade or God-made. If you don't get out of the way, you can get hurt. The boom in climbing has continued since 1996, although I don't know for how much longer. But even on Denali and Everest, fewer people are getting frostbitten, getting hypothermia, or freezing to death.

In my early days on Denali, one of my trademarks was a big, bushy beard. I started growing it in high school and it made me recognizable. I finally had to shave it because of a job where I had to wear an air mask. Then I was working on oil platforms, and hydrogen sulfide was a potential threat so nobody was supposed to grow one. I had to cut it off so my mask would be air tight. It took me several days to get used to not having it. My first reaction was that I didn't like being told what to do. But some gray was coming in, and somebody said I looked ten years younger. I still shave my head. I've been doing that for a long time. Sometimes people think I'm on medicine for cancer and lost my hair. Ultimately, I'd rather look crazy than old, so I've kept shaving. It worked with girls, at least for a while. Now I'm old and crazy.

Early in my days on Denali, I was on a climb of the Northwest Buttress with three other guys. One turned back and was accompanied by his friend. Two of us continued to the top. We climbed west of the top of the Kahiltna Glacier, dropped over the pass, and crossed the Peters Glacier to the right-hand side of the Wickersham Wall. The Wickersham Wall was the site I fell in love with when I first saw Denali, so I had come full circle to be climbing on it. Others, including Heinrich Harrer, had made the first ascent of the Northwest Buttress route, but we went to the true South Summit. I'm very proud of that first full ascent. A lot of people don't know it ever happened, or care, but it is important to me.

At base camp, I ran into a strong climber named Marty Schmidt, and although it was not planned, he asked if I wanted to climb the Cassin Ridge. We had extra food and fuel because some people had left the mountain. I was getting ready to fly out and was supposed to rendezvous with my girlfriend of the time. Although she was beautiful, he talked me into it. I confess he did not have to twist my arm too hard. The Cassin is a phenomenal climb, and I was acclimated. We skied over to the Northeast Fork, the area is sometimes called the Valley of Death because so many people have been buried in avalanches there and never found.

There are hanging glaciers on both sides, and when they calve, they tend to fill the whole valley.

One day later, I was putting a belay stance into the seventy-degree slope of the Japanese gully. I chopped a ledge for my feet to stand on and was almost finished placing an ice screw, which I would then clip into, when the ledge broke away. The one screw I had placed halfway up the pitch actually arrested my fall. When my vision finally cleared, I was hanging upside down looking at Marty. He was five feet away, frantically turning in a screw. Apparently he had pulled his belay anchor anticipating I was just about off belay. Then I fell. That jump of the gun could have killed us both if that one remaining screw I was dangling from had popped when I dropped. Chastened, we climbed on.

We hauled ourselves up and bivouacked that night. Marty took the outside and I lay on the inside of a ledge about three feet wide. Don't roll over in your sleep and don't nudge your buddy. Above that, it was a series of mixed rock and ice, but I was still in bunny boots from the other climb and they are quite useless for technical climbing. They were warm, though. However, being made out of rubber, they offered no support. You can't lean your lower leg forward to rest on the cuff of the boot, so you hold your weight with your calf muscles.

I was putting all of my weight, including the pack on my back, on my calves, and they were starting to burn. Marty wanted to do a ninety-degree pitch. It was dead vertical. The snow had melted on the rocks and run down, turning things into a vertical waterfall. Marty wanted pictures. I said I would take them, but he had to lead because I definitely couldn't while wearing bunny boots. He pulled off the climbing moves and belayed me up with a rope.

My legs were on fire before I got up to him, ever thankful for the belay. The beauty of following is safety. It's not safe for the leader. That's the challenge of leading. If something goes wrong and you fall, you're going to see God in the process. It's going to be exciting. I was on a snug rope, so if I fell it would only be like five feet. I did not fall, but boy, my calves were screaming at me.

I took the camera out, shot a picture, and put it back inside my jacket to keep it warm, and did it again. Though I took a mess of photos of Marty on the crux, they were rather disappointing. Putting the cold camera in my warm jacket was a bad idea. Condensation never rests.

In those days, there was a hanging glacier on the Cassin. I was leading across it when I saw this oak dowel sticking up out of the blue ice. Italian Riccardo Cassin and his partners made the first ascent of the Cassin Ridge (definitely a difficult route) in 1961. It was amazing to think they may have placed this archaic anchor. I thought it had been there for thirty-something years. However, it was free protection, so I clipped my rope to it as I climbed past. No more than two steps later one of my boots squirmed out of the crampon. Bunny boots are so flexible that they are known to do that. Maybe that is what happened to Naomi on Denali Pass. It was quite spooky, but there was this old dowel I could rely on to help put my crampon back on. *Grazie*, Riccardo.

We continued our climb and eventually topped out. It was really blowing at the top of the ridge. All we could do was make camp. Over the next few days, we got three or four feet of snow. The wind whipped at us. Marty had chosen a camping place in the shadow of a serac that helped protect us. It was just the right angle so our tent did not get buried. Meanwhile, Marty was having trouble with a frostbitten toe that was really blistered up. We really needed to go down, but we were so close to the summit. It was only about forty-five minutes away. We were in good shape with little gear, so we took a shot at it. But we got hammered by the wind and turned back. On the fourth day, it was quiet. We ran up and tagged the summit. We were really booking it. Then we ran back to our camp, scooped up our stuff and started down.

The storm had been so fierce that no one else was on the upper mountain. There was no trail. We had to plow our own path. We changed our route over to Fantasy Ridge so we didn't start an avalanche. We were going down, so we had gravity on our side. But there was deep snow. It was up to our waists and we had big packs on. We descended all of the way to 15,000 feet, to the bottom of the head wall with its fixed ropes, before we saw anyone else headed up. It was only then that I started thinking maybe we wouldn't get caught and die in an avalanche. I got home about a week-and-a-half late for my date with my girlfriend.

A little later, after she started to talk to me again, Marty, our girlfriends, and I went down to the Delaney Park Strip in downtown Anchorage for a kite day. We were just laying around on the grass watching all of the kites in the air. This little boy, about seven years old, was guiding his kite. He kept backing up without looking anywhere but the sky—you could not have choreographed this better—he backed up and stepped right on Marty's bad toe really hard. Marty screamed. The frostbite blister exploded. There was pus and blood everywhere. If his girlfriend wasn't there, I think Marty would have throttled the kid. He was in excruciating pain, but he lived through it and kept all his toes. The kid was probably scarred for life.

One year, I decided I wanted to see if I could do a speed ascent of Denali on my own. Someone had set a record. They did it round-trip from the Kahiltna Glacier to the top and back in around twenty-three hours, with about fifteen hours, twenty minutes of it spent going up. I just wanted to see if I could do it faster. Alex Lowe had been on pace to break it once, but he stopped to carry an injured climber down, and that slowed him.

The first time I tried it, I got to the top in fifteen hours, forty minutes, about twenty minutes behind the record. I passed some National Park Service rangers when I was running, and they seemed a little resentful that I was flying past them. They wanted to know what I was doing and I did not want to stop for a chat. I was trying to make time. They change the rules about climbing permits all of the time, and I made sure I was legal and acquired a permit for this solo.

However, on the way down, a snowstorm came in and I could barely find the 14,200-foot camp. By then, I was worried about avalanches because so much new snow had come down. I had to go over to the ranger tent and ask, "Uh, you guys got a spare sleeping bag?" Fortunately, they were very understanding. Another guided group had some extra food. My original goal had been to sled all of the way down to base camp. Now it was just to survive. It never pays to get too smug in the mountains.

I tried it another time with a buddy from Hypoxico, the makers of special tents you can sleep in for altitude training. You can set it up at home, or in a hotel room while you're traveling, and it will deprive you of oxygen so that you are training in thinner air while you are sleeping at sea level. My friend Brian lived in New York City and I was impressed how strong he was at altitude. You breathe more nitrogen and the oxygen is reduced in those tents. There is a canopy over it and a hose running inside. We tried speed climbs twice and both times we had issues that interfered with going fast. The second time we skied down from 14,000 feet. We just ripped it and had a great time. Best run of my life. The snow was perfect. But my speed ascent attempts never really paid off. Eventually, the record got faster and faster, beyond anything I could have come close to, and I was thinking that yes, eventually you do slow down when you get older. Though none of my speed attempts broke records, I learned I could cover the thirteen miles and 13,000 feet pretty fast. It did let me know what I was capable of doing.

Although the main guiding season on the West Buttress is pretty much May through July, given my winter ascent and guiding trips on the edges of the season, I have been on Denali eight different months of the year. I've never been there in October, November, December, or January. I've been there in September, but only leaving the mountain. Mostly, the severe weather dictates you not be there in the deep winter months. And you don't want to climb later in the summer when twenty-four hours of daylight has been beating down and causing melting. Snow bridges melt, crevasses open up, seracs slump and fall. The snow gets saturated with water and doesn't hold together well. Being there in August was doubtful, but lately, August weather has moved into July. July has warmed up. Just a couple of years ago, it was so warm in June we had people on the climb dropping into holes.

There are also more rocks falling down, especially in the Windy Corner area. A couple of climbs ago, we were at 14,200 feet, and a group was coming behind us. We heard some noise and looked down the ridge. It seemed as if a bunch of big mining trucks had dumped a load of rocks down the face; there were tons of rock. I got on a satellite phone and we alerted the Park Service about what happened. Rangers took a helicopter up to look at the situation. Things that had been in a deep freeze for 10,000 years were thawing. A few years earlier, rock just let loose and killed a couple of guys at Windy Corner.

From a distance, you can also see water on top of the glaciers, blue water forming lakes or ponds. For a while, they were at 5,000 feet. Now they are at 6,500 feet. More recently I have seen them up past Mount Francis. That's another half-mile higher. I've been going there for thirty-nine years, so I can see changes. I see rocks fall. I see the water ponds moving higher on the glaciers. In 1989, when I went to the top of Denali as part of a measuring program for Dr. Bradford Washburn, we stuck a pole on the summit as a benchmark. I always thought someone would steal it, but no one did. For years it was buried in snow, but for the last couple of years, it's been sticking out. More than a foot of snow has disappeared. At 17,200 feet, there's more rock exposed. There's less snow higher on Denali.

Since I have seniority, I can pick and choose when I want to guide on Denali. For a long time my sweet spot was June. I wanted to be up there for the Summer Solstice on the longest day of the year. We had lots of sun and it felt good. But over the last ten years, it has been getting warmer and warmer in June. When it was minus-forty in June, you didn't see melting snow bridges.

My definition of warmer is minus-twenty. I do wear a lighter wardrobe. If you are moving, you are not going to be cold. You don't want to hang out at the summit for an hour dressed lighter at minus-twenty. You will get cold. In my lifetime, that temperature difference is a huge amount of change. Glaciologists have said we are going to see more crevasses open up on the Kahiltna Glacier. It will no longer be just a straight ski hill. There is one crevasse there I used to see periodically over the years. Now it's open every year and is bigger. I worry about it because it could actually swallow a guy pulling a supply sled.

This does not mean climbing on Denali is going to come to an end. Climbers adapt. If there is a wide crevasse, they will just put a ladder across it. There will be more danger from falling rock. Also, if the snow cover has melted, it will be tougher to dig in and make a snow shelter in a storm. More snow bridges will melt during the earlier part of the season. Climbers will take up the challenge and find a way to get through it all. But worldwide, what are we doing about it? We are the cause of it. I don't care what the politicians say. This is happening all over the world.

I have seen photographs that compare the same places on terrain between fifty and seventy-five years ago and the present. You can see the stark changes. Hundreds of feet of ice fields have disappeared in a generation. What happens when there is no more water coming out of the Himalayas? There are three billion people who count on that to water their crops and to drink. The ocean waters are rising, and there is going to be a collision in the middle. We have to wake up as a species and realize we are changing the planet. We're going to be overwhelmed by the lack of water where we need it, and a profusion of water where we don't want it. There will be a sandwich between drought and flooding. That's not a good combination. We've got to figure out something. Hopefully, the light goes on. We have changed the world so much, that now we have to change.

Denali can still be a great adventure for people. There are so many known quantities in the world. You go to the right school, get the right job, punch the clock, get your paycheck, watch your TV. In the mountains, so many things are weather-dependent. I think sailors face some of the same factors of not being in control, of facing unpredictable weather conditions. The environment dictates if you have success on whatever mission you undertake. When you are no longer in control is when the adventure begins. Things happen that you didn't count on. I cannot make dreams come true, but I can help. I am a facilitator. I can make it more fun, and I can help take some of the risk out of the adventure. I promote the camaraderie, tell the jokes, play the harmonica, and make sure you get to enjoy the vistas. I try to settle the soul down a little bit.

In my earlier days on Denali, I played the fiddle. Marty Raney and I made music together. We put together a CD called *Strum It from the Summit*. That was great fun. We are one of the finest glacier bands in the world if you are planning a mountain wedding.

Many people are basically risk adverse, but they still want to do things. Denali is the big mountain with the reputation, but it is actually more difficult to climb Mount Foraker and Mount Hunter in the Alaska Range. Foraker stands 17,400 feet high. Its native name is Sultana, and it is referred to as Denali's wife. Hunter is smaller yet, but very demanding at 14,573 feet. Up close, they both look forbidding to a climber. Some climbers take a look at them and go, "Maybe I'll get back on the plane." Really. I've seen it happen on three occasions. It's intimidating. I saw a soloist turn back right away saying, "I'm in way over my head. There's too much risk here for me to be comfortable." There's nothing like the reality of a mile-and-a-half vertical mountain towering over your head to put things in perspective. All of a sudden, you seem really, really, really small.

Why go to the mountains? I go for the sheer joy of it; that's what keeps me going back. There's a delicate balance between risk and reward, and that determines how you choose to live your life.

You can say Denali is a sort of my specialty because I have climbed it more than anyone else. Trips are planned for three weeks, but you can adjust a little. When we are flown into the Kahiltna Glacier, we are at 7,200 feet. Then we camp at 8,200, 9,500, 11,200, 14,200, 17,200, and then at Denali Pass at 18,200 feet. The first day, I typically don't take the group all the way to 8,200. I advance to a half camp, about three miles, to 7,800, because otherwise it would be five miles and the climbers would be hurting. That way their bodies are not overwhelmed by the altitude right away. I buy an extra day of acclimating. I do a skill review. I go over rope knots, anchors, and pulley systems. We learn how to place anchors, set up tents, take down tents, demonstrate how to pack a sled and set it up so it is efficient and won't flip over. We've got a day to do all kinds of things. From Half Camp to Camp I at 8,200 feet, it's a short and easy haul.

My Camp II is higher, at 9,500 or so because it is less likely to be hit by storms than the regular Camp II. I'd also rather have my group camp away from a large number of people. It helps me focus on my team. We also get one additional day of acclimating. We spend two days at 11,200. Once you are above 10,200, you are no longer on the Kahiltna Glacier and have turned onto the West Buttress. The spot at 13,500 would be a great place to camp, except that is Windy Corner, the windiest place on the mountain. A big jump day is between 11,200 and 14,200, a 3,000-foot elevation gain. The area at 14,200 is a big camping area and it is flat. It is usually protected, but on a 2016 trip we had eighty miles per hour winds through there. That's the biggest camp. There are rangers and a weather station, plus a heliport. People hang there. Once, I think an Air Force team was there for eleven days because of storms. That is way, way too long. Below 14,200 is the lower mountain. Above it, all of the difficulties loom. That camp is right about as high as the other tall mountains in the rest of the United States.

Spots above there include the Autobahn, the Football Field, which I take credit for naming some thirty years ago, and Washburn's Thumb. Pig Hill is the last place before you get onto the summit ridge. Guide Nick Parker called it that. That's because it is such a pig to get up. You just suck it up. Most people go for the summit from the 17,200-foot high camp. Going up from 14,200, gaining 6,000 feet in one day, is just too much for most climbers. The old-style way of trying for the summit was to get up at 3 a.m. and go for it. Not me. My groups start at 10 a.m. now. The sun is up, and it is not as cold.

There is more room at the summit than on many mountains. It's like a group of rooftops put together. It is not a steep angle. You can take off the ropes and walk around, although you've got to stay away from the South Face. You can walk twenty or thirty feet in most directions. Long ago, I installed a brass disc benchmark that reads "U.S. Geological Survey." It doesn't say it is the tallest point in North America. There is no elevation number on it, either. At the time, the height was referred to as 20,320 feet, but it has been changed to 20,310. The top of the mountain is right where it has always been. At one point people left mementoes at the top. Dolls, trinkets, belt buckles, and stuff like that piled up at the summit. Climbers did the same thing at the tops of other mountains. But I think the Park Service cleaned it all out on Denali. And I think somebody does that on other mountains, too. There used to be a trip log on Vinson and when I guided a group up there I put everybody's name in it. Somebody decided to take personal responsibility to remove the historic "trash." Something was lost and something was gained. There are ashes on summits, too. I have taken people's ashes to mountain tops.

I would like to spend more time on Denali's summit, although often it is a fifteen-minute reward for a three-week trip. But it can also be freezing and other groups might be edging their way in. I'd like to be able to hang out—it always feels like too short of a stay—but you have to move on.

Vern Tejas

The Summit Ridge of Denali has become a familiar place for Tejas

The most dangerous part of the climb is often the descent because you are exhausted. People move a little faster and they get sloppy and forget to breathe. If your boot squirms out of your crampon, that can present a problem, especially on a downward slope. You can fall a thousand feet off the Autobahn. You can usually survive frostbite, but not a fall like that. We don't take as many breaks on the way down. You are trying to get to lower altitude and avoid any brewing storms.

I do take a break before descending the Autobahn because that is the place most likely for people to slip. I make them eat and drink. Then I slow things down and give a lecture about self-arrest use of ice axes. I want people fully energized, not gasping for air. We remind our climbers that a lot of people have died there. We clip into fixed ropes for safety. Typically, I prefer moving quickly on the descent, but for that part it's worth dialing it back.

Sometimes at the very end of the descent back to base camp, hauling two sleds, I am pulling 100 pounds. You traverse a short uphill stretch, Heartbreak Hill. In 2016, I was pulling hard and I was tired. I told myself I was getting old because I was really feeling it. But I have been saying that since my twenties. I'm not going to admit my age may finally be catching up to me. But man, I could never remember working so hard up that hill. Turned out when I flipped over one sled, there was a rope caught underneath it. I was pulling the sled with the brake on. It was like pulling a truck all the way up the final hill.

Decades ago, there was a scientific expedition studying cosmic rays, and they needed lead bricks as filters. Nobody in their right mind is going to carry lead bricks up Denali. So they dropped them by parachute. On one of my climbs at 18,200 feet, I saw a bright outline of cloth under the snow. The nylon parachute was so frayed that it broke apart in my hands. Beneath it was a cache of lead bricks. I thought it was nuts. There were some tools there like screwdrivers and saws as well. The cache may have been dropped in 1932, or in 1947, on one of Brad's climbs. I think it was from the 1932 expedition because those guys died lower on the mountain on their climb and never made it to the bricks. I thought one brick weighed twenty pounds, but one guy in our group wanted one for a souvenir and put it in his pack. We were making a long traverse of the mountain. Days later, we were cutting across the mushy tundra, and he couldn't carry it anymore. Somewhere out there on the tundra near the Muldrow Glacier is a lead brick lost to history.

About eleven years later, I was on another climb where some guys from Alaska Pacific University were doing some altitude measuring. While we were up there, I asked if they wanted to see a scientific cache and I took them to the bricks and tools. I buried a saw in the area just in case some day I needed one to cut snow blocks in a storm up there. One of the guys went, "A lead brick. Cool. I'm going to keep it." I said not to do it and definitely not to leave it along the way. At least we were not on a traverse, so our descent was going to be much shorter. "I'll carry it all of the way," he promised. "I've got it covered." A few days later, I was paragliding off the edge at 17,200 feet, and they were to carry my pack down since I couldn't fly with it. Flying is why I went. They agreed to carry my stuff if I flew. I did fly and then was way below them waiting. And waiting. Hours passed. I was starting to get cold and I was wondering why it was taking them so long to pack up and get down to 14,200. I started walking back up to meet them. I went up 500 feet. Nothing.

I kept going. Finally I was almost at 17,000 feet when I met them. They said they made breakfast and then had crampon problems so they were delayed. But now, as long as I was there I could help carry stuff down, they said, so I inherited a sled to lower down. As soon as we started going I couldn't believe how heavy it was. I was fighting with it all of the way. They were moving faster than me. The sled was practically pulling me over. They got thirty minutes ahead of me. I clipped the sled to the fixed line thinking I could catch up fast on the steep downhill. I let it go and the sled zipped down to the next anchor and blew up. Stuff flew all out of the sled over the place. There was a down snowsuit and I watched it roll down the hill like a medicine ball. It kept right on going like a pool ball into the corner pocket of a crevasse.

There was crap all over the mountain. The guys ahead of me didn't even notice. I was having a bitch of a time. They were going along, dum dee dum. "Hey, I could use a little help up here, boys." They had to see me. I was picking up parts, tent poles, the food bags. I was going along and saw this hole in the snow. I stuck my hand into it and it was that damned lead brick. That's what unbalanced the sled and tore it apart. The contents vomited themselves all over the snow. I was pissed off. I picked up everything, including the lead brick, and repacked the sled. When I got down the next camp, I let them have it. I also made the lead brick guy go back up with me, go into the crevasse and fish out the down suit. And I made that guy carry the brick the rest of the way.

When we got down, the calculations were studied. We revealed the new height of Denali over dinner. Brad Washburn was there and very pleased to hear our measurements were so close to what he calculated in the 1940s. The brick guy whipped it out asked Brad to autograph it.

At this stage of my guiding career, I do one trip a year on Denali. That is plenty. Of nine climbers on a recent trip, five of them had requested me personally as their guide. They either knew me or my reputation. Two of the guys signed up with me specifically because they knew I would be slow and deliberate on the slopes. They felt that was the approach they needed. The other four climbers, I suspect, were just plain lucky.

I have had people who really study the situation and want to invest in hiring the best guide for Denali. They researched it and chose me. I'm honored they thought that way. Somewhere along the way, I became determined to become the best high-altitude mountain guide. I'm pretty close to where I want to be. I've done each of the Seven Summits at least ten times, most of them many times more, and no one else is really in that category. It's a self-defined niche for me. I'm happy with it. I want to be known as a quality guide who can get you where you want to go and have fun doing it.

THE FUTURE

More than a decade ago, Vern Tejas suggested that his days of guiding many of the world's tallest peaks might be nearing an end. He said perhaps he would build his own guiding company and supervise guides that traveled to the same mountains he was so familiar with. However, he never pulled the trigger on that venture.

Instead, he kept climbing the Seven Summits and leading climbers to the tops of the Seven Summits. Time kept passing and Tejas kept up the arduous task. He never seemed to age, retaining his fitness into his sixties, long past the time many guides give up the adventurous lifestyle. He never found his way to a desk job, because even being the head of an adventure company was more likely to entail paperwork than adventures. He seems at peace with his decision to avoid the world's 8,000-meter peaks—with one possible exception down the road.

Stoking his competitive nature, Tejas appeared on reality TV shows of an adventurous nature, sometimes with teams of Alaskans, sometimes as a solo act. If he has cut back on guiding Mount Everest, he still maintains a seasonal annual schedule so that certain months of the year find him in Alaska, other months find him in South America, and still others in Antarctica.

He still loves the mountains. He does not tire of being out in the hills, high above cities and other landscapes with beautiful vistas spread before him. Tejas has joked that he probably will retire from guiding when he is eighty. That leaves plenty of time for new adventures, as well as repeat visits to the grand high points on each continent, except for Asia, where Everest reigns supreme. Never say never.

During his long guiding career, Tejas has been recognized with many honors. He broke the speed record for climbing the Seven Summits, which really included all eight peaks to satisfy both the Bass and Messner lists, by completing the circuit between January 18, 2010 and May 31, 2010.

He was recognized as one of the top fifty athletes in Alaska history by Sports Illustrated in 2000. Tejas was chosen as a member of the Alaska Sports Hall of Fame in 2012 and his achievement of making the first winter solo ascent of Denali gained him recognition a second time in the Hall's Moments category.

In 2012, Tejas was presented with the Governor's Award as the Alaskan of the Year. He is a lifetime member of the American Alpine Club. He completed the Explorer's Grand Slam by climbing the Seven Summits and skiing to the North Pole and South Pole.

In 2014, I was invited to participate in a thirteen-episode, National Geographic reality show called *Ultimate Survivor Alaska*. One of the other competitors was young Dallas Seavey. He is a third-generation dog mushing champion from Alaska who has now won the 1,000-mile Iditarod Trail Sled Dog Race between Anchorage and Nome four times before his thirtieth birthday. He is a hardcore athlete.

It was interesting on many levels. One thing the producers did was make me grow my beard back to show the passage of time during the show. I had shaved it off long ago, but when it grew back, it showed quite a bit of gray and white that I had never had before. Another intriguing element was that we were pretty much sequestered in Alaska without being able to contact people so that we couldn't leak the results of the shows.

If someone had told the shy me of the sixth grade who could barely talk to people, never mind engage in public speaking, that I would be in a TV show with a speaking part, I never would have believed that. Just like in mountain climbing I realized slow can be good. I didn't want to rush and trip over my tongue.

Now I talk to elementary school kids. They go, "Wow, you've climbed the highest mountain." They're all over it. They're bouncing off the wall. But high school kids are cool, too. You have to move around. Communication is about more than talking. Use your hands. You want them to stay awake. Sometimes they're trying to look up the girl's dress across the room and not even listening to you. I don't talk to high school kids that often. I have now given enough talks that I know I am not going to die from fright doing it. It's even better if there's money on the end. You mean I get paid to talk? How rad is that? I am hoping to do more public speaking and appearances as I gradually spend less time on high mountains.

I have accumulated stories, and I can tie them into lessons to be learned. Another speaker told me that the biggest deal is to keep them awake. If you've got them laughing, you've got them. If you get them laughing and make some salient points related to your sponsor, the sponsor will be happy. The woman who told me that is someone who

makes a substantial amount of money each year just by speaking.
She was a story teller to begin with, and you know Norman Vaughan
basically financed his trips to Antarctica by telling stories. Expeditions
are story-driven. I heard many of Norman's stories eight, nine, ten times.
It didn't matter. A lot of it was the delivery. You have to share your
experiences in a way that is entertaining.

I was in some other TV things earlier. When my son Cayman was a
little boy, I sat him down in front of the TV and started rolling a video of
Denali. John Waterman, a former Denali ranger, was in the room, and he
said, "Hey, your dad is a stud."

Cayman said, "I want to watch cartoons." That will keep you humble.

I helped guide a trip on Denali that was being filmed. My friend
Marty Raney was involved, too. It was fun and we got paid. On the
mountain, I started getting some more camera time. I wasn't scripted.
There were some skiers I zoomed past on a sled, carrying more weight
than them and laughing, and they decided they should put me on film.
John wrote a book called *Surviving Denali*, so that's what we named the
show. We spent a month on the filming on the mountain, and then rafted
the Tokositna River. I've got a copy of the film in a can somewhere. I
don't think it played much, but it was a delight to make.

As a guide, I do a pretty good job of entertaining clients, but it is
different in front of a camera. I try to remember to use humor and get
into the role. I typically understate. I might be standing there with tons of
mosquitoes buzzing around my head and they stick a camera in my face
and say, "What do you think about the mosquitoes?" I might just say,
"There's a lot of them." I'd be better off making some stuff up like, "This
is the most mosquitoes we've seen in Alaska since 1903." That would sell
a lot better.

Ultimate Survivor, which involved three months of filming, was a
wilderness race. Crazy things were involved. You have to get to a flag.
The gun goes off and sometimes you have to cut through a swamp to
advance. Sometimes you're going up the side of a mountain. There was
an ice-covered lake with the ice so thin you would break through if you
try to walk across it. Putting you at risk, making you use your wits, all of
that was intentional.

If you got to an intermediate flag first, you got maps and the first
choice of equipment. That's your reward. If you come in later, you get
what's left. You try to get to the finish line first each week, but the points
accumulate. The racers that get to the finish line the most times out of
thirteen, win. We spent three to five days on each segment. We did a lot

Vern Tejas

Tejas grew his beard back for
National Geographic's *Ultimate Survivor* TV show

of running and a fair amount of walking. Guess what? The cameraman
can't keep up with a fast team with a big camera on his shoulder. There
is a lot of footage of us running through the woods, but you have to talk
about what you're doing for the camera. Other things affected progress.
If a big rainstorm was coming, you had to go back to camp because
they couldn't film in the rain. Sometimes the safety guy would interrupt
because of conditions if a river was getting too high, or we were getting
hypothermic. It was only reality TV to a certain point. They maintain
the premise that you are out in the woods all by yourself, but you're not.
They are filming you. They are keeping track to make sure you don't kill
yourself or something.

The Future

We had teams. I was on Team Alaska. My friend Marty Raney and Tyler Johnson were two of the others on my team. Dallas Seavey was on the Extreme Team, not Team Alaska. There were younger athletes than us on the Extreme Team, and Johnson was a couple of decades younger than me and Marty. The young kids did eventually kick our butts. There was also tension on the show at different points between individuals on the same team and individuals on other teams. People got testy. Dallas Seavey was a huge success on the show. He won three shows in a row. He's a winner, highly competitive; you can tell a lot about a man by who he competes with.

Dallas is way ahead of the curve for marketing himself as an outdoor adventurer for the rest of his life. He grew up dog mushing, was a star wrestler who almost ended up in the Olympics, and then turned back to mushing and has become a great champion. His grandfather Dan helped get the Iditarod started and was in the first race. His father Mitch has won a couple of times. He was a shrewd, strategic competitor. He wins those races for a reason. Another Alaskan on the show predicted Dallas would become governor of Alaska in twenty years.

We were sequestered for most of the three months. We weren't even supposed to make phone calls. Yet, from time to time, depending if we made it near a city, we would hitchhike into town and get a pizza. At one point, we were in a camp near Portage on the Seward Highway. There is a wild animal preserve on the highway just down the road and somebody went over there. They invited all of the workers, especially the girls, to come over to our camp. We have musical instruments. They brought us beers. We had a couple of days off from shooting. All of the guys who had done the show before did not take the sequestering very seriously.

The whole show was a good time. Basically, I got paid to run around and do the same outdoors stuff I love to do anyway. I got to surf a bore tide. I had always wanted to do that. They gave us canoes and told us to go catch a wave. I caught the wave and rode it. Unfortunately, Tyler and Marty flipped. If we had all caught the wave, we would have moved into first place. Instead, we ended up third in that episode.

Other teams chose quadricycles and ATVs, but we actually won one segment on horseback because the horses were good at crossing the river. I had a fair amount of horseback background, actually, from growing up in Texas. I also worked as a cowboy in Oregon and rode in Patagonia, so I knew my way around horses.

In one segment, they wanted grizzly bears, but the bears weren't interested in being filmed. They sent us out into the woods hoping we would find the bears. You could say we were chasing grizzly bears. We were on an island north of Kodiak Island, on an island that has more bears per square inch than anywhere on earth. They avoided us. We went there for three days without seeing a bear. We saw bear scat. We saw hair rubbings on trees. We saw scratch marks. Everything but bears. There were safety guys with us carrying shotguns and pepper spray. It's hard to sneak up on bears when there were so many of us. Bears are no dummies.

We went fishing off of Kodiak in a little kayak. We caught some halibut, but didn't want them to be so big we couldn't get them into the boat. It was beating the crap out of the boat. Once Marty took out a gun and shot a monster halibut in the head and the shot went right through the boat, so we politely asked him to put away his firearm. Another time, we were paddling across an iceberg-filled lake. Somehow Marty poked a hole in his raft and sprung a leak. The camera wasn't on us. Too bad. We had a rescue situation.

After it all aired, my friends and family thought I was a hero. They were all bragging about me. There was a little buzz.

I did some other TV shows at different times. Way back after the late Jay Hammond was governor, he had a show called *Jay Hammond's Alaska*. We talked about mountaineering and climbing, and right at the end we played a harmonica duet of "Old Susannah." A life highlight, jamming with Governor Jay Hammond.

Also, I hosted on a show called *Tasting Alaska*. It was a small production for the Food Network. It was a special. I had to eat sourdough pancakes, and we set that up at the Talkeetna Roadhouse. People were bragging about how old their sourdough starter was and how good it was. One guy walks in, throws his down on the table, and goes, "This goes back to the Gold Rush." Mine actually came from California from the other Gold Rush.

We ate some Cajun food out on an oil rig. We caught salmon in Kodiak and made caviar out of its eggs. We did a segment on the giant cabbages that people grow for the Alaska State Fair. We opened the show with video of me flying off Denali with my paraglider. The next thing you know, I was in the Ruth Amphitheatre looking up at the mountain and cooking something. They liked the idea I would have this big, massive beard and look Alaskan, but I shaved off the beard for a job six months before they called me, so I had to grow it back.

The Future

One reason I went to the mountains in the first place was because I was not exactly socially adept. Then I became a guide and became really good socially with small groups of people. Next thing you know, I have to talk with a script on TV to an audience of a million people. I was not as good with a script. Some people are natural in the social graces. I have to work at it. I have worked with many groups since then, and you know what, the more you work at it the better you become.

The first time since sixth grade that I did anything in public was the day after I got home from the Denali winter solo. There was a St. Patrick's Day dance, and I wanted to take my girlfriend Gail. She loved dancing. To obtain tickets for the dance, I stopped in a music store and the lady recognized me as the person who had just finished the climb. My frostbitten nose was probably a clue. I was really attracted to the traditional Irish drum. So I picked up, saw the price, and put it back. It is surprising what imported products cost.

Later that night, this lady was at the dance, called me up to the stage, and presented me with the drum. Suddenly, they were talking about me and 500 people were giving me a standing ovation. I was embarrassed, beet red. The band wanted me to play on stage, which of course I did. I acted as if I was enjoying myself, but I was mortified. Afterwards, I took a Dale Carnegie course just to get myself more comfortable. Just a few days later, I gave a slide presentation on the climb at the University of Alaska Anchorage. I don't know how they got my film back so fast. I also didn't have many good shots. On a solo climb that can happen. Especially if you get caught in a storm and you are risking your life. The paucity of the photos meant I really had to talk since I couldn't rely on the pictures to carry the show. The line for the talk stretched to the parking lot. So many more people came than the auditorium held so I had to do it twice in a row: a double-header. I walked down the aisle to the stage and the first thing I said was, "Shucks." Everybody broke up laughing. I thought I was being modest. At the time, the presentation seemed harder than the climb, but now I actually enjoy giving talks.

Doing more shows like that, giving motivational speeches, making public appearances would be fun. Sooner or later, I will have to slow down guiding. Nobody can do it forever. I still enjoy my trips all over the world and going back to the mountains I know so well. But looking ahead, my body is slowing down. I've got to make a conscious effort to treat myself right, eat properly, stay hydrated, train, stretch, all that good stuff. I have to be more consciously aggressive in preparing myself for climbs. You lose body mass as you get older. I used to have bigger guns, but those arm muscles are getting a little smaller. Oh well, lighter is righter.

I really am trying to keep my act together. I am doing different kinds of guiding, some exotic trips that are not on the Seven Summits. I take people to Peru, Italy, Greece, and the Everest base camp. I have been into kayaking for a long time, but now it is whitewater kayaking. Paddling in the Greek Isles was one of the best decisions I've made in a long time. It's in a warm weather place. I'm usually traveling in such harsh environments and you have to worry about getting killed. Paddling in Greece is just the opposite. When people go to climb mountains it's like a mission. When they go to paddle kayaks in Greece, it is a real vacation. I can see a long and enjoyable career guiding that way.

During World War I and II in the Dolomites, soldiers camped in the mountains. They set up all of these steel ladders with climbing pegs and rocks. You can clip into cables. They call it going the Iron Way. You get the same kind of thrill of exposure you do on a mountain, yet it is a lot safer. I heard about them a long time ago and only recently got to check them out.

I have made other adventure trips and climbs that aren't part of the Seven Summits. One trip I am proud of was a journey to Greenland as part of a nine-member group in 2001. It was called "The Return to the Top of the World Expedition." I was one the climbers who made the second ascent of Helvetia Tinde, and the first one since 1969. That is in the mountain range the farthest north in the world. We also made an ascent of the second highest peak in the range and named it after our hero John Denver. For the fun of it, we climbed the northernmost mountain in the world. When I get the opportunity, I wish to climb Mount Howe, the southernmost mountain.

One thing that has been on my mind is to climb the second Seven Summits, the second highest mountain on each continent. I have done some of them. You also get back into the debate of what is a continent, so there are eight nominees. In North America it is Mount Logan in Canada. Others are Mount Townsend in Australia, or Puncak Mandala in Indonesia; Ojos del Salado, on the Argentina-Chile border for South America; Dykh Tau in Russia, for Europe; Mount Kenya for Africa; Mount Tyree for Antarctica; and K-2 for Asia. K-2 is the second tallest mountain in the world at 28,251 feet. It is also a far more difficult challenge than Everest and is climbed much less frequently. K-2 would be the biggest challenge. I have been asked to guide a K-2 trip, but I do not know if it is going to work out.

The Future

One great honor for me was being selected as a member of the Alaska Sports Hall of Fame, actually twice. I had not anticipated mountaineering being considered as a sport. To me it seems more of a lifestyle. Don't get me wrong. I think it was a wonderful honor to be acknowledged as a noted sportsman. Certainly, we are athletes. Some of the strongest people I know are mountaineers. You can say mountaineering is an athletic activity of the highest degree, pun intended. It is a great honor for Alaskans to consider mountaineering a sport, and for Alaskans to choose me. Mountaineering is an adventure sport. You don't know the outcome. Making the summit is not a foregone conclusion. You may make headlines or get killed instead.

Alaskans as a people are unique people. They have a little bit different definition about what life is about. For all of my travels that take me away from my state, I consider myself an Alaskan in spirit. That's one reason I was so happy they officially changed the name of McKinley to Denali in 2015. I think I signed my first petition for that thirty or forty years ago. I feel vindicated by the change. Very pleased. I felt the circle was connected to the first peoples of Alaska.

With so many mountains under my feet, I always seem to identify with the naturalist John Muir who said, "I hear the mountains calling and I must go. I am hopelessly and forever a mountaineer."

I read a book by R. Waldo McBurney called *My First 100 Years*. It is an inspiring book. Maybe someday I can look back in the same manner. Helen Keller did not climb mountains, but she is inspirational to adventurers nonetheless.

"Security is mostly a superstition," she said. "It does not exist in nature, nor do the children of men as a whole experience it. Avoiding danger is not safer in the long run than outright exposure. Life is either a daring adventure or nothing."

You can never predict what's out there and what you can do. I'd like to think I still have a lot of miles to cover all over the world and a lot of adventures still in me.